Heresy and the
English Reformation

Heresy and the English Reformation

Bogomil-Cathar Influence on Wycliffe, Langland, Tyndale and Milton

GEORGI VASILEV

McFarland & Company, Inc., Publishers

Jefferson, North Carolina, and London

BR
377
.V37
2008

LIBRARY OF CONGRESS CATALOGUING-IN-PUBLICATION DATA

Vasilev, Georgi, 1944–
  Heresy and the English reformation : Bogomil-Cathar influence
on Wycliffe, Langland, Tyndale and Milton / Georgi Vasilev.
    p.   cm.
  Includes bibliographical references and index.

  ISBN-13: 978-0-7864-3005-5
  softcover : 50# alkaline paper ∞

  1. Reformation — England.   2. Heresies, Christian —
England — History.   3. England — Church history.   I. Title.
BR377.V37   2008
273'.6 — dc22   2007033765

British Library cataloguing data are available

On the cover: *The Angel Michael Binding Satan ("He Cast him into the
Bottomless Pit, and Shut him up")*, William Blake, watercolor, ink and
graphite on paper 14⅛" × 12¾", c. 1802

Manufactured in the United States of America

*McFarland & Company, Inc., Publishers
  Box 611, Jefferson, North Carolina 28640
  www.mcfarlandpub.com*

To the memory of my teacher,
the great writer and humanist Stefan Gechev

Contents

Contents

Preface

The Latin proverb *habent sua fata libelli* states that *books have their fates*. This book reveals fascinating and unprecedented fates in the course of a journey through European life and literature during the Middle Ages. We will explore little-known historical and cultural aspects of Britain, France, the Netherlands, Italy and Bulgaria, in particular the constant revolt against religious dogma during the period in question. This struggle against harassment and persecution is a hallmark of the centuries-long fight for the right of men and women to think freely, and to communicate with God in their native language.

The spiritual influences, secret connections, hidden activities and efforts to that end were condemned as acts of heresy. They essentially represented reformist movements of the Bogomils and Cathars, whom American Baptist historian L. P. Brockett (in 1879) proclaimed the Early Protestants of the East. In Britain, these people were called the Lollards, and were the first to pursue a reformist initiative in Albion. These early reformist groups reflect a centuries-long process of self-enlightenment and self-evangelization through translations and preachings of the Scriptures in native tongues. Your journey inside these covers will make you participants in the reconstruction of history, as seekers and proponents of the truth. This text combines an asserted intellectual effort with an element of adventure: in order to reach these revelations, we shall have to pass through the labyrinth of the heretics' secret codes and connections, and their guarded interpretations and practices to protect themselves from the persecutors and the Inquisition. It is time for the shining light of spiritual achievement to illuminate the lurking shadows of burning stakes.

Naturally, when discussing this provocative subject and its developments several centuries ago, questions arise. What is dualism? Why did this philosophy attract renowned intellectuals and common people, alike, from the Middle Ages to the 18th century? True, it undoubtedly produced the first penetrating reformist trend in western Europe — the desire for direct communication with the Word of God. This challenging idea of direct communication with Christ was fundamental to Bogomils and Cathars. According to *The Secret Book* of the Bogomils, John the Evangelist reclines on the breast of Christ who reveals the secret of Creation. This direct communication with God and the Scriptures eliminated official priestly functions and made icons, rituals and liturgies superfluous for Bogomils, Cathars and Lollards.

Furthermore, Bogomil-Cathar philosophy offered another significant contribution. Its theology provided a psychologically convincing solution to the problem of all times — an explanation for the origin of evil. This issue has always plagued the doctrine of the Church: God created everything, so how, then, does the Devil, who is weaker than God, cause and impose so much evil?

According to Bogomil myths, initially Satanael was directly associated with the Lord, and some dualist versions even refer to him as God's first-born. However, he was filled with pride, and he sought to place his power above God, managing to involve one-third of the angels in his revolt. God threw the traitors in the abyss and removed the syllable "el," a symbol of divinity, from Satanael's name. Satan lost his light and his face became "like molten iron." Nevertheless, God was merciful and allowed Satan to create his own world — that was our Earth. Thus, Satan became the prince of the earthly world as the evil god. He devised and molded man in his likeness from clay, then entered angels' souls, once true to God, disguised as the bodies of men and women.

Therefore, Creation was divided between the heavenly, invisible, immortals that belonged to the Good God, and the earthly, visible, humans, controlled by the Evil God. Such is the dualist portrayal of the world. They believed that humans, subject to the power of Satan, bodies engulfing the souls of angels from the heavenly creation, constantly strive to leave the devil's creation to return to the Good Lord. For them, communication of the Word in their native tongue, the imitation of Christ (*imitatio Christi*), helped spawn a return to the kingdom of heaven. So, they did not fear the stakes — fire allowed these heretics to escape the sinful kingdom of Satan, the flesh of the bodies he created, to return to the kingdom of the Good God as free souls.

In this quest, Bogomils, Cathars and Lollards dedicated themselves to an exceptional aspiration for goodness and creativity, and denied coexistence with evil. They themselves became Satan's alternative world, as they emulated early Christian society. Historically and culturally, they established communities on Earth steeped in the spirit of love and purity, ensconced in introspection and education. They embraced peace and rejected violence.

The book's first three chapters are "Bogomils and Lollards," "Traces of the Bogomil Movement in the English Language," and "The Heresy and Women." They exhibit, using text comparisons, the strong parallel between Bogomils-Cathars and the religious practices of the Lollards through the myth of the fall of Lucifer and his legions, the direct confession to God, the denial of icons and the cross, and the right of women to preach and conduct sacred rituals and practices.

Chapter 4 explores the documented partiality of John Wycliffe toward the dualist philosophy. His renowned and loosely interpreted words, "Deus debet obedire diabolo," are actually a direct translation of the Bogomils' view of the devil as the impious steward of the world. Chapter 5 describes how William Tyndale, reformer and translator of the Bible into English, uses dualist arguments as a motivation to preach the Word in the English vernacular. Chapter 6 presents William Langland's famous poem *The Vision of Piers Plowman* in several passages that invoke Cathar treatises. The person of Piers Plowman is creatively modeled after the image of Christ Plowman from the Bulgarian apocryphal "Legend of the Tree" written by Father Jeremiah (10th century). Chapter 6 also delves into similar issues whereby the Bogomils' and Cathars' favorite myth of Christ's descent to hell to save human souls is thoroughly explained. Dualists' doctrine of destroying hell and denying purgatory's existence is intended to liberate the Middle Ages man and woman from paralyzing religious fears and blinding submission to the church's authority and dogmatism. The book provides two superb illustrations that illuminate the subject: one from the St. Alban's Psalter (created near London, 12th century) and the other from the Boyana Church (created near Sophia, Bulgaria, 13th century). Appendices follow each of these Chapters, and further illuminate particular facets of the topic under discussion.

Chapter 7 exposes the aspects of John Milton's keen attachment to the theology of the heretics. In some of his treatises, the great poet recommends the worship practices of the Waldensian communities as a model to reform the English Church. In his profound epics *Paradise Lost* and *Paradise Regained,* Milton introduces imagery from the Bogomils' apocrypha: *The Secret Book* of the Bogomils, *The Tiberiad Sea, Dispute between Christ and the Devil,* and *The Nicodemus Gospel.* The penchant for Bogomil-Cathar philosophy and imagery persisted as a formidable influence for centuries, including the works of poet and artist William Blake (1757–1827).

For the reader's edification, we should note that many of the sources used in researching the book are in the Bulgarian, or other languages that employ the Cyrillic alphabet. All Cyrillics have been transliterated, and in the text, translated. The bibliography has been divided accordingly.

I would like to note that I am not beginning this book with polemics in mind. Although alternative to the traditional position of English historiography, this interpretation would not have been developed over a relatively short period of time, nor would the abundant facts quoted here have been readily collected, if I had not received preliminary opinions and, most important, literature and published sources from the most outstanding British scholars Prof. Anne Hudson, Prof. Norman Tanner, Prof. David Daniell, Mrs. Janet Hamilton and Prof. Bernard Hamilton, Prof. René Weis, and Dr. Malcolm Lambert. This study is largely an additional interpretation of the information they have discovered and amassed. In other words, my work also relies on their research and their fellowship, which acquired a form of cooperation with an opponent. In turn, I hope that the discoveries regarding the continental connection of the Lollards with the dualist roots in Provence, Normandy and the Netherlands and, in the long run, with Bulgarian Bogomilism, which we have made with my respected colleague Krustina Gecheva,[1] will also serve our British colleagues. The clarification of controversial elements will be assisted by time and the interest of the readership, as there is already a new reading public capable of undertaking its own research and academically correct comparisons. It is not by chance that the Centre d'Etudes Cathares operates near Toulouse, France, as well as a cultural circle supported by the infrastructure of the virtual society at www.cathares.org.

Part of the materials in this book have already been published in my work in Bulgarian titled *Bogomil and Apocryphal Ideas in Medieval English Culture: The Bulgarian Image of Christ Plowman as Piers Plowman in William Langland's "The Vision of Piers Plowman"*; Koreni Publishing House, Sofia, 2001).

4

In expressing gratitude to British colleagues, I would like to take the opportunity to thank Prof. Valerie Hotchkiss, whose one-month hospitality in 2001 at the Bridwell Library, South-Methodist University, Dallas, allowed me to work intensively with the creations of William Tyndale and the reformist treatises of John Milton. I cannot but appreciate the responsiveness of Dr. Anne Brenon, France, who placed at my disposal her publications on Waldensian-Cathar literature in England in the 17th century. The same gratitude I extend to Dr. Jean Duvernoy, France, actually the best scholar on Catharism. I am also grateful to Prof. Thomas Butler, Harvard University, who supported my thesis even on Bulgarian soil, sending me a favorable opinion of my second doctoral thesis in 2000. I should also like to thank Mrs. Bistra Roushkova for her translations of my texts and her pertinent editorial recommendations. I express my gratitude to Dr. Boyka Sokolova-Leader, University of London, who translated Chapter 3, and also to Prof. Rumiana Zlatanova, University of Heidelberg, who sent me some important sources. I owe thanks to Dr. Linda Stillman for her support and pertinent suggestions. And I present my cordial gratitude to my mother, Stefana Vasileva, and to my cousin Prof. Antonia Shivarova, both of whom supported all my efforts.

Introduction:
The Dualist Heresy —
Bridging the Island to
the Continent During
the Middle Ages

European Genesis

When writing about the Lollards in England and their abundant literature, nearly all contemporary British medievalists perceive them as a local phenomenon, i.e., one that originated on British soil alone. It is from this point, however, that the contradictions begin. *Encyclopaedia Britannica* establishes a definition for the name *Lollard* which clearly speaks of a continental origin, or at least of a continental bond: "The term comes from Middle Dutch 'lollard,' a 'mumbler' or 'mutterer'; it had been applied to the Flemish Beghard and other continental groups suspected of combining pious pretensions with heretical belief."[1] One of the greatest authorities in the study of dualist movements, Ignatz von Döllinger, refers to a number of documents regarding the presence of Lollards in Europe, quoting a Bull of Pope Boniface IX, which explains that the "popularly called Beghardi or Lolhardi and Swestriones," spread in various parts of Germany, were "actually poor —*fratricelli*."[2] This occurred in the very beginning of the 15th century, as Boniface IX was pope in the period between 1389 and 1404. This text provides several pieces of important information. The first is that the Lollards were a variety of Beghardi and *fraticelli*, and the second

7

that the Lollards were in the sights of his predecessor, John XX (1316–1334).[3] In other words, the Lollards were definitely a phenomenon in the system of medieval heresies in Europe. The third is that, since the German Lollards were Beghards, then their origin lies in the 12th century, as Malcolm Lambert has had good reason to point out in his book *Medieval Heresy*.[4]

In his famous *Ecclesiastical History from the Birth of Our Savior to the Eighteenth Century*, Mosheim has collected an abundance of sources that prove the European origin and European proliferation of the Lollards. From there we shall only quote the information of Hocsemius "a canon of Liege," in his *Gesta pontificum Leodiensium*, lib. I., cap. 31 (in. Jo. Chapeavili Gesta Pontificum Tungrensium et Leodiensium, tom. II, p. 350 and c.) who wrote: "In the same year (1309), certain strolling hypocrites, who were called Lollhards or praisers of God (*qui Lollhardi sive deus laudantes vocabantur*), deceived some women of quality in Hainault and Brabant.... Thus this term acquired the same import with the term Beghard."[5] Mosheim definitely concludes that the English Lollards, the followers of Wycliffe, were called with an imported Belgian term — "be a vulgar term of reproach brought from Belgium to England, Lollards."[6]

This information is referred to and repeated in the three-volume *History of the Inquisition of the Middle Ages* by Henry Charles Lea. Again basing himself on the sources used by Mosheim, Lea mentions that Lollard associations were established in Antwerp around the year 1300 during the plague epidemic in order to take care of the sick and, above all, to bury the dead. They called themselves Alexians — "from their patron St. Alexis, and Cellits from dwelling in cells."[7] Reports similar to the Bull of Boniface IX and dating from the 15th century can again be found in Ignatz von Döllinger, this time in a document from the State Library in Frankfurt. This document mentions the Bull, but it also adds new and important details: some of the heretics were literate and won the sympathy of masters of theology and learned men. The heretics said they followed the life of Christ and the apostles and, what is specific, that they did not "accept any saints."[8] Moreover, they denied the right to consecrate of any priest who committed a grave sin.[9] The last three facts characterize the Cathars, who called themselves new apostles, rejected the existence of saints and the right of any priests who had committed a sin to officiate in church. The document then features other familiar Cathar characteristics, including that confession should be made directly to God and that indulgences do not count.[10]

In addition to the Cathar features, one can also quote echoes from the prime source — Bogomilism. The name Lollards or "mumblers" or "mutterers" (of prayers) leads us to the observation of Anna Comnena who, on the occasion of the sentence and burning of the Bogomil leader Basil, gave a short description of him in her *Alexiad* and mentioned the Bogomil custom to mutter — *kai mehei rinos skepetai*.[11] In turn, the definition given by Hocsemius — that the Lollards were praisers of God (*qui Lollhardi sive deus laudantes vocabantur*) — echoes of the very name of "Bogomil" — "dear to God." The next summary of heretical contacts between the island and the continent is found in the dissertation of the Swiss scholar Johann Conrad Fueslin, *Dissertatio de fanaticis seculo XII in Anglia repertis* (Bern, 1761).

At the end of the 19th and the beginning of the 20th century, various authors made discoveries mainly regarding the transfer of dualist apocrypha to the island. These were Ivan Franko in his remarkable collection "Apokrifi i legendi z ukrainskih rukopisiv,"[12] as well as Nikolai Ossokin with his excellent work on the history of Albigensians and their time,[13] which gave important details about these relations, and Moise Gaster, who published his *Ilchester Lectures on Greeko-Slavonic Literature and Its Relation to the Folklore of Europe During the Middle Ages* in London in 1887.[14] In fact, the belated isolationist notion of the categorical Englishness of the Lollards probably repeats an old Catholic thesis that the island was saved from continental heresies. This was noticed even by Conrad Fueslin, and in more recent times one can see it repeated in the *Catholic Encyclopedia*: "Till the latter part of the fourteenth century England had been remarkably free from heresy. The Manichean movements of the twelfth and thirteenth centuries which threatened the Church and society in Southern Europe and had appeared sporadically in Northern France and Flanders had made no impression on England."[15]

The Dualist Pre-Renaissance

Now what is the meaning of clarifying this problem? Quite significant, it turns out, for since the 12th century, when the presence of dualist apocrypha in England is clearly denoted, right until the 17th (i.e., the works of John Milton) there was a significant cultural and philosophical trend in English medieval culture, which was born on the basis of dualist Bogomil-Cathar heresy. The Lollards and their iconography, the reformers John Wycliffe and William Tyndale, the poet William Langland, the apocryphal volumes *Cursor mundi, Aenbyte of Inwite*, as well as the Anglo-Norman variants of *The Legend of the Tree of the Cross* and *Les enfaunces de Jesus Christ*, and John Milton's great poems *Paradise Lost* and *Paradise Regained* fall within this section of time, in this context of ideas and specific figurative thinking. Speaking of Milton, one should not forget the fact that he was also a reformer of the same temperament and dualist notion as Wycliffe and Tyndale, also expressing his continuity of ideas from Wycliffe. Therefore, we are faced with a chain of events, works and persons who were frequently also a pinnacle in English culture. Its study will necessitate both a more careful interpretation of known facts and the addition of new ones.

One cannot but notice such a peculiar need for greater precision in the perception of the "heretical" heritage among our British colleagues. David Daniell has done a lot to distinguish more clearly the reformist work of William Tyndale so that his exceptional contribution to the development of the English language could be seen. It was clearly said that the translation of the *Authorised Version* of the Bible (1611), known as the work of King James and a circle of scholars commissioned by him, actually used 80 percent of Tyndale's translation.[16] True, such an opinion was vouchsafed earlier by other authorities in England,[17] but now it has been said so clearly and distinctly for the first time, and the British and American public show definite interest in this historical specification.

Generally speaking, it seems this is where we should recall a thought of principal significance for these studies belonging to Dimitri Obolensky, for whom the study of Bogomilism and related heresies meant above all to establish connections:

> This connection, if successfully established, would in its turn enable Church historians to regard the Bogomil sect as the first European link in the thousand-year-long chain leading from Mani's teaching in Mesopotamia in the third century to the Albigensian Crusade in southern France in the thirteenth. Moreover, the study of the Bogomil movement has its own, and by no means negligible, part to play in the investigation of the cultural and religious links between eastern and western Europe, the importance of which is increasingly perceived at the present time.[18]

The phenomena mentioned here acquire the features of an early hidden Renaissance in British society. This phenomenon is one of particular beauty, for it was both a Renaissance at the apex (Wycliffe, Langland, Milton) and a grassroots Renaissance, in other words, the literary activity and the iconography of Lollard communities.

In conclusion one is faced with the question of what these unusual interactions mean, when ideas from one culture, Bulgarian, additionally developed in the Cathar culture of Provence, prove a permanent presence in a third culture, in this case English. The first conclusion is that lofty cultural aspirations are indestructible; even subjected to persecution, they migrate from one country to another, stimulate an upsurge everywhere, reincarnate and resort to mimicry until the time of full-fledged expression finally arrives. The second conclusion is probably that dualist, i.e., Bogomil-Cathar imagery and philosophy, should be viewed as a driving force of pan–European pre–Renaissance,[19] as well as a principal ingredient of English Reformation. And third — that we could presume to expect that the cultural potential of this unique philosophy has not been exhausted, that aspects of it could be resurrected, for they feature a unique example that is also necessary for our time, managing as it once did to convince millions of people to place spiritual needs above material needs. In other words, it developed as a culture of the masses, as grassroots amateur creative activities, an alternative to mass culture. Here the interaction between the elite culture of theology and academism and the self-expression of the broad public enjoy a surprising harmony. Nor should one overlook yet another majestic aspect of this phenomenon — it is *par excellence* international while it also contributed to the germination of national literatures, and consequently it was a pan–European bridge of creativity.

CHAPTER 1

Bogomils and Lollards

Spring
And all the flowers resurrected
with the colors of Easter eggs.
— Stefan Gechev

Penetration into England

There are two early references to disembarcations of heretics in England about 1162. The first comes from William of Newbury (Guillemus Novoburgensis) and has been commented upon by the well-known historian Stephen Runciman. He has pointed out that the visitors came from Germany on the crest of the heretical wave mentioned by Eckbert, later Benedictine abbot of Schonau.[1] Arno Borst and Milan Loos also mention the tragic fate of this group: most of the heretics were tried at Oxford, branded, chased away, or starved to death.[2] Thus we are left with the impression that the heresy failed to get a foothold in England.

The other view, upholding the idea of the serious penetration of the Bogomil-Cathar heresy into England, was expounded by Alexander Veselovski, Moses Gaster and Ivan Franko. The facts analyzed by them are from after the 14th century.[3] They study mainly how themes from the heretical apocrypha were taken over and interpreted in English culture. The central one of these themes is the "Harrowing of Hell," which reproduces chapter 18 of the *Nicodemus Gospel*, the favorite reading of the dualists. Gaster and Franko discuss the influence of the *Nicodemus Gospel* on the miracle plays and Langland's *Piers Plowman*. The proofs are numerous. It is really surprising that these finds have been overlooked by serious authors

13

like M. R. James, E. Chambers and E. Partridge, thus completely isolating medieval English literature from contacts with the heresy. Even Dmitri Obolensky's abundant commentary, which proves that the numerous apocrypha that spread all over Europe were, if nothing else, used by the dualists, has been neglected.[4]

Some change of attitude is marked by A. Baugh and K. Malone, who point out that the apocrypha were brought over to England via France in the 13th century.[5] They also note the important presence of the *Nicodemus Gospel*. In our opinion the presence of the "Harrowing of Hell" theme in the *Exeter Book* (10th c.) can be seen as a heretical influence. In this scene Jesus delivers from hell not only Adam and Eve, "but a countless multitude of folk," which is typical of the Bogomil-Cathar vision. The "Fall of Lucifer" and his angels found in the *Caedmon Ms* is another typical dualistic theme.

The odyssey of dualistic apocrypha in England has not found a satisfactory explanation and raises an important question: was the heretical presence durable enough so that it could propagate a type of nonorthodox culture, standing apart and often opposed to the official Church; could it create a milieu which could produce its own conceptions of life and patterns of behavior in the general cultural development? Put in the terms of sociology, we shall have to find whether the heresy could create its own social and cultural infrastructure in England.

The heretical communities of the Lollards of the 14th and 15th centuries have been well documented. They took part in John Ball's rebellion and were connected with the reformist efforts of John Wycliffe.[6] However, the Lollards have been regarded as a local phenomenon, though their very name suggests a continental origin.

As mentioned in the introduction, a number of documents about the Lollards in Germany have been collected by I. von Döllinger and Henry Charles Lea, and it bears repeating that the *Encyclopaedia Britannica* (1970) also points to the Lollards' European roots: "The term comes from Middle Dutch 'lollard,' a 'mumbler' or 'mutterer'; it had been applied to the Flemish Beghard and other continental groups suspecting of combining pious pretentions with heretical belief."[7]

Older dictionaries suggest a typology of the ideas connected with the Lollards. The respectable Du Cange, who used 14th century chronicles, describes the Lollards as heretics from Germany and Belgium and adds that "they hide in many parts of the English kingdom" (*in pluribus partibus regni Angliae latitabant*). John Oldcastle is referred to as "Lollardus." Du Cange provides us with the important reference to a chronicle from 1318, according to which "they called the Lollard also a Waldensian" (*Lollardus quoque dicitur haereticus Valdensis*).[8] Thus, the outlined spiritual kinship between the Lollards and Waldensians directs our attention to the roots of the Waldensian doctrine which lie in Catharism. In fact, Waldo adopted from the Cathars their social vision and organizational model but abandoned their complicated dualist mythology.

In his *Dictionnaire historique* the erudite Louis Moreri (17th century) also pointed to the German-Flemish-English triangle by referring to older sources, which he named carefully, and which reveal the beliefs of the Lollards:

> These sectarians said that Lucifer and the angels that followed him were condemned wrongly, that is rather Archangel Michael and the good angels that deserved this punishment. They [the Lollards] added inadmissible blasphemies against the Virgin, they said that God does not punish us for the faults we commit here. The authors [of the sources] say that a girl, member of this unhappy sect condemned to perish on the stake, when asked whether she was a virgin, answered that she was one on earth but would not be under it. They [the Lollards] taught also that the Mass, baptism and the extreme unction were useless; they also denied penance and refused to obey the Church and the secular authorities.[9]

In his *Encyclopédie des sciences religieuses*, F. Lichtenberger mentions also the Lollard prediction that "Lucifer and the demons unfairly chased away from Heaven will some day be restored there."[10]

From this we can conclude that the Lollards professed a dualistic creed marked in some cases by Luciferianism. It is hard to say, though, whether these allegations were the result of accidental contacts with continental Luciferians or came from the official Church, which sought to discredit the Lollards by presenting them as having a greater affinity for Lucifer than for God. The Luciferian turn is not typical of the English Lollards.

We shall go a step further in asserting that there is a great similarity of doctrines between the Lollards and the Bogomil-Cathars, which can be proved by comparing their writings. Excerpts from the scripts of the Norwich Heresy Trials (1428–31),[11] as well as quotations from other documents, reveal a commonality with Bogomil writings on the following topics:

I. Beliefs and Rituals of Bogomils and Lollards
1. *Common myths*— The fall of Lucifer; Satan as creator and ruler of the visible world
2. *Ritual practices*—baptism in the Holy Spirit; preference for the prayer Pater Noster; direct confession to God; negation of hell and purgatory

II. Social Ideas
1. *Preaching social justice*
2. *Negation of legal authority and oath taking; condemnation of bloodshed*

III. Anticlericalism
1. *The official Church is seen as a community of Herod, or of the Anti-Christ*
2. *Church buildings are thought of as synagogues, crossroads or waste-lands*

IV. Rejection of Official Church Ritual
1. *Negation of transubstantiation*
2. *Negation of the crucifix*
3. *Negation of icons (images) and relics of saints*
4. *Refusal to worship the Virgin and the saints.*

On comparing the texts one might well ask whether it is possible that phrases written in Bulgaria or Asia Minor in the 10th to 11th centuries can be repeated in England in the 14th through 16th centuries. An explanation lies in the habit of medieval thinking concerning religious writings, which relied on stereotypes. It is interesting to note, however, that the heretical writers, who also used such phrases, were allowed to adapt, change and interpret them. Unlike the official religious texts, these formulae were used as aphorisms to initiate the novice and could be developed and retold from a personal point of view. This important point was made by M. D. Lambert in his *Medieval Heresy: Popular Movements from Bogomil to Hus*.[12]

In the pages that follow we shall compare parts of Bogomil (Cathar) and Lollard texts.[13] The former come from the *Treatise against the Bogomils* by Presbyter Cosmas, *The Secret Book* of the Bogomils and the *Panoplia Dogmatica* by Euthymius Zigabenus. Some of the material also comes from the collection *Sources of Bogomilism in Bulgaria, Byzantium and Western Europe*.[14]

Text Comparison

I. BELIEFS AND RITUALS OF BOGOMILS AND LOLLARDS

Common myths

The Fall of Lucifer and His Angels

Bogomils

And with his tail he dragged away one-third of the angels of God, and he was banished from the throne of God and from the overlordship of the heavens [*Interrogatio Johannis*, or *The Secret Book* of the Bogomils (Carcassone version), translation T. Butler].

Lollards

Devils who fell with Lucifer from the sky, who falling on earth entered in the icons in the churches, and who continue to lie hid there [Depositions against Margeria, wife of William Baxter].[15]

Satan as Creator and Possessor of the Visible World

Bogomils

Now they say that the great king is the devil, because he is cosmocrator [Euthymii Zigabeni,* *Panoplia Dogmatica* § 40, *Patrologia Graeca*].[16]

Lollards

That God has to obey the devil [John Wycliffe, XXIV Conclusiones damnatae Londoniis in synodo, Fasciculi Zizaniorum, p. 278].[17]

Ritual practices

Baptism in the Holy Spirit

Bogomils

They say that ours is baptism of John, being accomplished in water, but theirs is baptism of Christ, achieved, as they think through the Spirit [Zigabenus, § 16].[18]

Lollards

That the sacrament of Baptem doon in water in fourme custumed of the Churcheys litell to be pondred for as muche as whan the child cometh to yeres of discrecion and receyvyth Cristis lawe and hys commaundments

17

he is sufficiently baptized and so
he may be saved withowtyn ony
other baptem [Depositions of
Richard Grace of Beccles].[19]

Preference for the Prayer Pater noster

Bogomils
They say that the only prayer is
the one the Lord handed down
in the Gospels, that is our Father
[Zigabenus, § 19].[20]*

Lollards
Also that no prayer shuld be said
but only Pater Noster [Deposi-
tions of John Kyngent of
Nelong].[21]

Direct Confession to God

Bogomils
The heretics confess and absolve
themselves although they are
chained by the devil. So do not
only man but women and that is
to be blamed [*Treatise against the
Bogomils*, Presbyter Cosmas].[22]

Lollards
Also that every confession only to
God is to be done, not to other
priest [Depositions of Matilda,
wife of Richard Fleccher of Bec-
cles].[23]

Also that every good man and
good woman is a priest [Deposi-
tions of John Skylan of Bergh].[24]

Negation of Hell and Purgatory

Bogomils
Also, they say, there is no purgatory [Rački, "Prilozi za povijest
bosanskih patarena"].[25] They say
that people of this sort (bogomils)
do not die, but are changed, as if
in sleep. They take off this cov-
ering of clay and flesh without

Lollards
Also that Richard Belward was
saying that this world is the place
of the purgatory, and all souls
who quickly are getting out of
their body without any interme-
diary go strait to heaven or to
hell. So useless were prayers and

All translations of Euthymius Zigabenus in English, except note 44, are according to "Euthymius Zigabenus against the Bogomils," in Christian Dualist Heresies in the Byzantine World c. 650–c.1405, *selected and annotated by Janet Hamilton and Bernard Hamilton (Manchester University Press, 1998).*

pain, and put on the incorrupt-
ible divine robe of Christ.
Becoming like him in form and
body, they come with an escort
of angels and apostles to the
kingdom of the Father, and their
abandoned body dissolves into
dust and ash, and will never rise
again [Zigabenus, § 22].[26]

masses done for dead people
[Depositions of John Burell, servant of Thomas Mone].[27]

II. SOCIAL IDEAS

Preaching social justice

Bogomils
They scold the rich, they teach
their own folk to disobey the
masters, they detest the king,
they blame the boyards, they
suppose that people working for
the king are odious to God and
they instruct any servant to stop
working for his lord [*Treatise
against the Bogomils*].[28]

Lollards
Also that the temporal lordis and
temporal man may lefully take
alle possessions and temporel
godys from alle man of holy
Churche, and from alle bysshops
and prelates bothe hors and har-
neys, and gyve thar good to pore
puple [Depositions of Hawisia
Moone, wife of Thomas Moone].[29]

Negation of the legal authority and oath-taking; condemnation of bloodshed

Bogomils and Cathars
Do not swear by Jerusalem,
because it is the city of the great
king. Now they say that the great
king is the devil, because he is
cosmocrator [Zigabenus, § 40].[30]

Lollards
Also that is no leful to swear in
ony caas [Depositions of Riccar-
dus Knobbyng de Beccles].[32]

19

Bogomils

Also say that is not allowed to defend one self, that is permissible to the invader to destroy. Also say that earthly power is not allowed to use a sword to execute a sentence of criminals [Döllinger, p. 323].[31]

Lollards

The tenth conclusion is that manslaughter by battle or law of righteousness for temporal cause or spiritual with out special revelation is express contrary to the New Testament, the which is a law of grace and full of mercy [Twelve Conclusions of the Lollards].[33]

The next item shows that the anticlerical vocabulary of the Bogomils, Cathars and Lollards was rich in repetitions — the anger of the heretics generated a vivid language, which traveled almost unchanged across countries and centuries and was later borrowed by the Protestants for their discourse with Rome.

III. ANTICLERICALISM

The official Church seen as a community of Herod, or of the Anti-Christ

Bogomils

They think that Herod is our Church, which tries to murder the Word of Truth born among them [Zigabenus, § 28].[34]

Lollards

Also that Y held, afermit and taght that the pope of Rome is Antechrist, and bisshopes and other prelates ben disciples of Antechrist, and that the pope hath no poar to bynde ne to lose [Abjuration of John Skylly of Flixton].[35]

Church buildings are thought of as synagogues, crossroads or wastelands

Bogomils

They call the churches crossroads and the holy mass and other divine services done in the

Lollards

Also that all material Churches are but synagogues. They have not to be in reverence because churches they treat as wasted words [*Treatise against the Bogomils*].[36]

God hears prayers said in the fields as well as he hears prayers said in such a synagogue [Depositions of John Godesell, parchemyn-maker].[37]

IV. REJECTION OF OFFICIAL CHURCH RITUAL

Negation of transubstantiation
(transformation of the Eucharist into Christ's body)

Bogomils
The eucharist is not commended by God, rather is God's work, as you tell, but is like every other food [*Treatise against the Bogomils*].[38]

Lollards
Also Y held and afermed that no prest hath poar to make Christis body in forme of bred in the sacrament of the auter, and that aftir the sacramental wordys said of a prest at messe they remayneth pure material bred on the auter [Abjuration of John Skylly of Flyxton].[39]

Negation of the crucifix

Bogomils
Because the Jews, crucified on it the son of God, so the cross is really offensive to God. If somebody has killed the son of the king with a cross of wood should this wood be pleasant to the king? [*Treatise against the Bogomils*].[40]

Lollards
And no more worship ne reverence oweth be do to the crosse than oweth be do to the galwes whiche man be hanged on [Depositions of Willelmus Hardy de Mundham, tayllour].[41]

Negation of icons (images) and relics of saints

Bogomils
They do not honor the venerable icons, saying, "call them heathen idols, silver and gold, made by human hand" [Zigabenus, § 14].

Lollards
No honor is due to manifest to any sort of images sculpted in the Churches by human hands [Depositions of John Burrel].[43]

To the relics of the blessed fathers demons are adhering [Zigabenus, § 12].[42]

Also that the relics of the saints are just (mean only) flesh and bones, so no need to be hold in reverence by people [Depositions of John Skylly of Flixton].[44]

Refusal to worship the Virgin and the saints

Bogomils

They do not venerate the glorious and pure Mary, the mother of our God Jesus Christ and say malignant gossips against her [*Treatise against Bogomils*].[45]

Lollards

Also that no honor is due to manifest to any sort of images of the cross, neither to the blessed Mary and to any of the other saints [Depositions of Johannes Reve of Becles].[46]

The great number of coincidences can be enriched even further. The appellation "good man" (boni homini), "good Christian" (boni christiani) is the title of the Perfecti, the spiritual leaders of the Bogomils and Cathars. This address is unique in the whole spectrum of medieval heresies and is typical only of the dualists.

This formula can often be found in the records of the *Heresy Trials in the Diocese of Norwich, 1428–31*. We read that "every good man or good woman is a prest" (p. 142) or, the variant phrase "good Christian man" (p. 153), and, again, the expanded version "every man and every woman being in good lyf" (p. 142). Even the well-known Latin appellation of the leaders of the dualists — *perfecti* — exists in the proceedings of Norwich: the "moost holy and moost *perfit* ... is very pope" (p. 141). Another Latin version is "Item quodlibet bonus Christianus est sacerdos" (p. 177) and the same sentence is also given in English translation: "Also that every good Christene man is a prest" (p. 179). To these the Latin paraphrase "fidelis homo" (p. 205) can be added.

An explanation of this appellation is provided in the proceedings which brings us back to the well-known Bogomil assertion that only the "good people" who have acquired by virtuous moral life the power to be priests should be allowed to teach, because a priest with an imperfect moral life can corrupt his disciples. The defendant Edmund Archer maintains "that every good Christian man is a good prest, and had as muche poar as ony prest ordered, be he a bysshop or a pope" (p. 166). The same assertion can be found in paragraph 2 of the address of the Lollards to Parliament (*Conclusiones Lollardorum*) and is confirmed by Wycliffe: "Also if a bishop or priest is in the state of mortal sin, he can not ordain, neither serve, neither chisten."[47]

In addition to the proceedings of the Norwich Trials, Norman Tanner gives a detailed and convincing reconstruction of the beliefs of the Lollards. He, however, does not comment on the phrase "good man," "good Christian," which might be due to the fact that he was not aware of its specific doctrinal meaning. It is clear that even to the clerks of the Inquisition "good man" had not been very clear, and sometimes they rendered it descriptively. Thus, for example, in the depositions of John Skylly de Flixton we find such a descriptive version of the phrase: "Also that every man who exists in true love is God's priest, and that no priest has a bigger power when administering sacraments in Church than whoever non ordained laic."[48] Here instead of "good man" one comes across the descriptive "homo existens in vera caritate," which echoes precisely the Cathar meaning of the word "caritas" (love). Rene Nelli stresses the lack of "caritas" in the visible world of Satan in which the absence of love causes the annihilation (Fr. neantization) of Satan's creatures.[49]

There exists yet another link between John Skylly's words and Bogomil-Cathar practices. In stressing the spiritual authority of the "whoever non ordained laic" (aliquis laicus non ordinatus) he reproduces the radical position of the Bogomils according to which the clergy is superfluous (Euthymius of Peribleptos). Moreover, in giving the right of women to become *perfecta* (a spiritual leader), the Bogomils, Cathars and Lollards were unique in the Middle Ages for allowing women the same spiritual function as men, an emancipation forerunning the ideas of social equality which appeared much later.

John Thomson proposes a successful interpretation of the appellation "good man": "Some held that every good Christian or a man who was living in charity was a priest of God, and this was carried to its logical conclusion by those who held that the true vicar of Christ was the best man."[50] The author obviously takes the expression literally, without relating it to its continental history. In this way he removes it from its religious context and intuitively reveals the basic cultural characteristics of the heresy, the fact that it enables its followers to abandon to some degree the religious myth by presenting them with an objective of self-perfection, an element anticipating the rise of Renaisssance rationalism.

The rationalist overthrow of the Orthodox ritual as undertaken by the Bogomils is parallel to the rationalist attack of the Lollards against the Catholic Church. There are records proving that among the favorite occupations of the advanced learners were literary and philosophical activities. M. D. Lambert notes the spontaneous formation of reading circles.[51] He mentions as an example the cultivated tastes of Sir Richard Sturry, who "had a copy of *Roman de la Rose* and was acquainted with Chaucer and Froissard."[52] Lambert's list can be continued with the impressive documentation collected by Margaret Deansly in *The Lollard Bible*.[53]

Another comparison is also pertinent in speaking about the rationalism of the heretics. The approach used by the Bogomils for explaining Christ's miracles is similar to the objections raised by the Lollards against the magic scenery of Catholic mass.

Bogomils	*Lollards*
They do not believe that the people were nourished in the desert with five loafs super only. They say these were not loafs but the gospels of the four Evangelists and the fifth — the Acts of the Apostles [*Treatise against the Bogomils*].[54]	That exorcisms and hallowings, made in the church, of wine, bread, and wax, water, salt, oil and incense, the stone of the altar, upon vestment, miter, cross, and pilgrim staffs be the very practice of necromancy rather than of the holy theology [*Conslusiones Lollardorum*].[55]

John Thomson has underlined the rationalist way of thinking of the Lollards, and Norman Tanner has paid attention to the fact that the heretics tried at Norwich "were accusing the Church of using magic, thus reversing the roles played in the trials of witches."[56]

These almost perfect coincidences and astonishing similarities point to the common roots of Bogomilism and Lollardy. Yet, it is surprising that given the well-studied problem concerning the views and beliefs of Lollards, there has been no attempt to trace down their Bogomil-Cathar roots. Here we would like to present the results of our survey and analysis.

First, we should mark the achievement of the brilliant trio A. Veselovski, M. Gaster and I. Franko, dating back to the previous century. In this field it is really they who first formulated the problem of cross-cultural influence.[57] Their achievement deserves to be brought to light again.

It was only in 1960 that M. A. Aston took a step in their direction by trying to discover resemblances between Lollards and Cathars in her study of their social conditions and dissemination: "Lollards, like Catharists and earlier continental heretics, and like friars themselves, flourished along the main roads, and found supporters among the trades people of large towns."[58] The proximity of certain basic Lollard ideas with those of the Bogomils was stressed by M. D. Lambert: "In East England the crucifix was attacked in terms oddly reminiscent of the Bogomils; 'no more credence should be done to the crucifix'[59] it was said, 'than to the gallows which thieves be hanged on.'" This author succeeded in establishing a long line of indirect but real links between the Bulgarian and the English heresies. According to him the heretics described by Eckbert of Schonau are "blended with Bogomil influenced group."[60] Let us recall here the fact that the German-speaking sectarians who landed on the English coast in 1162 have been supposed to be an affiliation of the community mentioned by Eckbert.

Certainly, the movement across countries and ages produced visible distinctions between the views of Lollards and Bogomils. *La couleur locale* is a deviation regarding the origin. Here we shall outline some of those differences.

First, the Bogomil assertion that the world of the Old Testament was the world of Satanael did not appear in Lollard thought. There was a predominant appeal for mercy and denial of bloodshed as motivated in the *Conclusiones Lollardorum* as "expressly contrary to the New Testament" (expresse contraria Novo Testamento).

While the Bogomil and Cathar *perfecti* denied marriage as a carnal continuation of the human race in the material world created by Satanael, the Lollards were not inclined to dogmatic abstinence. They only removed matrimony from among the regulative functions of the church by saying that "only consent of love in Ihu' Christ betuxe man and woman of Christene beleve ys sufficiant for the sacrament of matrimony withoute contract of wordes or solemnisation yn churche."[61] Nor do we find the Bogomil-Cathar restriction to the consumption of meat; rather, the Lollards showed their independence to the official church by saying "that no Cristen peple is bounde to taste in Lenten time, Ymbrin Days, Fridays, vigiles of seyntes ne other tymes which ben commanded of the Churche to be fasted" and even "it is leful ... to ete flesche" as often as appetite comes.[62]

Another local feature can be detected in the replies of some of the defendants in Norwich who asserted that while the sacrifice of Christ is "precious and profitable" the death of St. Thomas is unprofitable.[63] Can this disagreement over the holiness of St. Thomas be read as a sign of the temporal coalition between the Lollards and the royal institution against the papacy?

Cultural Activity of the Bulgarian and English Dualists

Perhaps the most attractive aspect of the heresies was their ability to develop imaginative thinking—both Bogomilism and Lollardy involved their followers in cultural activity which was surprising for the Middle Ages. Catharism was a major creative stream in the Provençal culture of the twelfth century. As different authors have pointed out, the Bogomils "contributed particularly to the advancement and propagation of literacy" (D. Mishev, p. 70); there were schools in practically all of their communities and they loved lecturing (S. Guéorgiev, p. 71). According to D. Angelov, these medieval dissenters were one of the principal intellectual forces that brought about major democratization "of letters and education in Bulgarian society during the 9th–10th centuries."[64]

During the past century V. Jagič concluded that by its intensive effort of copying texts, literary and educational activities and by imbibing the broader views of the apocrypha and views wider than the dualistic tenets, Bogomilism transformed the cultural effort of Simeon's and Climent's age into a popular enlightenment.[65]

Books had a prominent position with Lollards as well. In the records of the Norwich Trials there is ample information that the heretics practiced reading in secret societies or at home, and that many of the texts were translated in English. The Pater Noster, Ave Maria and the Credo were translated into English.[66] Robert Cavel reports that he had seen the heretics "in their private schools" (in scolis privates eorundem).[67]

Margery Baxter, "known as a Lollard and heretic" (notata de lollardia et heresi), mentions a Carmelite friar expounding the gospel in English.[68] According to Norman Tanner, "clearly schools existed in which heresies were taught systematically" (Colchester, London and other places).[69] Malcolm Lambert also treats the Lollards first of all as "a reading community, stimulating self-teaching,"[70] and mentions a small group of "academically trained" Lollards such as Nickolas Hereford, Philip Repton, John Aston and John Purvey, who was Wycliffe's secretary over the last years. More detailed research is necessary to illuminate the relations between this highly educated group and the Lollards of the lower strata. Its presence, however, suggests the existence of a well-developed Lollard culture which had real summits. Given these facts, it is possible to assert that the Bogomil Cathar and Lollard heresies generated important literacy. We can also say that in Bulgaria, France, England, as well as other countries, the heretics brought about cultural innovation and, in our opinion, they can be recognized as one of the driving forces of the Renaissance of the twelfth century.

Anne Hudson mentions a Lollard library, containing three types of books: "schedule," "quaterni" and "libri," though she does not specify their nature because it "can only roughly be asserted from episcopal and chancery records."[71] John Thomson has been less hesitant and has produced, according to Margaret Deansly (another excellent scholar of Lollardy), "an excellent and up-to-date bibliography of all printed and unprinted sources."[72] This is how Thomson describes the collection of James Willis from Chilterns in the mid-fifteenth century: "St Paul's Epistles, the Apocalypse, and St Luke's Gospel." Another Lollard possessed "a book of St John the Evangelist"; there is a reference to a copy of the Epistle of St. James.[73]

Margaret Deansley provides information about a Lincoln Lollard who used the *Nicodemus Gospel* in English.[74] This gnostic book also suggests a Bogomil-Cathar circulation.

Concerning *The Book of St. John the Evangelist* we would like to note that this might be the other title of *The Secret Book* of the Bogomils since *The Secret Book* contains the revelation received by John personally from Jesus Christ. In favor of such supposition is the notice of M. Gaster from a century ago: "The Apostle John, the author of the *Apocalypse*, which answered so well to their system, was the beloved apostle of the Bogomils, and many a book and revelation is ascribed to him."[75]

The culture of the heretics was an open one; the Lollards knew not only the strictly dualist selection of writings. There are numerous references to other texts such as the Old Testament, to a book of Solomon (perhaps Proverbs, or the Song of Songs as John Thomson suggests), a copy of Tobit, and so on. John Thomson mentions also perfectly orthodox books and that one suspect person owned a copy of the *Canterbury Tales*.

The heretics' affinity for books emerges as one of the inherent characteristics of their culture, accounting for their poetic feeling and rich imagination. According to A. Galahov, "the apocrypha were overflowing with poetic details and answers to most curious questions."[76] M. Gaster has observed that for their imaginative minds, "the Biblical story becomes a biblical romance: truth and fiction are inextricably mixed."[77] This is a sure mark of individual interpretation. Bogomils, Cathars and Lollards were not simply literate but were aware of the creative dimension of literature.

Let us at this point sum up the cultural similarities which have been discussed. First, the literature of the Lollards, no matter how scanty the information about it, coincides in its principal titles with the literary heritage of the Bogomils and Cathars. Second, the aspiration of the Lollards to read and preach in English (lingua Anglicana) made translation one of their major occupations, which was an important contribution to their national culture. The culmination of this process was reached with Wycliffe's translation of the New Testament, a turning point marking the official recognition of the English language as an ecclesiastical tongue. The heretical inspiration behind Wycliffe's efforts can be detected also in his translation of the well-known gnostic *Evangelium Nicodemi*. J. Gairdner quotes the exclamation of a chronicler of that time: "This Master Wycliffe translated into the English, not angelic tongue the gospel (in anglica linguam, non angelicam)."[78] In this way the Scriptures could be administered "to the laymen and infirm persons according to the requirements of the time and their individual wants and mental hunger."[79]

This, in our opinion, is a major achievement of the heretics on a European scale: almost everywhere they translated the New Testament into the vernacular, adding to it the apocrypha, and thus helping the processes of formation of a national literary language, the new letters for the laymen. Thus for instance, Provençal became so subtle and rich that Dante was deeply impressed by its beauty and wrote sonnets in it.

One of the successful attempts to place the English biblical translations in their European context was undertaken by Margaret Deanesly in 1920 in her impressive work *The Lollard Bible*. She compares the early English versions of the Scriptures with the translations of the French, Italian, German and Flemish heretics (see the appendix to this chapter). Her approach is authoritative particularly given that at the beginning of the fourteenth century the famous inquisitor Bernard Gui had registered in his manual *Practica Inquisitionis* that the translations into the vernacular were the most certain way of unveiling the heretical activities of Cathars, Waldenses and Beguins.[80] About the Cathars he writes that "they read the Evangelia and the Epistles in the vernacular" (legunt the evangeliis et de epistolis in vulgari).[81] The remark about the Waldenses reads: "they possess commonly the Evangelia and the Epistles in the vernacular" (Habent autem evangelia et epistolas in vulgari communiter).[82] Similarly, the Beguins are referred to as users of the vernacular though their books are not differentiated: "the mentioned Beguins have the books of Brother Petrus Johannis put into popular language" (habent libri ... ex latino transpositos in vulgari).[83] The practice of the Lollards to "teach God's precepts in English" (precepte Dei in lingua anglicana)[84] resembles closely practices described by Inquisitor Gui, who could hardly imagine that his notes would ever become the object of a comparativist study.

The spiritual awakening brought about the heretics had another important behavioral consequence — in the atmosphere of cultural revival there began a process of an initial awakening of the interest in human personality.

The leading personalities among the heresiarchs have been remembered in history along with sovereigns, conquerors and the fathers of the Church — Bogomil, Jeremiah, Nikita (the leading person at the Council of Saint-Felix de Carman), Jean de Luglio, John Wycliffe, and Jan Huss. They define the prototype of the human being who has found realization by his free thought and creativity. Malcolm Lambert's observations concerning England speak of the impulse of the Lollard "to search out the truths of Scripture for himself" by way of which the individual acquires the ability of self-teaching.[85] The first step is to inculcate the primary aphorisms and gradually, when becoming more learned, to make one's way to interpretation, ask questions and find answers. The way in which Lollards attracted new sympathizers and guided them to the depths of knowledge is similar to the one practised by the Bogomils and described by Euthimius Peribleptos (early eleventh century). They first gave a small piece of their knowledge to the neophyte and they increased the portion until they revealed the full scope of their knowledge.[86]

The heretic Margery Baxter presents a case in point, as her statements, eloquence, and the richness of her language all testify to the high quality of Lollard culture.

Given the vast scope of the problem, it might be helpful to suggest the directions in which more research needs to be done.

First, in spite of the work dedicated to Wycliffe and his ideas, as yet no detailed and convincing explanation of the origins of his dualistic views has been given. It will also be interesting to look into the durable interest of Sir Thomas More in the heretics sustained under the cover of a controversy with them.[87]

Second, the profound knowledge of the accused Margery Baxter of Martham of dualistic myths should direct attention to the higher level of Lollard culture, the translation of numerous apocrypha in English, a layer of literature left almost without scholarly attention for many years. It is enough just to mention the influence of the *Nicodemus Gospel* on *The Vision of Piers Plowman* and the miracle plays.

Finally, an endeavor that deserves to be undertaken is the elucidation of the problem of the Lollard contribution to the Reformation, where "by the time that the Roman establishment was succeeded by the Anglican, the Lollardy was developing into Puritanism"[88] (Max Weber has stressed the importance of Protestant ethics for the development of capitalism and its social role).

The material discussed in this chapter seems to suggest as a final conclusion that Bogomilism, the Bulgarian spiritual ferment, in its indirect and modified ways left a mark on the spiritual climate of England in fourteenth and fifteenth centuries.

Appendix to Chapter 1:
Cathars and Waldenses

According to M. Deanesly, the Waldenses were the first to start translating the Scriptures and the Cathars "borrowed from them a devotion to the study of vernacular versions of the Bible."[89] In return, the Waldenses should have adopted from the Cathars the "consolamentum." This view contains two inaccuracies. The first is that the Waldenses did not practice the consolamentum. The second, and more important, is the assigning of the priority of the translation into the vernacular to the Waldenses, since the Cathars historically and culturally precede them. Waldo started preaching at the very end of the twelfth century, while at the Council of Saint-

Felix de Caraman in 1167 the relations between the numerous and well-established Cathar sects were settled. The Cathars did not translate the whole Bible, but especially the New Testament, which they considered their spiritual guide.

Attention should be paid to one very significant detail, which is mentioned by many authors. The prayer Pater Noster (Matt. 6) in its Cathar version ends with the words: "For thine is the kingdom, and the power, and the glory, for ever. Amen." This phrase is missing in the Vulgate.

C. Schmidt explains this as follows: "The biblical versions that were in Cathar service in Italy and in France were translated not after the Vulgate, but from an original Greek text — the same which was used for the Slavonic version accomplished by Cyril and Methodius. The apocrypha that came in the Cathar sect were again of a Greek provenance."[90] The same conclusion is reached by Y. Ivanov.[91] C. Schmidt and N. Ossokin, backed up by other historians, remind us that some of the *perfecti*, the Cathar leaders, were highly educated people who knew Greek and Hebrew. Waldo did not know Greek, nor is there any information that any of his disciples did.

CHAPTER 2

Traces of the Bogomil Movement in the English Language

The Linguistic History of the Word "Bugger"

A traditional way of checking how far a certain phenomenon has become involved with the history of a given country is to see whether that phenomenon has left any traces in its language. In our case the answer is simply yes — there is such a word as "bugger" in the English language, a transformation of the French *bougre*, as the Cathar heretics in Southern France were called. The *Oxford English Dictionary* also quotes other variants of "bugger," as well as "buggerie," which is connected with the first entry. The whole lexical nest includes "bowgard, bouguer, buggerage, buggerer, buggar, buggeress and buggerly." "Buggery" also has several forms: "bugery," "buggerey," *-arie,* -one, "boggery," "bowgery," "bockery" and so on. This chapter deals with the topical meaning of "bugger"— a sodomite (a buggery — sodomy), particularly as it is also a legal term or, to quote the *OED*, "In decent use only as a legal term."

Naturally, this most prestigious dictionary of the English language also provides the etymology of the word "bugger": "Bugger. Also bowgard, bouguer (ancient French — bougre): Latin — Bulgarus, Bulgarian, a name given to a sect of heretics who came from Bulgaria in the llth c., afterwards to the other 'heretics' (to whom abominable practices were ascribed), also to usurers."[1] The correct statement is also added that, in the said medieval period, "the name was particularly applied to the Albigenses."

This valuable reference, however, is mainly left for limited academic usage, while the popular usage of "bugger" continues as a legal term for sodomite (as a technical term in criminal law — to quote the *OED*). In addition, this reliable information is not always given in the academic circles themselves. For example, *The Oxford Dictionary of English Etymology* quotes a similar form — "bowgard" (and "bouguer"), but claims that the Bulgarians were heretics "as belonging to the Greek Church, sp. Albigensian."[2] This is a serious mistake, because the Greek and the Albigensian churches have never been connected. What is more, if one follows the logic of events, the Albigensian church is a sort of opponent of the Greek one insofar as the Albigensians are genetically linked with the Bogomils who, in turn, are against the Orthodox (Greek) church on principle. A similar confusion of the Bulgarian Bogomil church and the Greek (Orthodox) church can also be found in *Webster's Third New International Dictionary*, where the word "bugger" is given only with the meaning of sodomite, "from the adherence of the Bulgarians to the Eastern Church considered heretical."[3] It is true that the Catholics accuse the Orthodox Church of heresy and vice versa — Catholics are considered a kind of heretics by Orthodoxy — but this controversy between the two official churches has nothing to do with the Bogomils and the Cathars, that is, with "the bougres," "the buggers."

Therefore, we are faced with the task of confirming the historically correct meaning of the word "bugger" ("bougre") as a variant of the national name Bulgarian; and determining what religious and political circumstances have loaded it with negative twisted meanings.

If the results of this study prove convincing, it is within the scope of the ability of English linguists and lawyers to restitute the initial meaning of "bugger" and, in the name of the new era of global communication, to free the Bulgarian national name of the hostile imagery of past antagonistic ages. There is natural evidence in this respect. In French, for example, the negative connotations of *bougre*, imposed by the Inquisition have been swallowed by the positive evolution of the same word with the meaning of "brave (or good) fellow." One finds a similar line of evolution in the English language, preserving almost the same meanings of "bugger." To quote *The Oxford English Dictionary*, there exist "often, however, in English dialect and in U.S., simply = 'chap,' 'customer,' 'fellow.'" It is interesting to reconstruct this cultural and historical development and the region and social strata which outlined it. One can assume that French linguistic practice has shed the negative connotations imposed on *bougres* because the French have reconsidered their attitude to the Cathars with the passage of time, perceiving them as the carriers of a highly developed (for the Middle Ages) civilization.[4] On the other hand, arriving in England under the negative stamp of the Inquisition, this word was locked in the artificially acquired negative meaning and the mass conscience lost its real history, nor did it have occasion to restore it.

To the best of my knowledge, the first, more comprehensive attempt to restore the historical truth in England was made by Moses Gaster in 1887. Quoting C. S. Faber, he wrote: "'Boggard' a Northern provincial appellation of a foul fiend evidently resolves itself into *Bulgard, or* Bulgarian, the very common designation *of the Albigenses,* whose dealing with Satan was notoriously a general belief."[5] As was already mentioned, in the next century *The Oxford English Dictionary* marked the connection of "bougres/buggers" or "heretics who came from Bulgaria in the 11th century" with "Albigenses" (Cathars). It is also pointed out that, according to R. Brunne Cron. of 1330, "bugger" entered the English language with the double meaning of sodomite and heretic: "þe Kyng said & did crie, þe pape was heretike ... and lyued in bugerie." The combination "þe bougre and þe heretike" is found in Ayenb. of 1340.[6] It is important that the *OED* admits that sodomy was ascribed to the heretics. The dictionary of Funk & Wagnalls uses a slightly stronger word to show the imposition of foreign meaning on "bugger": "Bulgarian heretics to whom abominable practices were imputed."[7] But it was Eric Partridge who finally pointed out the truth — that the "bougres" or Bulgarian heretics were vilified. He showed how "bugger" originated "from ML Bulgarus, a Bulgar, hence a heretic and, *by lay slander,* a sodomite"[8] (italics mine).

Who was the author of this slander? After the first two marches against the Cathars, undertaken by Pope Innocent III and the Northern French kingdom in the beginning of the 13th century, the populace of Provence and Northern Italy sympathized with the victims because of their education and moral purity. It was then, too, that the Catholic clergy launched a vilifying campaign against them.[9]

Why were the poor bougres, persecuted and burned at the stake, also presented as sodomites? Since the heretics and particularly their leaders were paragons of virtue and the fact that they did not spare themselves or their strict moral conduct was noticed by most of their contemporary chroniclers, an arbitrary allegation had to be found which could fire the imagination of the uneducated ordinary people by ignominious means so that they would substitute their admiration for complete denial. The psychological mechanism of this scheme seems well planned.

Yes, the Cathars, whose name means "pure" in Greek, were people who seemingly had no human weakness because they had given up the ways of the sinful world, like eating meat or shedding blood. Ordinary people thought of them as living saints capable of working miracles. But, the propaganda of the Catholic Church specified, the Cathars denied the carnal relations between people because they had such with animals.[10] But no one had seen such a thing, nor is there evidence of such actions. No one had seen it, the ecclesiastic "interpreters" explained again, because the Cathars fornicated secretly, in the night. And it was that fornication which wore them out, not the fast and prayer to which they claimed to have dedicated themselves.

Many authors including one of the most famous scholars of Catharism, Charles Schmidt, have pointed out that the church frequently resorted to calumny in dealing with the heresies. It is strange that in the past it was even taken up by creative personalities who were familiar with the depths of heretic philosophy, such as Joachim of Fiore. Nevertheless, objective scholars like Lev Karsavin, who had no personal sympathies for the Cathars and considered them a force destructive to medieval Christian civilization, wrote quite frankly: "It is not by chance that, beginning with Bernard of Clairvaux, many writers, saints, prelates and monks tried to discredit the morality of the heretics and spread rumours of how they sinned during their nightly gatherings. And if these allegations are few, this only proves one thing — their complete groundlessness."[11]

Therefore, the conclusion that comes to mind is that the word "bugger" entered the English language in the first third of the 14th century as an echo of the negative campaign the Catholic Church had launched in Southern France against *les bougres*, the Cathar heretics. That is why neither the Englishmen of the Middle Ages nor those that live today perceive it as the national name "Bulgarian" but as a negative epithet, frozen in signifying a perversion. It has undergone the greatest deformation in comparison to other words whose initial meaning was shifted when they entered the context of heretical culture. In 1931 J. L. Seifert gave two examples which confirm the pattern of such a shift. He pointed out that the national name "Fleming" (flamendr) entered the Czech language during the international heretical communications and remained there with the distorted meaning of "singer," while in the 16th century the word "Waldenses" (Vaudois) began to acquire the meaning of "sorcerer" under the influence of the mixing of late trends in the Waldensian heresy with subcultural phenomena like alchemy and astrology.[12] An additional, secondary designation of "bugger" as a result, as an echo of those events, can also be seen in the fact that in those times the usurers in Provence and Lombardy were called "bougres."

Hidden Identity

The logic of the linguistic quest presupposes another question: isn't there any other indirect trace connected with this or another encounter of the island with the dualistic heresy? Should one open *The Oxford English Dictionary* at the entry of "publican," one will find information about such an earlier arrival of a heresy on British soil in 1160. The evidence is provided by William of Newburgh (Guillelmus Novoburgensis) and is interpreted by Stephen Runciman and Milan Loos. It is the result of the wave which spread from Germany and was recorded there by Eckbert, Abbot of Schonau. A group of some 30 uneducated people who denied baptism, marriage, the Eucharist and Catholic unity and were led by one Gerhard came to England — these people William of Newburgh calls "publicani."[13] Stephen Runciman further adds that in 1167, heretics with the name of Poplicani or Deonarii were caught in Burgundy and tried in Vezelay on the charges that they denied the cross, holy water, churches, donations, marriage and the holy orders.[14]

Finding that the heretical group of "publicani" which arrived in England was related to Flemish and Burgundian heretical communities, Runciman has in fact pointed out the two main channels by which heretics and, more important, heretical apocrypha would again come to the island over the next two centuries. Those were actually the Flemish-German and French (Norman-Burgundian) ways of influence. But Runciman also cared to reveal the root of the name "publicani" or "poplicani," suggesting that this is a Latinized phonetic transcription of the Greek word for Paulicians. The Western followers of the heresy came into direct contact with one of the sources in Constantinople where the resident Paulicians presented the strictly dualistic or Dragovitsa branch of the Bogomil church.[15] And, according to Stephen Runciman and the majority of the scholars, it was the dualists from Constantinople who were among the propagators of the heresy in that period.

The view that the Cathars were called "poblicans" in Northern France and England was voiced as early as 1849 by the outstanding scholar Charles Schmidt, who also quoted a list of old chroniclers who mentioned that name.[16] Some of them are given in Du Cange's *Glossarium*. The latter notes the appearance of "popelicani" as early as 1017, while the *Chronicle* of Rodulphus Coggeshalensis from the time of Louis VII (1137–1180) says that it was thus that the "popular tongue" called the heretics who had spread to many parts of France.[17] At the Third Lateran Council of 1179 quoted by Du Cange, the names of the heretics Cathars, Patrenes (Patarenes) and Publicani were placed next to one another, with the explanation that they had spread in Albi, Toulouse and elsewhere.[18] From *Magna Chronica Belgica* of 1208, again after Du Cange, we learn that the Popelicani professed both principles, that is, they were dualists.

Among modern scholars, Stephen Runciman's opinion is shared by Femand Niel[19] and particularly by Borislav Primov, who pays special attention to this matter. Although he uses Du Cange's *Glossarium* most frequently, he has sufficient reason to conclude that all the forms of "Publicani," "Populicani," "Poblicani" and "Popelicani" originate from the Latin name of the Paulicians — "Pauliciani."[20] The Dragovitsa Paulician church around Plovdiv,[21] known for its extreme dualism, was a sort of rival in the infiltration of the Bulgarian Bogomil Church to the West. With time, regardless of the theoretical discussions between the adherents to the moderate (Bulgarian Bogomil Church) and the extreme (Dragovitsa Church) dualism, in western Europe the two religious communities began to be perceived as variants of one phenomenon — Catharism — both communities indicating that Bulgaria was the original source of that heresy.

Back on British territory, one sees that while the word "bugger" was pushed back because of its derogatory deformation of meaning, the heretics who found firmer foothold in England under the name of "publicans" and later on, maybe bearing in mind the tragic continental fate of the "bougres" (the annihilation of the Cathar civilization in Southern France), succeeded in adopting an aspect more acceptable to the Church in England. Although one could object that at the end of the 12th century it was "Publicans" who were tried, branded and chased out of Oxford, it seems that after several decades of persecution they contrived various means of adaptation and mimicry which to a certain extent led the heretic communities out of the sphere of direct conflict with the ecclesiastic power. A case in point is the fact that the heretics managed to "change" to a definitely positive aspect the etymology of their name by a skilfully translated parable from the New Testament.

To this end the Cathars and the "Publicans" used Christ's parable of the Pharisee and the publican (tax collector) (Luke 18:10–14), while the publican with his unpopular profession honestly admitted to his sins in the temple, the Pharisee placed himself closer to God and above the others. Christ condemned such hypocrisy and pointed out that the humble publican had greater chances for God's mercy. Identifying themselves with the publican (*publicanus* in the Latin translation of the New Testament), the "Popelicani" or "Publicans" succeeded in symbolically placing their much-suffering heads under the protective force of Christ's preference. At the same time, by the logic of this interpretation, their persecutors (inquisitors, Dominicans and bishops) proved in the place of the Pharisees. This comparison was used even in southern France, but there it was rather a means of polemizing than of mimicry. There is just such a quotation by the famous 14th century inquisitor Bernard Gui, who has recorded how the Cathars from southern France called their persecutors from the Catholic Church Pharisees and saw themselves in the position of the persecuted Christ and the apostles: "[they think] they take the place of the apostles ... and that they are good people and good Christians, persecuted just as Christ and his apostles were persecuted by the Pharisees."[22]

There are also facts indicating one of the ways in which this approach was transferred to England. It was frequently used by Guillaume de Saint-Amour (1202–1272), rector of Paris University, in his epic struggle against the tidewater of Catholic orders in the emancipated University of Paris. One finds that a sermon of his, reprinted four centuries later by an English Reformation publication, had the objective of using "old authors" to expose the "mistakes and malpractices of the Roman Church."[23]

The dauntless Guillaume de Saint-Amour, to whose courageous struggle nearly a whole chapter of the *Roman de la Rose* is dedicated, called his opponents from the religious orders "falsely pious" who loved the loftiness, fame, vanity, showiness and bows addressed to them. At the same time the "publicans" were presented as "men of the world who, even if they are sinners" do not pretend they are saints and admit to their sins. That Guillaume de Saint-Amour was familiar with Cathar mythology is also indicated by the following passage in the same sermon. He points out that the clerical Pharisees had become pseudo-apostles, just as the angel Satan was transfigured into an angel of light (angelum lucis, i.e., Lucifer).[24] This could be the shortest version of the Bogomil legend about the fall of Satan and at the same time a purely Bogomil-Cathar hint that the earthly order (including that of the church) was established by Satan.

This hereticized (or at least deviating from the canon) parable became a popular image in English literature: Wycliffe used it in his sermons; it is mentioned in the *Chronicle* of 1340 (Ayenb. 175) quoted above which speaks of "þe bougre and þe heretike," and the same sermon is mentioned by Chaucer. In its traditional and untraditional interpretation, the underscored image of the publican was used by Shakespeare, Robertson, Milton and Bunyan. In other words, when one looks at the respective page of the *OED* one sees that the publicistic-imagery meaning of this word has prevailed, its more frequent usage being connected with that anti-Catholic and Reformist spirit with which it had once been loaded by the "publicani" heretics in Southern France. This is a linguistic reflection of the ostensible change of identity with which the old "publicani" or "popelicani" covered their Catharo-Paulician origin and presented themselves as followers of the publican from the Gospel of St. Luke.

Thus the names "bugger" (Bulgarian) and "publican" (Paulician), which respectively started from the Bulgarian Bogomil Church and the Paulician (Dragovitsa) dualist Church near Plovdiv — in both cases from Bulgarian territory — traveled the long route through Bosnia, Dalmatia, Northern Italy, France, Germany and Flanders to be taken to the island and adopted by the English language with those changes, even distortions, which the long and difficult journey had imposed on them. The reconstruction of the cultural epic is a humanist task: in this way one leaves the layer of meaning imposed by the rule of the stronger (which is always deforming) and reveals the cultural and civilizational synthesis of ideas and conduct which took place during the Middle Ages, perceived as the age of introversion. In our case, the depth of philosophical ideas, the rich imagery and inventive discussion indicate that dialogue between cultures is a historical law. That that law today becomes a calling of mankind and that the real connection between the "ego" and the "other" is in the mutual revealing of their spiritual essence. Sooner or later this will happen — a stand which Tsvetan Todorov aptly defends in his well-known book *La conquête de l'Amérique: La question de l'autre* (1982). A similar kind of retrospection is applicable not only to the space that is external to Europe, but also within that of its own history. Thus the chronicle of some tragic centuries is substituted for, or at least complemented with its alternative —

the resurrection even today of important quests of the spirit which, one must say, were even then expressed in a surprisingly rational form.

Appendix to Chapter 2:
The Good Name of Bogomils and Cathars

The opinion of serious scholars coincides with the conclusions of L. P. Karsavisn about the moral purity of those heretics. Such is the stand of C. Schmidt and now N. Osokin; to sum up: "Even in the eyes of the strictest moral judgment the Cathars would be worthy of the name they have chosen for themselves" (in Greek *katharoi* = pure ones).[25] A whole list of recorded observations can be provided in this respect. First Euthymius of Akmonia (after 1034) wrote that the ungodly Bogomil leader Churila preached "He who does not leave his wife cannot be saved" and that, in addition, the heretics "teach the men to leave their wives and the women to leave their own men." It seems that to invalidate such asceticism Euthymius of Akmonia accused Churila of "raping a maiden in some abandoned mill." In his famous *Panoplia dogmatica* (the beginning of the 12th century) Euthymius Zigabenus described how strictly the Bogomils kept the fast. In addition to the Fast of Lent, they "on the second and the fourth day and the Friday of every week fast right up to the ninth hour." To throw a shadow on the strict conduct of the Bogomils and without quoting any facts, Zigabenus in turn makes the publicistic remark: "If, however, someone invites them to dine they immediately forget their instructions and eat like elephants. Hence it is clear that they also behave outrageously, although they denounce fornication as if they were without flesh and body." We find the same approach in Presbyter Cosmas (10th century). On the one hand he admits the ascetic self-denial of the Bogomils from this world and its pleasures: "they declare themselves inhabitants of the heavens and the men who marry and live in the world they call servants of Mammon." On the other, however, Cosmas did not miss the opportunity for an insinuating remark — without, of course, quoting facts — when he calls their fast "hypocritical": "Actually the heretics are like sheep: meek, submissive and quiet. Their faces are seemingly pale with the hypocritical fast."[26]

I quote two of the more popular Western sources: Salve Burce's description and that of inquisitor Bernard Gui. In 1235 Salve Burce wrote: "The Cathars say that marriage on Earth is fornication, that the bad god, the Devil, has ordered so."[27] Bernard Gui (early 14th century) describes how the Cathars keep strict fast and, in addition to the regular fasts: "the whole year they fast on bread and water three days a week.... Also they do not touch any woman."[28] There is no attempt at calumny in these documents and the facts are given as they are. In Salve Burce one finds an important detail which, either because of misunderstanding or because of the intentions of Catholic propaganda, served as the basis for a rumor against the Cathars.

The Cathars believed that they were children of the Good God, and it follows from this that they considered themselves brothers and sisters, members of one spiritual family. That was why they thought that cohabitation with one's own wife was equal to incest with one's mother or daughter.[29] It is with exactly this interpretation that Raynier Sacconi, for example, speculated. With the zeal of a renegade (a former heresiarch) he did not hesitate to use for anti–Cathar propaganda the twisted claim that "both men and women have no fear of having intercourse with a sister or a brother of theirs ... etc."[30] Still, considering the good name the Cathars enjoyed among the population, Sacconi stipulates that some of the Cathars did not do that because they were ashamed.

Until the end of the 14th century the populace in southern France retained the strong memory of the high morals of the Cathars, particularly of their leaders — the "perfect" (perfecti).[31] Jean Duvernoy quotes a number of opinions of ordinary people, recorded and published in his *Régistre de Jean Fournier.* A farmer who was led out of the secret Cathar meeting (around 1303) because he seemed slightly suspicious exclaimed: "But, sir, I too want to receive my part of the Good!"[32] Another 14th century exclamation has been recorded: "Since the heretics were chased from Sabartes there is no longer good weather in the area."[33] This is followed by the emotional statement that after the heretics were driven away "the land does not produce anything good."[34] Jean Duvernoy also quotes another document, dating from around the year 1300 — the "Régistre de Geoffroy d'Ablis" (Paris, Bibl. Nat., ms. Lat. 4269, f 16v) in which a similar belief has been recorded that the Cathars brought happiness and plenty and that one could not do evil on the day one had seen one of the perfects. Sometimes the goodness of the Cathars was given natural dimensions. A notary from Soual (Tarnes) says: "When the heretics lived in these lands we did not have so many storms or lightning. Now that we are with Franciscans and Dominicans the lightning strikes more frequently."

A similar collection of examples of the good deeds of the Cathars is provided by Richard Abels and Ellen Harrison in their study "The Participation of Women in Languedocian Catharism."[35] One of them, however, is particularly interesting in our case. The following has been recorded in the famous MS 609 (f 157v) about one of the witnesses with Catholic orientation: "he never believed that the heretics were 'good men'; he believed, however, that their works were good, even their faith was bad" (credebat quod heretici numquam fuerunt boni homines; opera tamen eorum credebat esse bona et fidem malam).

There are truly cases when the intellectual subtlety of denying marriage by comparing it to incest was sometimes wrongly interpreted by later deformed imitators. They were not familiar with the rich philosophy of Catharism and gave a more primitive expression of their anticonformism. Johannes Hartmann (1367) claimed that incest with mothers and sisters was allowed "because just as the calves were given for food to the people, women are given for the use of free spirits."[36] These, however, were no longer Cathars but the sect of free spirits. Finally, it is only fair to note the case of Belibaste (14th century) who really was known for his penchant for the flesh, although those were times when the Cathar church had already been destroyed by persecution and the self-control which the perfect strictly kept between themselves was no longer possible.

The spiritual purity of the Bogomils and the Cathars remains a high moral example for an age during which the dissipated clergy was extremely embarrasing to medieval society. Presbyter Cosmas used strong words against the "laziness and ignorance of the shepherds" and upbraided the Orthodox priests that they sheared their flock without caring about it.[37] Pope Innocent III sent special scorching letters and punished the steeped-in-corruption Catholic clergy in southern France. The rigorism of the "perfect" (Bogomil and Cathar leaders) was so consistent that they themselves were aware it could not be achieved by their ordinary audience. That was why the Cathar community allowed those ordinary people to have a family and live in the world within the limits of the rules in the Scripture. It was in fact the Bogomil-Cathar purity which attracted enthusiastic followers of the heresy, for they saw in it the opportunity to begin a spiritually dedicated, undivided and morally ennobled life.

CHAPTER 3

The Heresy and Women

Women's Emancipation
and the Bogomils

During the 12th century, if not slightly earlier, western Europe lived through a period of economic and social upheaval, termed by many historians the 12th century Renaissance. One of its aspects is the considerable emancipation of women, mostly in southern France, a development which spread to Italy, Flanders, and later, England. One can detect social zones where real emancipation was achieved. These were created in the socio-economic climate of the Cathar communities who followed heretical dualist ideas. Similar developments can be observed among the Waldenses, who were generically close to Cathar ideas. It is important to remember that the dualist streak came from Bulgaria, cutting across to the west through Bosnia, Dalmatia and northern Italy. One of the most important characteristics of the Bulgarian dualists, Bogomils and Paulicinians alike, was the complete social liberation of women.

Bogomilism has attracted much scholarly attention, but new research has come up with new questions — especially those concerned with the status of women. As we know, women achieved a high degree of emancipation in this movement.

This fact will be examined through consideration of a particular element of Bogomil theology and social practice, and by tracing some of the paths of transmission of these developments to western Europe.

Bulgarian heretics had a different conception of woman compared to official religion — they did not regard her as Adam's rib, nor as a creature inferior to man, nor as an object for material and sexual domination. This difference underlies the central myth of Bogomil heresy, according to which the human soul was an angel of God placed within its mortal clay wrapping of a body by scheming Satan. That is why the idea of spiritual growth among the Bogomils required a complete ascetic denial of this world, which was imagined as a secondary creation of Satan, not God; such was the way of returning to the heavenly realms of the Good Father/the Good God. By entering an evolution of purification in the form of strict asceticism, the adepts were offered the chance to "divest" themselves of their bodies as if the latter were merely clothes (stola), and thus set their souls free at the moment of the body's death. The body would remain on earth as ashes and would never be resurrected.

The Bogomil myth contains some remote echoes of the imagined greater responsibility of woman for the fall. According to it, women are incarnations of the souls of "angels of the second heaven" (angelo secundi coeli),[1] while men have incorporated the souls of the "angels of the first heaven" (angelo primi coeli). But all in all, the basic aspiration of the Bogomils to abandon everything pertaining to the material world (omnia corporalia and visibilia),[2] created by Satan (Lucifer), and get back to the real, yet invisible one, of things spiritual (omnia spiritualia et invisibilia), places both men and women in the same position of being able to deny earthly materialism.

This theologically motivated equality was supported by an equality in ritual — women had the right to be ordained and give absolution. In a word, women had the right to be spiritual leaders, which has always been a bone of contention for the Orthodox and Catholic clergy. Here is an early testimony of such a reaction coming from Presbyter Cosmas, an anti–Bogomil polemicist: "The heretics absolve themselves, though they are tied up with devilish fetters. This is done not only by the men but by the women also, which is most damnable."[3]

The equality of men and women also finds expression in the fact that women were allowed to become leaders, a role traditionally occupied by men; men, on their part, were granted the spiritual ability to give birth to God's Word, the Logos, which enabled them to adopt the position of Mothers. According to the Bogomils, both women and men could be Mothers of God's Word (theotokoi, in Greek).

Dimitar Angelov, the well-known scholar of Bogomilism, often comments on the high status of women.[4] A good example is the story of the heretic leader Irina of Thessaloniki, who lived in the 15th century.[5]

We are not trying to suggest that the genesis of the idea of women's equality is Bulgarian. The Bogomils inherited it from the Manicheans through the mediation of the Paulicinians. Yet unlike the Manicheans, who kept their teaching secret, locked in small, closed elite groups, this belief became a wide social practice among the Bogomils, who brought it later to the West. The civilizational aspect of this attitude can hardly be overestimated, for women were not just introduced to the sacrament of the religious ritual, but were given access to working with the Word, thereby achieving the full scope of their culture's potential. Their participation in an activity traditionally reserved exclusively for males is strikingly modern and marks the emergence of a humanistic streak in cultural and social behavior, a striking feature prominent in the practices of the Cathars of Provence and the Lollard circles in England.

In a dissertation defended in Lausanne in 1920, Archimandrite Stephan Gúeorgiev describes the collective discussion of sermons and apocrypha typical of the Bogomils. The Bogomil longing for the depths of literacy (as Presbyter Cosmas ironizes the heretics) includes women without any restriction. The bishop-monks Leonce and Clement, who had Bogomil convictions, were accused in Cappadocia (1143) during an official trial of allowing women-heretics to "read the holy gospels and to officiate together with Clement." As if this was not enough, these women were ordained as deaconesses by the same Leonce and Clement (see the appendix to this chapter).

This new reality, in the long run, brought about important changes, both in the Orthodox and, particularly, in the Catholic tradition. The impact of Bogomil practices was for the first time brought into focus by Stefan Lazarov, who noted that the Bogomils "encouraged even their enemies to think in a broader, more humane way in the sphere of art."[6] A significant change concerned the representation of the Holy Virgin, in both the Orthodox and Catholic traditions, a change caused by the impact of the popularity of the Bogomil conceptions of the place of women.

A basic Bogomil tenet is that all souls can be saved, so there is no need of the Day of Judgment. Such an idea seriously invalidates the power of the Orthodox and Catholic churches, which curb disobedience by threatening the sinners with the eternal fires of hell. Under the pressure of Bogomil ideas, the Church felt the need to introduce some degree of mitigation of such eternal punishment to prevent the growing sympathy toward the more merciful heretics. A degree of mildness was introduced into the system by borrowing an idea whose origins were in heretical literary imagery. The Orthodox Church started to propagate the apocryphal (better described as noncanonical) tale of *The Descent of the Holy Virgin*. This story, as Moses Gaster and others point out, is an imitation of the apocalyptic books written in defense of the Bulgarian dualists, especially *Visio Paoli* and *The Descent of Christ into Hell*.[7] In the same manner in which Apostle Paul descends into hell to describe the torments of the sinners (such as corrupt clergymen who persecuted heretics), the Holy Virgin is made to visit the underworld. Stirred by the suffering of the sinners, she asks her son Jesus Christ to give them some respite, from Maundy Thursday to Pentecost. The reinforcement of the female principal in the official Christian myth was the answer, or rather, the adaptation of the Orthodox Church to the conditions of the contest for women's emancipation so powerfully apparent in Bogomil spiritual and social life.

In the first part of this chapter we defined three major elements, rooted in the practices of Bogomils, which suggest a new place for women in society: full participation in religious ritual; the right to engage in literary activities; and a changed attitude of the official church regarding women, brought about by their emancipation in Bogomil communities. The heresies which followed in the wake of the Bulgarian heretical tradition preserved these three elements until, in the south of France, new opportunities for cultural realization appeared and brought about new modifications in the position of the official church.

Women in Catharo-Provençal Civilization

The place of women in Cathar communities in the south of France has been well studied. A few monographs deserve special mention; among them are the two volumes by Jean Guiraud,[8] which pay considerable attention to Cathar women. Koch's monograph[9] (1962) has also been of great use to the present study. R. Nelli's book *La vie quotidienne des Cathares au Languedoc au XIIIe siècle* (1969),[10] devotes an entire chapter to women. Le Roy Ladurie (1975) has also collected interesting empirical data about the social life of women under Cathar influence.[11] In 1979 R. Abels and Ellen Harrison published an excellent article, "The Participation of Women in

Languedocian Heresy,"[12] which is undoubtedly the best work in the field. One of the latest studies is Anne Brenon's *Les Femmes cathares* (1992).[13] Clearly, the problem has been studied in some depth, yet the empirical material also lends itself to interpretations somewhat different from those offered so far.

Starting with Ms 609 and having considered other sources as well, Abels and Harrison give the following figures concerning the number of women perfectae: "the ratio between sightings perfecti and perfectae would still have been three to one,"[14] and further, that "of 719 heretical ministers named in Ms 609, 318, or slightly less than 45% were women."[15] The authors apply the term perfectae-class, which suggests the existence of an identifiable, stable body of people. There is proof that the perfectae functioned among the women of the community and that, when there were no perfecti at hand, the women had the right to give the consolamentum, the last unction, to male Cathars (see Döllinger T.II, p. 165). Cathar women were the first to create charitable institutions which we find in medieval towns much later. Jean Guiraud describes their schools, boardinghouses, hospitals, and workshops for poor women. Anne Brenon has pointed out correctly that these charitable and caring activities, typical of the Cathar communities in Languedoc at the beginning of the 13th century, began to grow in French towns only during the late Middle Ages.[16]

Female Catharism had an institutional impact on the aristocracy. Guiraud speaks of the tradition among the lower and impoverished aristocracy to send their daughters, who were excluded from the inheritance of land, to Cathar pensions and boardinghouses so that they would be provided with a decent living. Abels and Harrison mention the same practice.[17] There is the curious example of Raimon IV (1194–1222), who, to get rid of his second wife, Beatrice, made her convert to Cathar asceticism. Similarly, Raimon-Roger de Foix "agrees" to let his wife part with him to follow the secluded life of Cathar nuns.[18] This is an example of the permeation of Cathar precedent into law, which helped solve problems raised by female inheritance, which suggests that Catharism was found acceptable when it came to solving social problems. Cathar hostels, of the type of nunneries, were established in various places — in 1209 there were six of them in Montesquieu; in Saint-Martin-de-la Lande there were ten. Such institutions were familiar in Le-Mas-Saintes-Puelles, Laurac, Vitrac, Villeneuve-la-Comptal and Cabaret.[19]

The strongest historical memory of the participation of women in social life is borne out by Provençal culture. Le Roy Ladurie remarks on its integration and rationalization of the place of women on the level of everyday life. Provençal culture was open to "an exchange of ideas," where a woman's words had the same scope and freedom of play as that of men. There is "an insatiable aspiration in Occitan women to acquire and preserve their language."[20] As in contemporary feminism, there is an attempt to overcome "the disempowerment through silence" and "to democratize access to the spoken and written word."[21] The complete encounter between the woman and the word was achieved in the literature of Provence, more precisely, in the *amour courtois* genre. There woman is not subject to man but is an object of veneration. This does not mean that feudal attitudes had completely changed, but that in spite of all, an unheard of enhancement of the status of women was achieved, though mostly as a verbal gesture. The realities of life were as if compensated for in a symbolic literary gesture. After the trouvères had sung Roland's glory in the chanson de geste, the Provençal troubadours raised the lady of the heart to celestial heights.[22]

This aesthetic emancipation might also be interpreted as a projection of the equalizing of the status of men and women among the Cathars. Scholars like Raul Manselli object to "any attempt to draw a parallel between Catharism and the amour courtois poetry."[23] Yet writers like Denis de Rougemont and René Nelli believe that such a link is legitimate, though they have not unraveled its complex convolutions and psychological motivations. A point which is important to remember is that most of the troubadours shared Cathar ideas. Piere Cardenal's poems often read as dualist treatises and Piere de Corbian, though he wrote a prayer to the Virgin in which he glorifies the mother of God, also believed that she had conceived through her ear, and that Christ had come out of her like a ray of light, without damaging her body.[24] These are traditional docetical views, typical of the dualists, by way of which they deny Christ's material nature, identifying him with the Word (the Logos), which every purified human being is capable of conceiving within him- or herself.

Bernard Sicart de Marvejols, like many other troubadours, leveled severe criticism against the Catholic Church, the major enemy of the Cathars. That the *amour courtois* poetry was rather an act of the emancipation of women is suggested by the appearance of women poets (trobaritz) like La Comptesse de Die, and Marie de Ventadour, who, in her poetic manifesto, declares *The Equality of Sexes in Love* (*L'egalité des sexes devant l'amour*).[25] The development of women's poetry was interrupted in the 13th century when Pope Innocent III and the French kings began a crusade against the Cathars in southern France. As Alfred Jeanroy, a scholar of troubadour poetry, has noted, these were not times favorable to the flourishing of new literature because "the Inquisition had a firm grasp on all spiritual life."[26]

When one considers the alternatives offered by the Catholic Church to the emancipation achieved by Catharism, the contrasts are striking. Unfortunately, the first of the Catholic measures was physical extermination — over one million people were killed. Mercy was not shown to women as an act of exemplary punishment. The well-known *Song of the Crusade Against the Albigenses* (*La Chanson de la Croisade Albigeoise*) tells of the woman ruler of the town of Lavaur — Dame Guiraude, thrown into a well on May 3, 1211, and stoned to death. The author of *La Chanson*, Guillaume de Tudèle, though in favor of the crusader's cause, could not refrain from praising her goodness and generosity.[27]

Later came a time of more peaceful methods. Dominique d'Osma, the founder of the Dominican Order, established Notre Dame de Prouilles, with the explicit intention to reeducate Cathar women from good families. This monastery was rather rich, as its documents testify, and had the support of the Vatican. But even then, according to R. Nelli, "women went on choosing the Order of Cathars, wherever it still existed, because it ensured their equality and made the oppressive nature of patriarchal power more bearable."[28]

Catholic literature about women was neither original nor attractive. The diversity came again by imitating its heretical counterpart. An example of such borrowing is the famous *Legenda Aurea* by Jacques de Voragine, a collection of lives compiled at the end of the 13th century. The book contains catholicized versions of some heretical apocrypha, including *Descent of the Holy Virgin*, which was the official reply of the Eastern Orthodox Church in its cultural struggle with the dualists. In this text, the Virgin begs the ireful Jesus Christ to have mercy on sinful mankind; as a result of her intercession he sends Dominique to begin working for mankind's salvation from heresy.[29] Jean Guitton also thinks that the rise of the cult of the Virgin is a reaction against "the mistakes" of the heretics, and was meant as protection against the "dangerous degeneracy of the amour courtois poetry" [*sic*].[30] Insofar as the Virgin was represented as benign to sinners, the possibility for mercy and forgiveness in the Catholic world became much wider and allowed for milder relationships among human beings. The appearance of a system of nunneries in this period became a way of making up for the shattered system of Cathar homes. These became the new centers of social care for women and their cultural needs, in spite of the limitations set on them by the dogma. Having destroyed the Cathar centers of women's social and cultural realization, the Catholic Church had to create analogous formations.

Lollard Women: Outstanding Personalities

The generic links between the dualist Bogomil and Cathar heresy point further in the direction of the Lollards and serve as a testimony to its pan–European nature, a question we have discussed elsewhere.[31] Here, we shall continue following the thread of the place of women in social groups, exposed to dualist ideas. Although there was a considerable distance in time between the Cathar civilization of the 12th and 13th centuries and the life of the Lollards in England in the 15th century quoted here, the cultural and historical role of women Lollards was the same in principle. The achievement of equality between men and women is best demonstrated by the permission granted Lollard women to conduct services, as the Norwich trials testify. This has been declared in the testimonies of women at the trial. As Hawisia Mone put it, "every man and every woman being in good lyf oute of synne is a good prest and hath [as] much poar of God in all thynges as ony prest ordered, be he pope or bisshop." A similar statement was made by Sibilla, John Godsell's wife.

These, however, are not statements made only by women. John Skylan, accused at the same trial, repeats Mone's words nearly verbatim: "Also that every good man and good woman is a prest."[32] Fifty-one men and nine women were accused of heresy. Yet in some respects, the women had the more active part in it. Norman Tanner writes that "Margery Baxter and Hawisia Mone appear to have been active Lollards and not mere followers of their husbands!"[33] He correctly places John Burrell and Margery Baxter as major characters in the trial. The inquisitor's notes from the interrogation of the latter clearly state that she was independently involved in heretical activities (ipsa tenuit, credidit et affirmavit articulos sive opiniones subscriptas; p. 42).

Hawisia Mone also revealed her talent to dispute well. Matilde, wife of Richard Fletcher, was described as a prominent heretic (notata et multipliciter diffamata de heresi; p. 131). Katerina Wryght, wife of Roger Wryght, was also described as a "well-known suspect as a fervent follower of heresy" ("notatata et vehementer suspecta de crimine heretice pravitatis") (p. 194). Isabelle Chapleyn was also proclaimed a "well-known" heretic (multiplicater notata; p. 198).

The Lichfield and Coventry trials of 1511–12 provide similar data about the activity of women. Among the 45 persons put on trial, one-third were women. Again, they were not just their husbands' followers, but were among the leaders. John Gest confessed that he had been persuaded for eleven years by his wife Johanna to enter the heresy: "circiter xi annos elapsos solicitationibus Johanne, uxoris sue incidet in heresim."[34] Another woman, Alice Rowley, "appears to have been one of the busiest and most important working members of the sect."[35]

The most outstanding personality in the whole of the three-year process in Norwich was also a woman. Margery Baxter transcends all the clichés typical of the discourse of both inquisitors and heretics. She was the only one who freely spoke of her religion in an outburst of spontaneity, telling the Bogomil-Cathar myth of the fall of Lucifer in her own rendition (p. 49) and the legend of the bee, which stings the tongue of traitors, which suggests a possible acquaintance with the *Physiologus*, an important literary and philosophic book of the Middle Ages. By abandoning the formulaic language of the dogma, Margery Baxter infused the trial with most surprising metaphoric expression, or as a modern feminist might say, hers was "a self-articulation within the subculture."[36] She provides a strong example of the link between liberal religion and literacy, typical of Lollard subculture, which, because of its greater openness, can be regarded as the avant garde cultural space of the times. According to Malcolm Lambert, the latter included the variants of the Wycliffe Bible, which was then translated into English, as well as other vernacular collections of the Lollard sermons, functioning of professional writing offices, etc.[37] The cultural significance of the translation can hardly be overestimated, given "how strongly the ecclesiastical authorities held the view that it was the translations of the Scripture that were the cause and root of all trouble."[38] This literary production had a high academic quality and is among the most important literary legacies of the period.

Documents testify to the active role of women in this field. Alice

Rowley confessed that she had used "good bookis,"[39] while her husband was in the habit of reading to her "from St.Paul's Epistles."[40] There are other records of such family readings in the proceedings of the Norwich trials. Authors as different as A. Lombard, M. Gaster, Yordan Ivanov, R. Abels and E. Harrison have pointed to the profusion of heretical literature, which was part and parcel of a wide and free literary context, shared by heretics and orthodox alike. In England, this also brought about a new understanding of women by the official church — the appearance of nunneries and a vast body of literature addressed to women testifies to this process. Such popular pieces are *Hali Meidhad, Seinte Margarete, Sawles Warde,* and *Ancrene Wisse* (or *Guide for Anchoresses*), two of them containing key motifs from the founding dualistic myths, disseminated by Bogomils, Cathars, and Lollards.

In their introduction to the collection *Medieval English Prose for Women,* editors Bella Millet and Jocelyn Wogan-Browne reconstruct this topic from *Hali Meidhad,* without discussing its heretical roots: "Had man been content to replace the angels in God's creation and not to imitate Lucifer's disobedience, our nature could and should have been like that of the angels."[41] This is a close repetition of the myth about Lucifer's rebellion and fall, as told by Margery Baxter, but already coming from the pages of the official religious literature. Another visible dualist quotation can be found in *Sawles Warde.* It concerns the descent into hell and the ascent to heaven.[42] This is a typical variant of *Visio Paoli* and the *Nicodemus Gospel,* apocalyptic writings distributed by the heretics. Such characteristic free compilation and reproduction is also visible in *Seinte Margarete,* which contains borrowings from the popular Eastern apocrypha about the virgin Juliana.

The fourth text, *Guide for Anchoresses,* also reveals traces of heterodoxy. There are some essential and stylistic reminiscences of *The Letter from Heaven* (also referred to as the *Legend of Sunday,* or *Lord's Letter*), which was widespread in the Middle Ages and was an essential book for the Flagellantes, with an Eastern provenance, as Moses Gaster explains. Jesus is called Paraclete (the Consoler) — a way of naming him used mostly by the Eastern dualists.[43]

Two important features emerge from *Medieval English Prose for Women.* First, the editors point out that these lives are set in the context of the debate of the official church with the heresies, the new realities created by life in their social groups, and the Islamic conquest. The Catholic

Church had used such compilations to create its own popular literature in its struggle against the Cathars — as is the case of Jacques le Voragine's *Legenda Aurea*, which includes apocrypha subjected to a pro–Catholic rewording.

Second, the enhanced interest in women in medieval England was a reflection of the dynamics of the Renaissance of the 12th century. The editors of *Medieval English Prose for Women* have avoided the temptation of specifying the developments included in it as typically English and see them as an "influence not only of the literary tradition, but of the French courtly literature and the Latin prose of the twelfth century Renaissance."[44] The authors prefer the formula "transmitter or transformer" (we shall say both), and pay attention to the element of Jewish and Eastern apocrypha.[45] It remains for us to narrow the focus to a clearer picture, as M. Gaster, I. Franko and D. Obolensky have already done, by specifying the heretical character of these apocrypha. Millet and Wogan-Brown have hinted at this by seeing in *Hali Meidhad* an apparent closeness to heterodoxy,[46] although they play down the importance of this fact.

A few rather clear conclusions can be drawn at the end. First, Bogomils and Cathars, as well as the heresies close to them, were a powerful force of change in the cultural and social processes in the way they placed women in religion in an equal position with men. As a result, women's cultural activities brought about an important element of mildness, mercy, elegance, psychological depth and an interest in finer literature to the life and literature of the period. Mores and behavior become milder; to be elegant in manners became a matter of prestige.

There is some truth in the observation made by Alfred Jeanroy, who noted that while in southern France the troubadours explored an unprecedented spectrum of literary genres, in the north, which was less affected by the heresy, the *amour courtois* was unknown, while the poetry of the trouvères was rather schematic, bearing testimony of the pride of the aristocracy in recounting the glories of battles, rather than the beauties of the world of emotion.

Ladies' attention toward the troubadours and the jongleurs created a more "open society" — the poets and the singers were accepted in the feudal milieu as equals. The emancipation of poets was parallel to that of women and is an example of a high degree of early democratization. In the north, the epic poem was the only flowering genre of the time (about 1160).

In the south of France, according to Alfred Jeanroy, there was a rich variety of literary forms, a sign of a cultivated taste.[47] The leading role of Provençal literature was admitted by Dante and Petrarch, who saw themselves as its followers.[48] In England, after the suppression of John Bull's rebellion, the dualist heresy lost the ground for free development but created social groups that brought about a peak in the literature of the period. As the proceedings of the Norwich trials clearly show, women were natural leaders in this literary revival.

Bogomil-Cathar and Lollard emancipation of woman is an undeniably important spiritual component of the 12th century Renaissance, helping the rise of a provisional cultural model — an early forerunner of modern civilization.

Appendix to Chapter 3: The Right of Women to Ordain and to Shrive

A. BOGOMILS

Tenth century

"The heretics absolve themselves, though they are tied up with devilish fetters. This is done not only by the men but also by the women which is worthy of castigation."[49]

Twelfth century

(1143): Heresy trial of the monks-bishops Leonce of Balbissa and Clement of Sasimes: "he ordained women for deaconesses letting them read prayers and the holy Gospels, and serve mass along with Clement."[50]

B. CATHARS

Beginning of the 14th century

Depositions of Raymunda Valsiera for the Inquisition in Languedoc, describing how Cathar women can practice the "Consolamentum," the sacrament of the Cathars: "that this power from the hands of the good men upon the good men, and from the hands of the good women upon the good women ... that the good women possess the mentioned power and they can receive it for exercising on men and women, and if so it is that good men are absent [the adepts] can by saved by good women, the same way as good men do" (quod dicta potestas transiret de manibus ad manibus bonorum hominum ad bonos homines; et bonarum mulierum ad bonas mulieres quia, ut dixit, ita sunt bonae mulieres, sicut et boni homines; quae bonae mulieres, sicut et boni homines; quae bonae mulieres dictam potestatem habent et possunt recipere in fine homines et mulieres, si tantum sit, quod non sint praesentes boni homines, et ita salvantur per bonas mulieres, sicut per bonos homines).[51]

C. LOLLARDS

Fifteenth century

Lollards' depositions at the heresy trials in Norwich: "Also that every man and every woman in good lyf oute of synne is a good prest and hath [as] much poar of God in al thynges as ony prest ordered, be he pope or bisshop" (Hawisia Moone, wife of Thome Moone de Lodne).[52]

"Item quod quilibet fidelis homo et quilibet fidelis mulier est bonus sacerdos " (also that every true man and every true woman is a good priest) (Sibilla, wife of Johannes Godsell de Dychingham).[53]

"Also that every good man and good woman is a prest" (Johannes Skylan de Bergh).[54]

Margaret Aston mentions that the Lollards produced some women preachers. The question, however, of whether there were Lollard women priests does not have a definite answer yet, according to her. Aston gives the case (after Henry Knighton, 1391) of a Lollard woman who had taught her daughter to celebrate mass but not to consecrate the sacrament.[55]

Note: 563 years after the trial of Norwich (where it was established that the heretics gave women the right to shrive), the Anglican Church, unique among the Christian churches, ordained 32 women as priests in March 1994; in this we can discern the distant influence of the tradition of the English heretics. In its centuries-old disputation with the Vatican, the Church of England used almost the same critical qualifications and epithets as the heretics who preceded it.

The rigid position of the Catholic Church against ordaining women was corroborated by Pope John Paul II on July 27, 1994. He explained that since Jesus had chosen only men for apostles, there is no justification for changing the situation today. It seems unlikely that the Church's position will change under Benedict XVI or in the foreseeable future.

CHAPTER 4

John Wycliffe
and the Dualists

Our Bread Over Another Substance

Thus far we have examined the daily life and ritual practices of the heretics, but the time has come to explore how prominent individuals charged the teaching with the potential for reformation. In order to do so, it is necessary to specify the usage of two basic terms. The "Cyrillo-Methodian version" of the Bible, and particularly the New Testament, signifies the text that was finally translated and compiled by the disciples of St. Cyril and St. Methodius. As we now know, the Slav apostles translated only a selection of New Testament texts dedicated to feast days and used in service (Aprakos),[1] while the complete version was the work of their disciples. One way or another, the approach of Sts. Cyril and Methodius and their school of translation remained a characteristic feature of the translation work done later in Ochrida and Preslav. It is this and copies thereof that are indicated when speaking of Cyrillo-Methodian versions.

Similarly, it is the now generally accepted opinion of British and American medievalists that, most probably, John Wycliffe himself was not directly responsible for the translation of the New Testament. Today, the idea that John Wycliffe was not the author of the translation of the New Testament into English prevails among English and American medievalists. In the introduction to her book, M. Deansely mentions a "median" version and texts created in the circles of Wycliffe's followers.[2] *The Cambridge History of English and American Literature*, in turn, mentions a translation by Nicholas Hereford, as well as a revision of the translation made by John Purvey.[3] The situation is most probably summed up best by V.

Hotchkiss: "Although often given credit of the translation of the Vulgate into English, it is now generally thought that Wycliffe was not directly responsible. Nonetheless, he certainly inspired his followers to undertake this project."[4] And, since it seems one should agree with the *Cambridge History of English and American Literature* that the history of those early translations should be deciphered and written about further,[5] this author has chosen a rather different approach. Besides adopting the more general concept of "Wycliffite translations" we shall concern ourselves with a later version, dating from the 1400–1450 period.[6] Presumably, as a result of the repeated copying and passage of time, in this case there will already be a distance from the original. Should one find characteristic features inherent to Wycliffe's philosophy in this text, they would be even more valid for the manuscripts considered to have come out under the direct supervision of or to have been edited by Wycliffe himself. One important observation in this respect is that repeated comparison between the later 1400–1450 version and the copy ascribed to Wycliffe's own hand[7] revealed a coincidence of the fundamental interpretations and peculiar terms used by Wycliffe. This proximity and concurrence, by the way, resounds in the theology Wycliffe expressed in other works. Generally speaking, this study is in the sphere of the underlying ideas expressed in and reflected in these and related texts and is the first of its kind. And there is still abundant material for studying Wycliffe's ideas and thought, regardless of the currently ongoing revelations about his literary heritage. In our case, the main approaches are frequency analysis and hermeneutics. Since the version we have used is on a CD, it allows a precise quantitative description of Wycliffe's specific vocabulary. For a number of objective reasons, this author could not use previous editions of Wycliffe or other direct sources connected with the Wycliffite translation circle.[8]

Open any modern official edition of the Bible in English (for example the *New Revised Standard Version*, Oxford, 1989) and read the Lord's Prayer and you shall see that there God is asked to give [us] "this day our daily bread." In Wycliffe's English versions of the Scriptures, however, begun about the year 1380, one finds a rather different text: "oure breed ouer othir substaunce" (Math. 6:9–13 — "give us this day our daily bread over another substance").[9] Why the difference? Why such an unusual sounding phrase in which, beyond the translation, there is obviously a small comment being made by the translator himself? The answer on principle was indirectly provided by Yordan Ivanov, a noted Bulgarian philologist and historian. In his well-known book *Bogomil Books and Legends*, he wrote that the Bosnian Bogomils read the Lord's Prayer in just such a way, pronouncing "give us our daily bread of another substance."[10] A similar version can be found in the Lyonnaise rendition of the Albigensian Scriptures: "E dona a noi lo nostre pa qui es sabre tota cause" (the bread that is above all else). Similarly there is one Old Italian version: "Il pane nostre sopra tucte le substantie da a nnoi oggi" (our bread over any substance). Since the Bogomils gave the Cathars the quoted version of the Cyrillo-Methodian translation of the New Testament (subsequently translated into the Latin by the Cathars), we shall turn to the idea that John Wycliffe did not translate the Scriptures from the Vulgate, as the printed editions of his version later stated, but from a Cyrillo-Methodian version. Even today the Bulgarian version of the Lord's Prayer reads "our daily substantial bread," which is much closer to the Greek original "tov artov hemon ton epiousion," where the word "epiousion" means literally "suprasubstantial." In other words, the Cyrillo-Methodian version is closer to the Greek original than the Vulgate "our daily [quotidianum] bread." The term "supersubstantialem" is used in the various Vulgate versions, in Matthew and in Luke (11:2–4), but it is practically excluded from the liturgical and sacramental practice of the Catholic Church. What is more, to pronounce "suprasubstantial" (supersubstantialem) instead of "our daily bread" (panem nostrum quotidianum) in the Lord's Prayer was considered a sure sign of heresy in the Middle Ages. According to *Collectio Occitanica*, Inquisition records from Carcassonne, in Lombardy Bernard Oliva, the heretical bishop from Toulouse, pronounced "panem nostrum supersubstantialem" (dicendo in oratione Pater noster: panem nostrum supersubstantialem) when he said the Lord's Prayer.[11]

Even in the 19th and the beginning of the 20th centuries, many authors paid attention to the fact that the Bogomils lay the stress on "our bread of another substance." In this case we shall list just a few of them because, both in Bulgaria and abroad, one encounters a conservative underestimation of this detail and an inability to decipher its theological significance.[12] H. Puech and A. Vaillant underscored the concept described by Euthymius Zygabenus that "Bogomils created their haven, the true eucharistic bread that is 'artos epiousios,' by which they acquire the blood and flesh of Christ everyday."[13] Zygabenus mentions the special word "epiousios" by which they characterized the bread: "tov arton gar, fesi, tov epiousion."[14] N. Osokyn also noted the "Greek practice" of the Bogomils and the Cathars: they sang the Lord's Prayer after the Greek fashion, substituting "our daily bread" (quotidianum) for the words "our supernatural bread" and adding at the end "Thy Kingdom come" etc., "adopted by the Eastern Church with good reason."[15] Jean Guiraud, a scholar who studied the Cathars and was their opponent centuries after they existed, claimed that "they dared to adjust even the word of Christ," taking the liberty to read the said part of the Lord's Prayer in their own way.[16]

At this point we will undertake a more comprehensive explanation of the Cathar concept of the Lord's Prayer that C. Schmidt made in 1849:

> they interpreted "daily bread" in the sense of food for the soul and, instead of the simple formula from the Scripture, "Give us today our supersubstantial bread," ending with the words "for Thine is the kingdom and the power and the glory in all eternity." Since these words cannot be found in the Vulgate, the opponents of the Cathars who were not familiar with the original text, accused them of misrepresenting the Bible in this particular place. This accusation the latter did not deserve because on this point their version, made on the basis of a Greek source, was more correct than the version of the Western Church.[17]

Schmidt's explanation was repeated a century later by Yordan Ivanov. He pointed out that in the Greek original, the expression from Matthew "tov arton hemon tov epiousiov," repeated also in Luke, was translated as "panem supersubstantialem" (Matthew) and "panem quotidianum" (Luke) in the Vulgate. He added that the latter expression "was more accepted in the [Catholic] Church than the former one."[18]

Dualistic Arguments in Wycliffe

One could actually say that Wycliffe's "oure breed ouer othir substaunce" is rather more than just a translation. It is a strongly accentuated comment, for it substitutes for the word "supersubstantialem" three whole words, "ouer othir substaunce," intended to endorse the supramaterial notion of the Word as spiritual bread. On other occasions, and in open polemics with the Catholic Church in England at that, John Wycliffe repeatedly supported the view that the Word was spiritual bread and true communion: "Teneamos ergo quod, virtute verborum Christi, panis fit" (We consider bread the virtue of Christ's word).[19] There is an undoubted coincidence with the dualistic thesis, to mention even Euthymius Zygabenus (early 12th century), according to whom the Bogomils called "the Lord's Prayer bread of the communion" (arton men gar koinovias onomazousi ten proseuhen tou, Pater hemon).[20] We have the same coincidence with the Albigensian thesis that "God's word is this bread," recorded by the Inquisition at the beginning of the 14th century.

Albigensians	*John Wycliffe*
The Lord's Word is this bread.	Thus, it remains to accept our
Verbum Dei esse ille panis	daily bread as spiritual, [as] it is
["Acta inquisitionis	God's daily precept that we con-
Carcassonensis	template and act.
contra Albigensis,	*Restat igitur ut panem cotidianum*
a. 1308 et 1409," in Döllinger,	*acceptamus spiritualem, praecepta*
vol. II, p. 28].	*divina cotidies opportet meditari*
	et operari [*Operis evangelici*, Lib.
	III et IV (London: 1896), p.
	285].

This definitely dualistic interpretation prompts one to look for other dualistic themes in Wycliffe. And there are so many of them and so well expressed that one wonders how they have not been noticed until now. To the best of this author's knowledge, none of the contemporary scholars studying Wycliffe has made even a single such observation. In the first third of the 20th century, Leo Seifert alone expressed the opinion that Wycliffe was very close to dualism.[21] To fill this void, we shall hereafter quote some of Wycliffe's fundamental dualistic theses, compared to those of the Bogomils and Cathars, and grouped by dualistic theogony; dualistic criticism of the Church and the rites; and social views.

DUALISTIC THEOGONY

The Devil as Master of This World

It was a fundamental Bogomil tenet that the Devil was creator and master of this world. This explains Wycliffe's well-known seventh of the twenty-four Conclusions refuted by the Synod in London in 1382, one that continues to amaze British medievalists.

Bogomils and Cathars

In 1211, the anti–Bogomil council in Tarnovo convened by Tsar Boril anathematized, among other things, "those who claim that the Devil is the autocrat of this world" [*Synodicon of Boril* (Sofia: 1928), p. 92].

John Wycliffe

That God ought to obey the devil

Item quod Deus debet obedire diabolo

["XXIV Conclusiones Wycclyf damnatae

Londoniis in synodo," *Fasciculi Zizaniorum*, p. 278].

The Fall of Lucifer and His Angels

The other part of the dualistic myth about the pride and fall of Lucifer and his angels also features repeatedly in the works of Wycliffe. True, he called upon Isaiah, obviously to defend himself from his numerous opponents from the Catholic Church. Both Bogomils and Cathars themselves also frequently quoted this theme according to Isaiah.

Bogomils and Cathars

And he was observing the glory which pertained to the Mover of the Heavens, and he got the idea of placing his throne above the clouds of heaven, and he wanted to be like the Most High

Et (Sathanas) obserabat gloriam, quae erat moventis coelos, et cogitavit sedem sua ponere super nubes coelorum et volebat Altissimo similis esse [*Interrogatio Johannis, or the Secret Book* of the Bogomils].

John Wycliffe

(on Lucifer's pride, quoting Isaiah, Ysa XIV. 13): I will ascend to heaven; I will raise my throne above the Stars of God

In celum ascendam super astra celi exaltatio solum meum [*Summa in theologia, Tractatus tertieus, De civili domino* (London, MDCCCXXV), p. 1].

It is known that Lucifer and his accomplices were initially in a state of innocence

Argumentum patet de Lucifer cum suis complicibus apostatis (Ysa XIV.12–15) *de primus parentibus in state innocencie* [ibidem, p. 373].

It is essential to know that the English reformer leaned on this myth to attack the Pope, comparing him and his court to the fall of Lucifer and his angels. In the commentary column in English on the same page, the publisher has summed up the result of the comparison thus: "Angels, our first parents and the apostles have sinned, much more may the pope with his whole college sin."[22]

Incarnation of the Souls of Angels in the Human Body

This important part of what is called "secondary" or Satanic creation in the West, to use the Bogomil terminology, also found a place in Wycliffe's views. He developed the thesis of the dual human nature, i.e. flesh and soul, explaining that souls were probably angels implanted in human bodies. Wycliffe did not reveal his source, mainly out of caution; he just said he had taken the idea *ex fide* scripture. By this expression he underscored both the orthodoxy of the source and the reliability of the knowledge.

Bogomils and Cathars	*John Wycliffe*
And in addition (Satan) devised and made man in his likeness, that is his own, and he ordered the angel of the third heaven to enter a body of clay. And he took from it and made another body in the form of a woman, and he ordered the angel of the second heaven to enter the body of the woman	Thus man has a double nature ... this means body and soul ... and speaking of the soul, a true writing gives it as being created as a completely invisible and immortal spirit, it being possible that it is an angel in itself
Et praeterea excogitavit et fecit hominem ad similitudinem ejus vel sui, et praecepit angelo tertii coeli intrare in corpus liteum. Et tulit de eo et fecit aliud corpus in formam mulieris, et praecepit angelo secundi coeli introire in corpus mulieris [Interrogatio Johannis, or the Secret Book of the Bogomils].	*quomodo homo est duaram naturam utraque* (p. 2) ... *scilicet corporis et anime* (p. 35) ... *Loquendo itaque de anima opportet ex fide scripture supponere esse spiritum creatum mole invisibilem et incorruptibilem possibilem per se esse ut angelus* (p. 3–4) [*De compositione hominis* (London, 1884)].

63

DUALISTIC CRITICISM OF CHURCH AND RITES

Wycliffe's Catholic adversaries persecuted him even after his death. In addition to the fact that his bones were exhumed and burned, there were claims by some Catholic authors that he was guilty of 700 transgressions against the Roman Church and its practices. Wycliffe's most attacked thesis was probably his rejection of transubstantiation, the conversion of the bread and the wine at the altar into the blood and body of Christ. As we well know, this rejection was a fundamental tenet with both the Bogomils and the Cathars.

Rejection of Transubstantiation

Cathars	John Wycliffe
that none should believe that the host the priest shows the people during Mass is the body of Christ for it is only bread	That the essence of material bread and wine remains [the same] after their consecration at the altar
quod nullus debebat credere quod illa hostia, quam Capellanus ostendit populo in missa, esset corpus Christi, et quod erat nisi panis ["Acta inquisitionis Carcassonensis contra Albigensis a. 1308 et 1309," Döllinger, vol. II, p. 18].	*Quod substantia panis materialis et vinum maneat post consecrationem in sacramento altaris* ["XXIV Conclusiones Wycclyf damnatae Londoniis in synodo," *Fasculi Zizianorum*, p. 278].

At that, the heretical Wycliffe made an important addition, one that should be acceptable to any reasonable theologian: that the bread and the wine of the host acquired the meaning of moral participation unto Christ, that they were *efficax ejus signum*. It is regrettable that the synod refused to accept this nuance, offered by Wycliffe on the basis of St. Augustine's famous interpretation of the three aspects of the communion.

Only God Giveth Absolution, to Him We Confess without a Mediator

This fundamental dualistic attitude to an internal communion with God, inherited by the Protestants today, was also a familiar position of Wycliffe's.

Cathars	John Wycliffe
They also believe that God alone forgives	Contrition belongs to the mind alone, and it is not an object of sense, inasmuch the contrite confesse to the Lord [*Great Voices of the Reformation*, p. 26].
Item credunt quod nullus possit pacere nisi Deus ["Tractatus de hereticis," in A. Dondaine, "La hiérarchie cathare en Italie," *Archivum Fratrum Praedicatorum* (Rome: 1950), p. 319].	That if one is forced to confess any exterior confession is super-fluous or useless
	Item quod si homo fuerit debite contritus, omnis confessio exterior est sibi superflua, vel inutilis ["XXIV Conclusiones," *Fasciculi Zizaniorum*, p. 278].

Wycliffe developed this view in severe criticism of the decree of Pope Innocent III, "Omnis utrusque sexus," according to which people who had not been granted absolution by Catholic priests could not be saved. The uncouthness and pointlessness of such an assertion were refuted categorically: "No one can believe that a man may not be saved without a confession of this kind, for other wise all the dead from Christ's ascension to the time of Innocent III are lost — a horrible thing to believe."[23]

Sinner Priests Have No Right to Officiate

Another dualistic rule, the belief that priests who sinned could not serve believers, was also adopted. To that Wycliffe added his famous assertion that earthly rulers who sinned lost their right of property and power. In other words, to use the modern political terminology, he created a situation of impeachment by the attitude to God.

Cathars	John Wycliffe
The priests of the Roman Church cannot unbind and bind as they are sinners; they cannot cleanse from anything	Thus it should be accepted that none may be a lord, none may be a bishop, none may be a priest while in a state of mortal sin
Sacerdotes Romanae Ecclesiae non possunt solvere et ligare cum sint	*Item asserere quod nullus est dominus*

peccatores; et cum sint immundi, nullum allium possunt mundare ["Collectio Occitanica," in Döllinger, vol. II, p. 6].

civilis, nullus est episcopus, nullus est prelatus, dum est in peccato mortali ["XXIV Conclusiones," *Fasciculi zizaniorum*, p. 280].

The Catholic Church Is Fornicatress

We know that John Wycliffe reached the point of complete rejection of the Catholic Church and the pope and recommended that the civil power deprive the Church of its endowments. He defended a similar opinion directly in a letter to Richard II, but with much sharper expressions in the spirit of the Cathar allegation that the pope was "involved with the Devil," that is, the Antichrist, that can be found in his other texts.

Cathars

That the Roman Church is not the Lord's Church but a whore

Item quod ecclesia romana non est Ecclesia Dei sed meretrix ["Tractatus de hereticis," in Dondaine, p. 318].

John Wycliffe

If the pope is known as a bad man and one related to the devil still then he does not have the right to the power given him over those who believe in Christ

Item quod si papa sit praescitus et malus homo, ac per consequens membrum diaboli, non habet potestatem supra fidelis Christi sibi datam ["XXIV Conclusiones," *Fasciculi Zizaniorum*, p. 278].

Rejection of Excommunication

Like the Cathars, Wycliffe rejected excommunication, one of the most severe sanctions of the Catholic Church, as invalid and immoral, thus rendering its authority ineffective to a certain degree. Wycliffe must have enjoyed considerable authority and social support, for although the London Synod of 1382 condemned his views, the reformer was not excommunicated.

Cathars	*John Wycliffe*
If the Roman Church excommunicates someone for refusal to make an oath or something else that excommunication should not be believed	Anyone that excommunicates shall himself be a heretic and excommunicated because of that

Si ecclesia Romana eum excommunicaret propter hoc, qui non vult jurare, vel alium, non crederat se esse excommunicatum [Döllinger, p. 231].

Item quod sic excommunicans, ex hoc sit heareticus, vel excommunicatus ["XXIX Conclusiones," *Fasciculi Zizaniorum*, p. 279].

SOCIAL VIEWS

Wycliffe's social views are a matter of such richness and complexity that they will probably be the source of plenty of studies to come. In this chapter we shall focus on two essential cases of ideas and practice shared by the dualists and the British reformer.

Rejection of Oath

Considering how underdeveloped medieval legislation was, the oath was an important legal tool to subject ordinary people to the worldly and ecclesiastic authorities. By rejecting the oath, the dualists actually refused involvement with the structures of authority in society that they considered unjust and subject to the Devil. Thus ordinary man was provided with social involvement as a democratic choice in a hint of the first modern right of civil society. One cannot but notice that John Wycliffe considered the oath "superfluous among the perfect," mentioning one of the fundamental terms of Bogomils and Cathars, perfecti. In other words, he used the language of the dualists.

Cathars (Patarenes)	*John Wycliffe*
And they deny the oath and say it is not permitted to make an oath either for justice or for injustice	See now that it makes sense to ban the oath for one can see that the oath is superfluous among the perfect

Item negat iuramentum, et dicunt: nec iuste, nec iniuste licet iurari

videtur ad sensum suum prohibere simpliciter iuramentum, quia

["Prilozi za povest bosanskih patarena," *Starine*, p. 139].

videtur iuramentum superfluere inter perfectos [Operis Evangelici, p. 188].

Rejection of Liturgy

Even the Bulgarian Bogomils called the liturgy something superfluous, a view that was later transferred among the Cathars. Wycliffe was also one of its radical supporters, being in harmony with the familiar Bogomil protestation that the apostles did not conduct liturgies.

Bogomils
You say that not the apostles established the liturgy and communion but St. John Chrysostom; that more than three hundred years passed from the Birth of Christ to the time of St. John [*Treatise against the Bogomils*, p. 36].

John Wycliffe
It is pertinent to assert that the Gospel does not feature an argument that Christ ordained mass
Item pertinater asserere non esse fundatum in evangelio quod Christus missam ordinavit ["XXIV Conclusiones," *Fasciculi Zizaniorum*, pp. 278, 281].

Rejection of Indulgences

Just like the Cathars, John Wycliffe rejected the sale of indulgences.

Cathars
And they do not believe one whit in the indulgences meted by the Roman Church
Item de indulgenciis quas facit ecclesia romana nuhil credunt ["Tractatus de hereticis," in Dondaine, p. 318].

John Wycliffe
There are no indulgences other than those given by our Lord Jesus Christ
Non sunt indulgencie nisi a Domino Jesu Christo [*Wyclif's Latin Works, Opus Evangelicum*, vol. II, p. 480].

Icons and the Cross

Quite naturally, there are some specific differences in this parallel. Although he was an adherent of dualism, John Wycliffe retained a certain desire to arrive at a compromise with the official church on some problems. For example, he did not reject the presence of images in church. Partially adopting the dualist criticism of icons and the cross, he only warned against extreme veneration of the latter and the former.

Cathars	John Wycliffe
They do not bow to the cross or to an altar, for they say these are replications made by man out of silver and gold	If it be meant that God and stone are identical, it is heretical and to be denied [*Miscellania philosophica*, vol. II (London: 1905), p. 104].
Nec inclinant cruci nec altari, allegantes illud: Simulacra gentium argentium et aurum ["Tractatus de hereticis," in Dondaine, p. 317].	

Persecution of New Testament Usage in the Vernacular

It is natural that this part should conclude with a comparison of the persecution suffered by dualists for disseminating the New Testament in the vernacular, and the repression of Wycliffe's work on the translation of the New Testament.

Cathars	John Wycliffe
(Author's note: This is how the famous 14th century inquisitor, Bernard Gui, described the "forbidden" literary practice of the Cathars)	As Anne Hudson has mentioned in her *"Laicus literatus": The Paradox of Lollardy*, "the Decree De heretico comburendo identifies the making of books as a typical activity of the heretics." In his *Constitutions* (1407), Archbishop Arundel forbade the use of Wycliffe's translations of the Bible without a special permission. In 1412 the same cleric addressed a letter to the Pope accusing Wycliffe that "to fill up the measure of his malice, he
Also they read the gospels and epistles on vulgar tongue, combining and explaining them in their own way, and constantly against the Roman Church	
Item legunt de evangeliis et de epistolis in vulgari, applicando et exponendo pros se et contra statim	

Romane ecclesie [B. Gui, *Manuel de l'inquisiteur*, T. I (Paris: 1926), p. 26].

devised the expedient of new translations of the Scriptures into the mother tongue" [M. Deanesly, *The Lollard Bible*, p. 238].

The Specific New Testament Vocabulary of Wycliffite Translations

The subject of New Testament translation is rooted in John Wycliffe's dualistic philosophy. The measure of that involvement, however, is a much stronger and organic one and it found a peculiar linguistic expression in the translation of the New Testament. It turned out that the formula "oure breed ouer othir substaunce" is accompanied by a certain vocabulary that carries traces of traditional Bogomil and Cathar interpretations of the Gospel. Dualism is the philosophy that gave birth to the initiative of translating the New Testament into English, and the translation carries in itself the imprint of that philosophy; in other words, a mutual motivation proceeds from the spirit of the "Bulgarian heresy." At that, we shall see that the Wycliffite approach to translation largely followed the Cyrillo-Methodian example. More specifically, we are speaking of daring coinage, of enriching and energizing phrases, the latter distinction originating in the Greek phrase. In other words the literature of Bogomils, Cathars and Lollards rested on the cultural tradition of the Orthodox Church. What we have here is not heresy but a popularization of the Holy Writ. It is this sense that Pope John Paul II discerned in the work of the Slav apostles, seeing in it "enculturation — the incarnation of the New Testament in local cultures — as well as their introduction to the life of the Church."[24] The dualists did the same thing.

The opinion supported by Margaret Deanesly that the Wycliffite translation is "the most revised and idiomatic form of the Earlier Version"[25] indicates that Wycliffe's strong propensity for the vernacular is well known among the English authors. This author, however has assumed the even more radical view of American researcher Fred Robinson, who introduced the expression "the Lollards' Englishing of the Vulgate Bible."[26] He pays special attention to the "General Prologue" included in nine Wycliffite copies, where ambition to render the Scriptures in the vernacular is declared, a proposition reinforced by the argument that such a translation would overcome some ambiguities in the Vulgate. The linguistic procedures of the English translation are commended as being richer in a discussion on the importance of using Middle English as opposed to Latin word order in the translation.[27]

Subsequently we shall quote some cases of intentional substitution of Latin words and roots for English ones, as well as impressive examples of creating new words, both of which indicate that John Wycliffe and his followers conceived and achieved a translation alternative to the Vulgate. Obviously, they wanted to render the Holy Writ into the spoken, vernacular language. Among other things, their achievement also differs from the biblical excerpts translated into Old English in terms of flexibility and lexical abundance.

To put it simply, the translation reveals a visible effort to replace the Latin with the Anglo-Saxon, the older and more widespread substratum of the English language. One example is a crucial notion and image, that of the resurrection of Christ. The word *vazkresenie*, used in Bulgarian, was absolutely new and bore considerable poetic charge. It was not a direct translation of the Greek *anastasis* that means "getting up, rising." The Bulgarian word means rising from the cross, ascension above the cross. The Bulgarian writer and medievalist Stefan Gechev assumed that the image originated among the earliest Slav converts to Christianity around Salonika and that the apostles of the Slavs, Cyril and Methodius, adopted quite a lot of that first Slavonic Christian popular vocabulary.

The Wycliffite translators repeatedly used the Latin term *resureccioun*, resurrection of Christ (Acts 1:22). Thus they share a vocabulary with the King James version (see the appendix to this chapter). Nevertheless, they preferred a purely English term, *agenrysing*, and used it in the key phrase where Christ says: "I am agenrysing & lyf" (John 11:25). True, according to the *OED* this word was used in 1380 in a variant of the Catholic Credo: agenrysing of fleish.[28] Its introduction as New Testament lexis, however, was a feature of the Wycliffite version. The *OED* also mentions that Wycliffe used the same word in 1382.[29] The word *agenrysing* appears on thirteen other occasions: in Luke 20:27, John 11:24–25, Romans 1:4, I Corinthians 15:12–13, I Corinthians 15:42, Acts 4:33, Acts 17:18, Acts 23:6, Acts 24:15, Acts 24:21, Acts 26:23, I Peter 1:3 and Revelation 20:6. It would be interesting to note that one sometimes finds a certain similarity to this phrase in the King James version. In Romans 4:25 we have "was raised again," almost a complete concurrence with "roos agen" in the Wycliffite translation. The only difference is that passive voice was used in the King James version while the Wycliffite translation uses the active voice. Wycliffe and his disciples did not achieve a richer image than that contained in the Bulgarian word *vazkresenie* (rise, ascend above the cross). With a similar desire to use their native language as much as possible, however, they achieved an expressive rendition of the Greek and Latin term into English. Instead of using Latinized lexis they created their own Christian vocabulary in English with the dedication and frequency the Slav apostles applied in creating its Slavonic equivalent.

John 11:25, "I am the resurrection, and the life"

Greek	Latin	Wycliffite	King James
Ego eimi he anastasis kai he zoe.	Ego sum resurectio, et vita.	I am agenrysing & lyf.	Jesus said unto her, I am the resurrection, and the life.

    Another example in this respect is that the Wycliffite translation uses the word *cristne*, i.e., christianize, instead of or parallel to baptize. Cristne is an old root in the English language. According to the *OED*, it was first mentioned in 890 (*cristenesta*),[30] and Wycliffe obviously used it to increase the presence of English vocabulary in the translation of the New Testament. His use of *cristne* is mentioned on the respective page of the *OED* that states Wycliffe used the word in 1380.[31] That, too, was the supposed date when the translation of the New Testament was begun, it being said in both the case of *agenrysing* and *cristne* that the words were used by Wycliffe himself.

Matthew 3:11–12

Greek	Latin	Wycliffe	King James
Aiutos iumas baptisei ev pneiumati agioi kai piuri.	Ipse vos baptizabit in Spiritu sancto, et igni.	He schal baptise or cristne you in the Hooly Gost, & fier.	He shall baptize you with the Holy Ghost, and with fire.

Another example: "Thanne Ihesus cam fro Galile into Iordan to Iohn, for to be cristened of hym. Sotheli Iohn forbeed hym & seide, I owe forto be cristenid of thee, & thou comest to me?" (Mt 3:13–14). The desire to anglicize did not stop even at the titles of the chapters. Instead of Acts of the Apostles, as in the King James version where it originates directly from *Actus Apostolorum* in the Vulgate, the Wycliffite version offered *Dedis of apostolis*, using the Old English word of *ded, dæd*. This ambition even went to the point of detail. In the Lord's Prayer (Mt 6:13), the Wycliffite translation follows "amen" with its translation — that is, "so be it."

Now we come to the dualistic tones. One can discern a measure of dualistic interpretation in the case of the verb *waische* (to wash). On the one hand, the Wycliffite translation uses this verb in its traditional meaning of "to wash," fully coinciding with its meaning in the King James version.

Matthew 15:2:

Wycliffe	*King James*
Whi brekenthi disciplis the tradiciouns of eldre men? For thei waischen not hondis, whanne thei eten breed.	Why do thy disciples transgress the tradition of the elders? For they wash not their hands when they eat bread.

When speaking of baptism, however, the stress lies on the fact that John the Baptist baptizes with water, that what he did was rather a ritual cleansing for repentance and ablution than baptism, while true baptism according to Bogomils, Cathars and Lollards was in the Holy Spirit.[32] In other words, we have an absolutely free introduction of the verb *waische*. No similar term exists either in the Greek or the Latin text, nor can it be found in the King James version. Hence what we have here is dualistic reediting.

Matthew 3:11–12

Greek	*Latin*	*Wycliffe*	*King James*
Ego men iumas baptizo en hiudati eis metanoian	Ego quidem baptizo vos in aqua in poenitentiam	I waische you in watir; into penaunce	I indeed baptize you with water unto repentance

One finds yet another usage of *waischun*, as a past participle, in order to underscore that John's baptism is "with water" (Mt 3:5):

Wycliffe	*King James version*
Thanne Ierusalem wente out to hym & al Iudee, & al the cuntre aboute Iordan, & thei weren waischun of him in Iordan.	Then went out to him Jerusalem, and all Judaea, and all the region round about Jordan. And were baptized of him in Jordan, confessing their sins.

This is another dualistic accent in the Wycliffite translation, and in this case not from John Wycliffe's dualistic texts in general, but a dualistic thesis in the translation of the New Testament, added as a commentary. This is an important thing to know because it leads to the thought that Wycliffe's translators could have used not the Vulgate as an original, but a version the dualists spread in Latin. The Prologue to St. John's Gospel mentions that he is more beloved of God than the other disciples (seid loued of God bifore othere disciplis). This is a familiar dualistic idea, directly embodied in *The Secret Book* of the Bogomils where John with head resting on the breast of Christ receives Christ's explanation of the origin and structure of the universe. With this detail we already have two indirect quotations of *The Secret Book*. As we have mentioned already, John Wycliffe called on *ex fide* Scripture in his work *De compositione hominis* and mentioned that human souls are borrowed from angels.

From *haeresia Bulgarorum* to *exemplum Bulgaricum*

Considering such obvious typological similarity between the dualists and Wycliffe, could one find proof of a genetic link between the English reformer, his supporters and *haeresia Bulgarorum*, the Bogomil movement? The answer is in the positive and, although we have mainly indirect evidence so far, this is still something unique. In other words, the evidence points at a single interpretation and it is difficult to find another one that would refute it. For example, the fact of Wycliffe's dualistic or geographically Eastern orientation is also supported by his special preference for

Greek lexis. To the best of this author's knowledge, English scholars have not yet commented on it.

John Wycliffe had a penchant for Greek. We find three characters in conversation in his work *Trialogus*: Alithia, Phronesis and Pseudis. However, Alithia, Phronesis and Pseudis are Latinized Greek words that mean truth, reason and fraud. A witness at the 1382 trial against Wycliffe reported that he considered antiquity as an authority and quoted names like Orpheus, Plato, Aristotle, Pythagoras, and so on.[33] When he proposed the idea of an English Church independent of the Vatican, the reformer called on the "Greek tradition" (more Graecorum), as it was usually called in the Middle Ages,[34] that is, the tradition of the Orthodox Church. When he argued against an opinion of Socrates Wycliffe relied on Aristotle.[35]

What we have in this case is a scholar who, by his knowledge of Greek philosophy and the Greek original of the New Testament, overstepped the Latin linguistic restriction imposed by the Catholic dictate over culture at that time. That, according to British author F. Hearnshow, was the earliest humanistic sway in medieval England.[36]

None of Wycliffe's biographers ever wrote he knew Greek, nor do his works (at least those this author has seen) feature quotations in Greek. The use of Greek words could mean that he had an erudite friend who directed him toward the Greek cultural heritage. According to historians, quite a few of the "perfect" (as Bogomil and Cathar leaders were called) knew Greek besides their native language and Latin. We also know about Bogomil missions from Constantinople to western Europe, quoted by Stephen Runciman. Therefore, such a man could possibly have been next to Wycliffe.

It is high time, though, to reveal the power and dynamics of the Wycliffite phrase, qualities that in a sense had a measure of Greek origin. Let us take the well-known place in Acts 26:23, "that Christ should suffer, and that he should be the first to rise from the dead," or "if Crist is to suffre, if he is the firste of agenrysing of deed men, that schal schewe light to the peple & to hethen men" in the Wycliffite version. While the King James version uses the verb "should suffer," the Wycliffite translation adopts an if clause that is almost identical with the Greek original *ei protasis* form, "*ei*" or the Latin "*si*." The act of the resurrection expressed by the gerund (agenrysing of deed men), is more emotional and more lasting than in the case of the simpler verbal form of the King James version that promises but lacks the same emphasis — "he should be the first that should rise from the dead." Generally speaking, when one compares the Wycliffite and the King James translation, one cannot but see that the former is a more masterly rendition of the Greek text. Last, but not least, the Wycliffite expression is more poetic and bears more sharing of the glory of the resurrection, while the King James version is a rational presentation of the final outcome.

Acts 26:23

Greek	Wycliffe	Latin	King James
Ei pathetos ho	if Crist is to	si passibilis	That Christ
Hristos, ei	suffre, if he is	Christus, si	should suffer,
protos eks	the firste of	primus ex res-	and that he
anastaseos	agenrysing of	urrectione	should be the
vekron	deed men	mortuorum	first that
			should rise
			from the dead

These lexical, stylistic and syntactic peculiarities were also noticed by some Western scholars. This was how, for example, Fred Robinson characterized them: "The General prologue also defends a more flexile translation of Latin ablative constructions, of polysemous words, of present participles, etc."[37] This approach is quite close to the linguistic results that, according to A. Schlötser and P. Lavrov, were achieved in the translations of the Bible in Slavonic languages.[38]

Translators from the Greek were forced to use "introductory sentences, ten different participles related to one another, rich resounding words," and so on.[39] In other words, this outlines a marked typology of translation characteristic of the Cyrillo-Methodian tradition. To put it more precisely, Greek has left the imprint of its system on the recipient languages. As we have already mentioned, C. Schmidt and Yordan Ivanov thought this typology was conveyed by the Cyrillo-Methodian copies that the Bogomils relayed to western Europe. Of all British authors, Bertrand Hamilton alone is interested in looking for such Greek reflections with a dualist flavor, and that in the sphere of lexis: "A faint memory of such a process may be preserved in the gloss on the Lord's Prayer in the Cathar Rituel of Florence: 'Quoniam tuum est regnum' — 'hoc verbum dicitur esse in libris greccis vel hebraicis' ('For thine is the kingdom' — this phrase is said to be in the Greek and Hebrew texts')," he wrote.[40]

When all of this is considered, a convincing case can be made that John Wycliffe and his adherents did not use the Vulgate as the source of their translation, but a Cyrillo-Methodian copy. The latter was most probably translated into Latin, but it had preserved to some extent the freedom of translation achieved by St. Cyril, St. Methodius and their disciples. In the earliest Slavonic variant of the Lord's Prayer, dating from the 10th century and discovered by Trendafil Krustanov in the Vatican palimpsest (Codex Vaticano graeco no. 2502), Ana-Maria Totomanova deciphered the word *hleb nash epiousion*, doubtless a direct borrowing from the Greek.[41] We know that this is not an isolated case: other Old Bulgarian translations of the New Testament have preserved *epiousion* in the Lord's Prayer.

However, one finds a preference for the Greek term *ephiusion* in John Wycliffe. At the synodal trial in 1382, Thomas Wyntirton tried to achieve a measure of condescension for Wycliffe because they both had a predilection for the works of St. Augustine. Thus Wyntirton's treatise was called *Absolutio* and he polemicized with his opponent much more subtly and intelligently than the other accusers. Without entering into detail we shall only say that, according to Wyntirton, Wycliffe said, "Panem dixit quidem, sed ephiusion 'hoc est supersubstantialem.'"[42] This evidence that Wycliffe used *ephiusion*, a Latinized form of a Greek term, outlines a visible chain of conceptual and lexical transfer. The chain begins with the Bulgarian transcription of ephiusion in the Vatican Gospel (10th century) and ends with the Latin transcription of this term, *ephiusion*, in Wycliffe.

This chain of transfer, the initial and final stage of which are clearly outlined at this point, lies in the context of Wycliffe's undoubted spiritual association with the dualists, as well as in the context of his marked interest in Greek culture. Detailed restoration of the vocabulary and the environment of the Wycliffite translation of the New Testament and the clarification of dualistic elements in Wycliffe's theology allow one to draw the following general picture from the separate facts:

1. John Wycliffe was an adherent of Bogomil-Cathar dualism. He and his disciples introduced specific dualistic tones into the New Testament translation.
2. The Wycliffite translation reveals similarities with the Cyrillo-Methodian approach to the translation of the Scriptures, including coining new words and extracting lexical material from the mother tongue, dynamic phrase and a variety of participles.

3. Wycliffe had a visible penchant for Greek lexis and for Greek culture. Although it is still not specified, this Greek source is a reality that warrants further investigation. At this point, the most acceptable assumption is that this could have been Bogomil "perfecti" who came from Constantinople or Bulgaria.

4. These data allow one to endorse the hypothesis that the Wycliffite translation could have been made not from the Vulgate but from a Cyrillo-Methodian version that was Latinized and transported by dualist Bogomils and Cathars. The least that can be said is that the Wycliffite translation was made with a knowledge of and a respect for the Greek version of the New Testament.

Thus, *haeresia Bulgarorum*, with its already proven pan–European diffusion and footing in the cultural life of many countries like Italy, France (particularly Provence), Germany, Spain and Flanders, became the *exemplum Bulgaricum* of popular translations of the New Testament, bearing the freedom of direct communication with the Scriptures.

One should also look at this phenomenon from the aspect of social and cultural change. One could definitely claim that Wycliffe, his circle and the popular culture of the Lollards achieved a sort of renaissance of the English language. That liberated culture even created its own social type, the educated layman or, to borrow the term from Anne Hudson, *laicus literatus*.[43] What she had in mind was the investigation against the Lollard Walter Brut in the period between 1390 and 1393,[44] opened by Bishop Trefnant of Hereford. The defendant Brut displayed broad culture, a knowledge of Latin and the ability to argue with the bishop's rather impressive team, including 15 officials, three masters and two bachelors of theology, and two doctors of civil and canon law. Although she still retained some doubts as to how widespread Brut was as a social phenomenon, Anne Hudson concluded that "Walter Brut may have been an extreme example of the Lollars *laicus literatus*, but he was far from the only one."[45] To her comments she added the fact that "the Lollard heresy was learned, indeed academic," and that "the immediate source of the heresy was the thought of John Wycliffe."[46]

That cultural upsurge was in harmony with the brilliance of the Cathar civilization in Provence, with the cultural and literary activity of the Bulgarian and Bosnian Bogomils. A phenomenon where evangelization, that grew into self-evangelization, developed into a national and popular self-education, into a proto–Renaissance.

Appendix to Chapter 4: Anglicization in the Wycliffe and King James Bibles

Why undertake this comparison between the Wycliffite translation and the King James version? First, the Authorized version of the Bible is really the most popular variant in England and the United States that performs the prime prescription "appointed to be read in the Churches." The translation of the Bible, done by 54 learned men under the aegis of King James in the period between 1604 and 1611, was designed as an alternative of the Vulgate in order to achieve "a more exact Translation of the holy Scriptures into the English Tongue" by a fresh interpretation of Hebrew and Greek originals.[47] That initiative also aimed "to offer a palpable defence" against the criticisms of "Popish Persones at home and abroad."[48] The *Cambridge History of English and American Literature* in 18 volumes specifies: "It is agreed on all hands that the English of the *Authorised Version* is, in essentials, that of Tyndale,"[49] who in 1525 made a translation of the New Testament from a Greek original. Other authors add that *Textus Receptus* by Erasmus was also considered when the version of King James was produced. For our purpose, we ask what the degree of Anglicization is when one compares the Wycliffite and the King James version? Andrew Sanders sees "inaccuracies and Latinate rhythms of the Vulgate" in the Wycliffite result,[50] meaning that the King James version is supposed to be more Anglicized. But when one undertakes a textological analysis one comes upon an opposite trend. The vocabulary of the King James version is more influenced by Latin than the Wycliffite one. Besides, the Wycliffite rhythm is more distant from the Latin than the former.

Another fact supporting this observation: King James version adopted the translation principle that "the old 'ecclesiastical words' (as 'church' for 'congregation' and 'charity' for 'love') were to be preserved."[51] That meant substitution of the English word love (ME<*lufu*, akin to OHG *luba*, Goth *lubo*) for the Latin root charity (ME & Ofr *charite* <L *caritas*). Commenting on Tyndale's work, Bishop Stephen Gardiner of Winchester gave similar advice — "that certain 'ecclesiastical words' should be left as they appeared in the Vulgate, chief among them being *ecclesia, episcopus, caritas and gratia*."[52] Thus, recurrent returns to Latin vocabulary is a practice in the King James version.

This author has no intention of implying some kind of rivalry when speaking of the Wycliffite and King James versions because both of them proclaim the defense and the development of the English language. This comparison is intended to reveal some visible specific features suggesting that Wycliffe and his followers may have used a Latin translation of the Cyrillo-Methodian version of the New Testament, a source more specific than the "corrupt text of the Latin Vulgate."[53]

CHAPTER 5

Dualist Ideas in the Works of Tyndale

Courage
A large white flower on its stalk
in the deserted garden
meets with the wind and has a talk.
— Stefan Gechev

Tyndale: The Covert Dualist

Two centuries later, William Tyndale reiterates to some extent the historic cause of John Wycliffe, while voicing a great respect for his predecessor. Revealing such continuity entails many surprises. It is already the 21st century, but new discoveries are still made in the history of the Middle Ages and sometimes established views are changed. William Tyndale is one such phenomenon the conception of which will seemingly become richer with time. The observation of David Daniell that "he has reached more people than even Shakespeare"[1] is well founded considering the quantities in which the Authorized Version of the Bible, which is based on Tyndale's translation, has spread across the world. Tyndale's translations enriched the English language with the "sounds and rhythms" and he himself became a sculptor of the language, going on to create "unforgettable words, phrases, paragraphs and chapters."[2]

While supporting the opinion of David Daniell on principle, this author also naturally retains the right of his own concept of the issue with some nuances. It seems to me that the first heightened level of the quality English language was accomplished by the circle around John Wycliffe with the translation of the New Testament. William Langland's *Piers Plowman* (c. 1360, text A) is practically contemporary to that undertaking, sharing the philosophy of dualism and using its imagery. In other words, just as the foundations of a rich and expressive English language were laid in the Langland-Wycliffe period, to which one should add the brilliant contribution of Chaucer (particularly the 1392–1395 period when he wrote the main part of the *Canterbury Tales*),[3] the English literary language emerged in all its richness and glory in the Tyndale-Shakespeare period. Chaucer is no mechanical addition here. There are grounds to pay attention to the information indicating certain sympathies in the founder of modern English literature, for it is also known that he translated the *Roman de la Rose*, in which Cathar moods are a proven presence. In addition we know what honor Chaucer paid to Piers Plowman in his prologue to *The Canterbury Tales*. Regarding the linguistic contribution of Wycliffe himself, Herbert Workman wrote that "Wycliffe's Bible was one only, not by any means the most widely read, or the standpoint of influence on the English language, the most important."[4]

This chapter has a strict focus: the presence of hitherto unstudied dualistic ideas in the work of Tyndale. It is not a biographical or critical literary study but an ideological and theological analysis or, more specifically, a case study of the history of ideas. Such analysis allows one to outline the origin of certain ideas and images; their transfer from their place of origin to the host country; and their interpretation adequate to a certain age.

Bogomilism — with its west European branches of Patarenes, Cathars, Beguins and Lollards — is probably the most outstanding example of transcontinental, pan–European proliferation and interaction between cultures. It was for such an approach that Dimitri Obolensky appealed even in the first edition of his excellent book on the Bogomils: "A detailed study of Bogomilism should help Western medievalists to shed new light on the still somewhat obscure problem of the historical connections between Asiatic Manichaeism and the dualistic movements of western Europe, particularly of the Italian Patarenes and of the Cathars or Albigenses of southern France" (p. 17).[5] Our starting point is the idea that William Tyndale relied upon Bogomil-Cathar philosophy in his motivation for the translation of the Scriptures, as well as in many of his interpretations of mainly New Testament material. Now let's move on to the facts. It is well known that Tyndale communicated with Luther, but in the thinking of the Englishman there is definitely something more specific than the influence of the head of the German Reformation. For example, one discerns Tyndale's own renditions in relation to the parable of the dishonest manager in St. Luke, which also impressed his authoritative biographer, David Daniell. Daniell compares Luther's famous *Ein Sermon dem unrechten Mammon Lu.XVI* with the manner in which Tyndale treats this parable in *The Wicked Mammon*. To quote Daniell, "Luther's printed sermon occupies only six leaves in quarto; Tyndale has six times as much.... Moreover, Tyndale alone sets out the whole parable — Luther's text is only the final verse."[6]

This preference turns one's attention to the fact that the same parable from St. Luke is an important part of *The Secret Book* of the Bogomils. It explains the beginning of Satan's treachery and the corruption of the angels who followed him. It explains how Satan became the impious lord of this world. In other words, for Tyndale this story acquired nearly the same importance it had in *The Secret Book* of the Bogomils.

Could this preference for the parable shared by Tyndale and the Bogomils be a coincidence, a mere chance? Coupled with the parable, chance seems unlikely when one considers a remarkable definition of Tyndale's whereby he expresses the foundation of the Bogomil-Cathar teaching: "God and devil are two contrary fathers, two contrary fountains, and two contrary causes: the one of all goodness, the other of all evil."[7] Now for comparison we shall give Bogomil and Cathar texts, which reveal complete cognitive and almost complete lexical correspondence:

Bogomils
Against him who says and believes that there are two principles, a good one and a bad, one the creator of light, the other of darkness, one of men, the other of the angels and other living bodies, anathema [Theophylact Lecapenus writes to Tsar Peter of Bulgaria about Bogomils].[8]

Cathars
I hereby wanted to speak of the two principles in honour of the Holy Father [*Liber de duobus principiis*, end of the 13th century].[9]

Such notable dualistic definitions are not an isolated phenomenon in English literature. When he wrote that he had called his *Cain* a mystery, Byron added that he had done so in accordance with the old "very profane" mysteries and *moralité*. And in *Cain* Lucifer reigns together with Jehovah:

> *Lucifer:* No we reign
>
> Together; but our dwellings are asunder....
>
> To the great double mysteries! The *two* Principles![10]

It seems that dualism was a certain trend in English literature and since Byron himself confided from where he had borrowed the dualistic theme and imagery, it is our turn now to reveal how it is present in Tyndale and how he chanced upon it. The dualistic views of the reformer find an even more comprehensive expression when he voices another important idea of Bogomils and Cathars, that this world is the kingdom of the devil. Acknowledging the power and the great hold of the devil on people's souls, Catholics and Orthodox Christians adamantly define the world and the creatures as God's creation while the dualists regard it as the creation and kingdom of Satan. This, too, is why Presbyter Cosmas reproaches them: "They should also be condemned because they call the creator of the sky and the earth father, but regard his creation as one of the devil."[11] Now here we find the same thinking expressed through the words of Tyndale: "Seeing we are conceived and born under the power of the devil, and we are hiss possession and *kingdom*, his captives and bondmen" (italics added).[12] We shall recall here yet another element of harmony with the dualists in the above phrase: Tyndale obviously shared their opinion that conception as essential to the flesh is subordinate to the devil.

Of course, these dualistic definitions in the works of the reformer are not placed one next to the other, nor do they comprise a comprehensive and consistent exposé. It seems that, as he was aware the dualist philosophy should be concealed, Tyndale made a fragmentary intertextual presentation, making it accessible to insiders, to those who had previous knowledge about it or who spread it secretly among sympathizers. This, by the way, is an old Bogomil method to which Euthymius of the Periblepton (11th century) devoted plenty of space and even earlier was described by Presbyter Cosmas (10th century): "ostensibly they do everything to avoid being distinguished from orthodox Christians," which attracted people "to approach them" and to think that they are "orthodox and capable of guidance to salvation."[13] The explanation is simple — as K. Radchenko has explained, it was an established Bogomil habit to mix canonical with noncanonical literature to enable the heretics to espouse their philosophy without trouble. Bogomils and Cathars were communities of nonviolence, they had no means to defend themselves and consequently used such mimicry to avoid attracting unwanted attention from church authorities. Tyndale himself said that "to lie also, and to dissemble is not always sin."[14]

Tyndale's method was so successful that not only his opponents but his researchers as well failed to discern the dualistic presence. Consequently, we shall hereafter bring these fragments to the fore and connect them in the comprehensive dualistic exposé that they form. This will be accompanied by comparisons with well-known Bogomil and Cathar formulas to reveal to what extent they overlap with Tyndale's theses. For example, Tyndale repeatedly used the definition "good man," which is what Bogomils and Cathars called their dualist leaders: "good men," "boni homines," "boni christiani," "perfecti."

To make the direct comparison, the Cathars said "and thus they call themselves good Christians, good men and holy."[15] Tyndale, in turn, used "good and learned man," "a Christian man is a spiritual thing and hath God's word in his heart,"[16] "and God make thee a good man."[17] On a single page of his *Doctrinal Treatises* he mentioned the root "perfect" four times exactly in the sense of achieving the dualist status of spiritual elevation: "For *perfecter* we be, the greater is our repentance, and the stronger is our faith. And thus, as the Spirit and doctrine on God's part, and repentance and faith on our part, beget anew in Christ, even so they make us grow, and wax *perfect*, and save us unto end, and never leave us until sin be put off, and we clean purified, and full formed, and fashioned after the similitude and likeness of the *perfectness* of our Saviour Jesus" (italics added).[18] One finds a constant usage of the same definition with the Lollards (good man, good woman, true man, homo fidelis, perfit man). According to studies of this author (which carry abundant evidence), the Lollard communities definitely professed the dualist philosophy. The scope of this chapter does not permit us to go into more detail, but the evidence leaves little doubt that the Lollards were the last, most Western branch of the Bogomil-Cathar heresy.[19]

Just as Bogomils, Cathars and Lollards say that the state "good man" and "perfect" is acquired through the act of consolamentum, by the descent of the Holy Spirit on the ordained Tyndale describes the same sacrament as more powerful than papal ordination: "but prayer as when we say God make you good man, Christ put his spirit in thee."[20]

The Reformation Potential of Dualism

The next major chapter in the parallels between Bogomil–Cathar theology and Tyndale's interpretations pertains to the problems of direct communication between believers and God (respectively, the Scriptures), and specifically focuses on the denial of saints and icons; the denial of service; the denial of confession; and on the role of the priest.

The Bogomil position regarding the saints is categorically negative. As Euthymius of the Periblepton succinctly put it, "The blasphemers say no one is or should be called holy; only God is holy."[21] Tyndale's opinion is equally unequivocal: "Take Christ from the saints and what are they? What is Paul without Christ?"[22] Or "not the saints, but God only receiveth into eternal tabernacles, is so plain and evident, that is no to declare, or prove it."[23]

One should underscore here the coinciding beliefs of the Bogomils as expressed by Euthymius of the Periblepton and Tyndale. The former say "only God is holy" and five centuries later their British follower repeats "but God only receiveth into eternal tabernacles." The personal nuance with Tyndale is that he is inclined to a little concession: he is ready to take the saints for an example only,[24] naturally not as mediators between God and believers. Once the cult of the saints is removed there is no longer need to revere their icons, or as Presbyter Cosmas wrote, "the heretics do not revere the icons and call them idols."[25] Tyndale is a bearer of the same attitude, calling the reverence of icons "false faith, superstitiousness and idolatry and damnable sin."[26]

Tyndale enhances the reprimand, objecting in God's name against the depiction of God's images: "For nothing bringeth the wrath of God so soon and so sore on a man, as the idolatry of his own imagination."[27] Tyndale's last phrase and Bogomil–Cathar criticism of the icons are also in harmony with some texts in the New Testament. "It is not as though Christ had entered a man-made sanctuary which was only modelled on the real one; but it was heaven itself, so that he could appear in the actual presence of God on our behalf" (Heb 9:24). Here we encounter a tendency to which we shall return later in this study. Although they had a philosophy complicated by Manichaeism and Gnosticism, the dualists practically strove to identify themselves with the early Christian communities with evangelical type of conduct. Considering that the Bulgarian Bogomils and the Cathars, representatives of mitigated dualism, reinstated the reverence of the cross and called themselves fashioned after the manner of Christ, one can see that the activity and the spiritual efforts of these communities constituted a spontaneous return to the initial form of Christianity. This is essentially an example of reformation, of shedding the depravity amassed in the church as an institution.

Rejection of liturgies logically follows the rejection of icons. The Bogomils, as Presbyter Cosmas wrote, considered them "many worded," maintaining that it was not "the apostles who established liturgy and communion, but John Chrysostom."[28] One should recall here that the critical expression "many worded" corresponds to Matthew 6:7: "In your prayers do not babble as pagans do, for they think that by using many words they will make themselves heard." One finds similar views and definitions in Tyndale: "Subdeacon, deacon, priest, bishop, cardinal, patriarch and pope, be names of offices and services or should be, and not sacraments."[29]

In other words, the superfluous and profuse ecclesiastic bureaucracy was not in service of the sacraments, did not contribute to the spiritual development of the people, did not Christianize. William Tyndale pointed out that the hearing of mass, matins and evensongs, and receiving of holy water, holy bread and the bishop's blessing and so forth[30] did not make one love one's neighbor more, be more merciful or more thirsty for the spiritual. This seems to launch the thesis of the Bogomils (according to the letter of Euthymius of the Periblepton), "what is a priest"[31] something useless, but in this case developed in lengthier form. Tyndale added his own commentary, according to which the priest should be the elder and more experienced preacher, as it had been in early Christian communities, which in turn was also to be the image of contemporary church.[32] Tyndale often makes a definition in this sense in his *Table of the Book*: "in Greek called presbyter, in Latin senior, in English an elder" and "priest is to say an elder."[33]

To the Bogomils and the other dualists God is the sole recipient of personal confession. In this case, too, we have many observations to make. According to the 15th century *Summa contra haereticos* (Cod. Monac. Lat. 544), the dualists thought believers confessed their sins directly to God and received forgiveness from Him.[34] This, too, was the opinion of the Lollards, featured in the 15th century Norwich heresy trial records: "the same Margaret claims confession is made only before God and no other priests."[35] William Tyndale also literally rejected the opportunity for a priest to be "a mediator between God and us."[36]

One also finds the respective coincidence in the other, the public variant of dualist confession. We know that Bogomils and Cathars also practiced the so-called collective confession, a 14th century description of which we can see again in Döllinger's collection of documents: "This confession is preferred in public where the prelate holds the Scriptures above his head while the rest lay their right hands with prayer."[37] Tyndale's definition of the two models of confession repeats the dualistic in both spirit and letter: "Confession, not in the priest's ear (for that is but man's invention), but to God in the heart and before all the congregation of God."[38]

The practice according to which the actual function of the priest is above all either in the sermon or in leading collective confession, or in spiritual guidance makes these activities also achievable by the ordinary but spiritually elevated man. This is the common stance of the Bulgarian and the European dualists, of the Lollards, Wycliffe and Tyndale, and it offered outlets for the religious activity of women.

Margaret Aston has pointed out quite correctly that "in the fourteenth and fifteenth centuries, as earlier," Cathars, Waldenses and in general "unorthodoxy offered women outlets for religious activity that were not to be found in the established church."[39] Thus this tradition was introduced and spread by the Bogomils even in the 10th century, as Presbyter Cosmas wrote. The letter of Euthymius of the Periblepton mentions the heretic leader Churila who split with his wife because of the Bogomil requirement for abstinence from marriage and made her a "mock abbess."[40] When discussing the place of women in the Lollard community, Margaret Aston pointed out that there women used to study, read and preach the Scriptures and were some sort of evangelists, although she couldn't take it upon herself to say definitely whether women were given the role of priests.[41]

It seems to this author, however, that we can rely on the records of the heresy trials in Norwich, where several heretics categorically stated that "every trewe man and woman being in charite is a priest."[42] Aston herself quoted the same thesis voiced by Wycliffe. Such categorical positions give grounds to assume that, although we do not know a name of a Lollard priestess to this day, such a document could be discovered one day, particularly as there are numerous recordings of the phenomenon of "perfect" Cathar women in Provence. In addition, Döllinger's collection features a 14th century document of the Inquisition in Provence, according to which "perfect" Cathar women officiated at the supreme sacrament of the dualists, consolamentum, i.e., baptism in the name of the Holy Spirit.[43]

Since precedents abound so much, they could possibly have found their concrete expression somewhere in England, too. In addition, one should not forget that preaching God's Word, public reading of the Scriptures in the native tongue and their explanation are the real priestly functions according to the dualists. In other words, the role of evangelist, which Aston agrees was granted to Lollard women, according to the dualists means acting like a priest. The question is whether English women heretics had the right to give consolamentum, the supreme unction. The fact that this has not been recorded does not mean a negation in itself since the abundant archives on the Lollards to the best of this author's knowledge do not feature a description of consolamentum. The reason seems understandable — the Lollards hid their dualistic essence (and consolamentum was their supreme sacrament) and rather presented the structure and creed of their church, defending them as direct conformity to the Scriptures to generate respect in the official Church. Nor did the Inquisition surmise that the English heretics were a continuation of the continental dualistic heresy.

About a century later Tyndale in turn placed the high sacrament "to bind and loose" (which according to the Catholic doctrine proceeds from the pope) in the hands of "every man and woman that know Christ and his doctrine."[44] In other words, his continuity with the dualists is doubtless because he shared the then extremely unusual idea, for Orthodoxy or Catholicism, of female clergy, which today bothers the Orthodox and the Catholic churches.

While nothing external has been introduced here and only thoughts and images of Tyndale have been used, one could pose the question of whether the stress is not laid extremely on some of his separate views and whether they actually have the weight they are allotted. Such focusing in our case is not only allowed; it is a necessary process, as we can thereby reconstruct actual material which had the meaning of at least concealed narrative. Besides, although it is concealed, the narrative is of primary, not secondary, significance. Therefore to distinguish it — which has not been done so far — is an important academic task. As one can see, it bore the personal, confessional and functional philosophy of the reformer. Things become much clearer when the new narrative is related to two important religious discussions, which British scholars in most cases treat as a product of English national life. True, they are part of the cause of the national church, but in their foundation they were imported from the dualist movements in eastern and western Europe.

At places — for example in *The Obedience of a Christian Man* — Tyndale did not launch any sharp discussion involving transubstantiation, obviously with the intention of concealing his negation. In his *Doctrinal Treatises* he compared various fundamental views on the issue ending exactly in the spirit of the dualists and directly expressing his negation. To him the idea of transubstantiation is false: "through the eyes and other senses perceive nothing but bread and wine ... and thereof, no doubt, came up this transubstantiation through false understanding."[45]

And, of course, transubstantiation is defined as a papal mistake: "The pope confirming transubstantiation did purchase his own gain to the overthrow of the right use of Christ's sacrament."[46] In the place of the idea of transubstantiation Tyndale raised an extremely free interpretation of his own. To him the cup of the New Testament should be understood as the cup holding the blood of Christ: "this cup is 'my blood of the New Testament,'" or even more directly "my blood of the New Testament."[47] This, however, is in harmony with the Bogomil metaphor recorded by Euthymius Zigabenus: "The 'new wine' they say is their teaching."[48]

One should also mention that Tyndale's refusal of equating the Eucharist with "the blood of Christ" harks of the Bogomils' early objections to the cross, that the memory of Christ's suffering cannot be accepted as His symbol. "Now the testament is, that is his blood was shed for our sins; but is impossible that the cup or his blood should be that promise," wrote Tyndale.[49] In essence he emulated the style and the words of the Bulgarian dualists: "But how can we bow to it? Because the Jews crucified His son on it the cross is most hated by God. That is why they teach their own to hate it, not to bow before it, saying thus: If anyone murdered the prince on a cross of wood could that wood be beloved of the king? The same is true of the cross and God."[50]

One could also add another borrowing. The Bogomils and the Cathars were authors of a sarcastic attitude, familiar in the Middle Ages, against the Eastern Orthodox and Catholic belief that the body of Christ is in the Eucharist. Here we shall quote it according to Bernard Gui's 13th century *Manual of the Inquisitor*: "The body of Christ, they say, is not there [in the Eucharist], for if we assume it could be compared to the greatest mountain then the Christians would have eaten it all by now; the Eucharist is born of straw, passes through the tails of stallions or mares. In other words when the flour is cleansed of this filth through the sieve it goes down to the end of the stomach and excreted through the dirtiest organ. That is why it is impossible, they say, for God to be there."[51] Now here we have the similar phrase — and with the same image of the horse at that — pronounced by Tyndale on the same occasion: "If thou bring a bowl of blood and set it before God to flatter him, to stroke him and curry and claw him, as he were a horse, and imaginest that he had pleasure and delectation therein, what better makest thou of God than a butcher's dog?"[52] One should explain here that such detailed quotation does not aim to recall the emotions and the character of the discussion between the dualists and the Catholic Church. It provides two proofs on principle of the relation between the dualists and Tyndale not in ideas alone but in imagery, style and sustainable individual vocabulary. In other words we have one and the same theology, born in Bulgaria and transferred to England, expressed in the 16th century with an almost identical vocabulary. The study of these details is a procedure of comparative analysis, whose evidential powers increase with the respect for detail, for cliché images and expressions. In the Middle Ages they were typological indicators, something akin to the fixed epithets in Bulgarian folk songs.

Here we shall quote a series of examples of traditional dualist criticism against the official church starting from the Bogomils, passing through the Cathars and Lollards, and preserving a very characteristic imagery also shared by Tyndale. This criticism pertains to the church itself and to the liturgies and sacrifices. One should also add here the enrichment of this criticism by the dualists in western Europe during their battle with the Vatican. Ideas new to the fray were the declaration of the pope as the Antichrist and his prelates servants of Satan; the rejection idea of Purgatory; and the rejection of indulgences. These ideas will be discussed one by one, starting with the rejection of the official church.

The words with which Presbyter Cosmas said the Bogomils denied the official church were the following: "The churches they consider crossroads and the liturgies and other services in them — many words."[53] Euthymius Zigabenus added: "They think that Herod is our Church, which tries to murder the Word of truth born among them."[54] Because in the case of the Cathars the conflict with the Catholic Church was more severe and the persecutions more systematic, this negation was graded. On the one hand they declared their community the true and benign church, "*benignam, quam dicunt esse sectam suam*," while the church of Rome was bad, the "mother of fornication, the great Babylon, mistress and basilica of the devil, synagogue of Satan."[55] The formulations of the Lollards were equally categorical and sometimes even more temperamental. The parchment maker John Godesell declared at the heresy trials in Norwich (1428–1431) that the pope was "Anti-Christ and the head of the dragon mentioned in the Scriptures and that the bishops and other prelates of the church were followers of Anti-Christ, and the mendicant orders — the tail of the dragon."[56]

Such, too, are Tyndale's position and language. At first he pointed out that preaching was the essence of the first Christian churches (the dualists practiced this extremely modest churchgoing without any special church building) and declared that the church is not material but spiritual: "The Churches at the beginning were ordained that the people should thither resort, to hear the word of God there preached only, and not for the use wherein there now are."[57] By the way, this type of "internal worship" was expressed in another way by the well-known Bogomil instruction on how to pray: "When you pray, go into your room." They say that the room is the mind.[58]

This Bogomil instruction was reproduced by Tyndale: "Of entering the chamber and shutting the door to ... the meaning is, that we should avoid all worldly praise and profit, and pray with a single eye and true intent according to God's word."[59] This is a paraphrase of Matthew 6:6: "But when you pray, go to your private room and, when you have shut your door, pray to your Father who is in that secret place, and your Father who sees all that is done in secret will reward you." Thus the "private" churchgoing of Bogomils, Cathars and Lollards and Tyndale actually followed the prescriptions of the Scriptures verbatim.

After he outlined the image of the true modest church of direct communication with God in the heart of man, Tyndale took up the fiery criticism of the dualists against the Catholic Church. Even in the tables of contents of his books one finds expressions like "Pope ... a sure token that the pope is antichrist."[60] The quoted subtitle of Tyndale's *An Answer unto Sir Thomas More* is reproduced in nine variants bearing a similar antipapism. One even finds the attack "the pope is the whore of Babylon,"[61] which is yet another literal coincidence with the Cathar anti–Catholic speeches. The Catholic prelates are presented as a greedy group "whose God is their belly,"[62] as "murderers" and "liars."[63]

"Destitute of the truth they corrupt minds." Tyndale used the vocabulary of the Cathars and Lollards to attack donations and indulgences: they "beguile God's word ... to establish their wicked tradition,"[64] "with such glosses corrupt they God's word, to sit in the consciences of the people, to lead them captive, and to make a prey of them: buying and selling their sins to satisfy their unsatiable covetousness."[65] And that this truly was the language of Cathars and Lollards one can see from a quotation of the same polemic vocabulary set down in the minutes of the 15th century trials in Norwich. Margery Baxter, probably the most outstanding defendant at the trial, claimed that the bishop of Norwich and his ministers were "members of the devil who spread the false indulgences given them by the pope" and that indulgences taught the simple people "damnable idolatry."[66] One could ask here whether similar rhetoric couldn't have been used in other circles. The answer is unequivocal: in the Middle Ages only the dualists took the liberty of polemicizing temperamentally against the Catholic Church openly and consistently, in the course of several centuries. They always felt theirs was a separate large world, they had an idea of the scope of their presence, particularly as they saw it under God's direct guardianship. It is only in their case that such a line of conduct was amassed and passed down from generation to generation with the respective emotional vocabulary which, by the way, was also taken from critical New Testament passages against the heathens and the Pharisees. Thus it became a sort of autocharacteristic feature which can hardly be mistaken.

Naturally, one can sense the time and *couleur locale*. In the case of the Bogomils it is clear even in their *Secret Book* that they regarded this world as Satan's creation and therefore as hell. In western Europe, however, a new element entered this explanation: the Cathars and their affiliates were forced to give their own answer as to the location of purgatory and what it was, as purgatory was invented by the Catholic Church.

The earliest answers belonged to Bosnian Patarenes since they were the first to have direct contact with Catholic influence: "they say there is no Purgatory."[67] Similar opinion was recorded in the minutes of a 1387–1388 heresy trial in North Italy: "there is no other purgatory nor other hell but this world."[68] This was also the opinion of the Lollards tried at Kent, with the added warning that "there was no purgatory but only in this world, and aftir that a man was decessid he shulde go straight to heven or to hell."[69]

And while the above-mentioned objections against purgatory seem rather doctrinal in the sense that the dualists who expressed them considered that this world was actually purgatory or declared it an unreal, fabricated construction that did not correspond to God's creation, two centuries later Tyndale denounced the avaricious aspect of purgatory. He described it as a zone invented as a result of the commercial and power-lusting ambitions of papacy: "but have created them a Purgatory, to reign also over the dead and to have one kingdom more than God himself hath."[70] This artificial kingdom acted as a customs office, for untold riches were collected through it from the relatives of the deceased who paid generous sums for the expurgation of the souls in purgatory and their "ascent" to heaven.[71] There were also elements of "economic" or rather anticorruption criticism of purgatory on the continent. Döllinger quoted a document according to which, in addition to denying the existence of purgatory, the heretics claim donations are unclean, good only for the priests who ate them and lived in luxury.[72]

Tyndale was nevertheless rather more global, closer to the idea of modern times and civic society: he rejected purgatory not so much with theological arguments as denouncing it as a totalitarian scheme, an open tool of unprecedented social dictum and manipulation, of economic exploitation through which the clergy take away "faith, hope, peace, unity, love and concord then house and land, rent and fee, tower and town, goods and cattle, and the very meat out of men's mouths. All these [the clergy] live by Purgatory."[73] The pope and his pardons are grounded on purgatory, Tyndale giving the cross of Christ as an alternative to that rapacious theology.[74] A powerful gesture indeed, which summed up Tyndale's idea of a national church where all could read the Lord's Prayer in their mother tongue; where all should know that churchgoing was above all the preaching of God's word by modest servants, a church whose signs were Christ and the holy cross. In fact this was the image of early Christian communities.

By returning to the cross Tyndale surpassed the tradition of clandestine heretical communities and offered an open, general national church reformed in the best of dualist spirit and practice. Although the examples we have quoted are unequivocal evidence of Tyndale's predilection for dualist theology, he wanted the edifice of his church to be one for all society, for the entire nation. The return to the cross, in fact, is a trend of internal evolution of Bogomilism and the Cathars, which was discerned by authors such as A. Solovjev, Dmitri Obolensky, Rene Nelli and Stefan Lazarov.

Tyndale's determination to elevate the significance of the cross corresponded to that trend, but it also emerges as his personal initiative in England when one recalls that the bulk of the Lollard defendants at Norwich (1428–1431), who were obvious staunch supporters of absolute dualism, rejected the cross. One can also discern Tyndale's new attitude to the cross in the fact that he used imagery and rhetoric whereby the Bogomils denied the cross but without the very act of rejection. Therefore Tyndale was also a reformer in the hard wing of dualist tradition, suggesting that it come out of its self-isolation and converge with the institutionally and historically established Christianity but shed corruption and other deformities by reform. Considering that most of the texts used by Tyndale stem from the books and formulas of absolute dualists, his officially declared reverence for the cross overcomes some internal dualist dogmas, which sound like extreme speculation to the general public.

In this sense Tyndale's position was an expression of humanism, of liberation from the faith of dogma and ossified perception, of toning down excess confrontation. This was a return of Christianity to its calling to be the moral and motivation of love open to all, to that divine bounty which can be called individual emotional life and individual imagination in the perception of the Word.

At the same time the reproaches he levied against the Catholic Church were the result of doctrinal disagreement for he saw a tendency of dehumanism there, although he did not use this term. Above all he claimed that by using a foreign language the church terminated the process of Christianization, of spreading the teaching of Christ and familiarizing people with it, which meant the introduction of love. Without the native tongue there was no connection to Christ or complete appreciation of His kindness: "How shall I prepare myself to God's commandments? How shall I be thankful to Christ for his kindness?"[75] In addition, by corruption the church underwent a process of mammonization, which was an antipode of Christianization, and introduced the fashion of greed.[76] As a type such criticism was a position modern for those times, for Tyndale saw evil not only in the mythological figure of the Devil but also in socially removable roots like the implantation of greed, of the bad passion for plentiful, excessive wealth as an end in itself, of the easiest corruption of people.

Dualist Influence in the Two
English Translations of the Scriptures

Now that we have seen that the philosophy of William Tyndale shared fundamental Bogomil-Cathar doctrinal positions it is pertinent to ask by what ways the dualist philosophy actually reached him. On the one hand, things are complicated because he lived in the 16th century, his connections with the familiar writings of dualist culture were indirect and he was, so to say, a third-generation dualist. What we have in mind as the first generation of dualists of Albion are the German-speaking heretics described by W. Novoburgensis who were branded in Oxford in 1166. The second generation consisted of Wycliffe and the 14th century Lollards with their abundant literary work. Naturally such periodization is conditional and can only be finalized with the addition of new data. For example, Henry Knighton quoted Higden in his *Chronicle* and wrote: "Mony of the heretikes Albigense, commyn into Ynglonde, were brent in lyfe." It was difficult for this author to decipher the exact date of this report precisely because it retold Higden, and based on the context I date it to 1209.[77]

On the other hand the high degree of presence of clearly defined dualist theses in Tyndale's works cannot be explained without systematic contacts with the dualistic heritage in England or in Europe. I would like to mention here four of the many cases on which this relation was discussed. In 1906 W. Summers saw undoubted continuity between the English Reformation and Wycliffe's work.[78] Eighty years later Charles Nauert, Jr., saw the possible relation between Tyndale and the Lollards as an occasion to underscore the national character of Tyndale's work and to extract him from the notion that he was "merely an English disciple of the Saxon reformer."[79] David Daniell also assumed such closeness, stating that "his memory was still green" at the time when Tyndale studied at Oxford. Daniell added that in 1520 "Lutherans as well as Lollards were now sought out for punishment."[80]

The conviction that Tyndale had familiarity with Wycliffe's work — and that means with Lollard writings — is most powerful (and I think quite rightly so) in D. Smeeton.[81] In addition to the quantitative indicator, Smeeton also discerned a visible conceptual continuity: "In view of the recent availability of critical editions of certain Wycliffite writings, it is possible to examine Tyndale's writings in light of parallel passages from Wycliffite literature. It would be difficult indeed to show that Tyndale used a particular version of a particular treatise, but compatibility, approach, language and general theological themes could certainly be indicated."[82]

In the opinion of this author, Tyndale was not only familiar with Wycliffe's writings and work, but also melded in the significance of apostolic example, which he himself wanted to follow. In other words, he quoted Wycliffe as his predecessor in the national anti–Catholic cause: "Wycliffe preached repentance into our fathers not long since. They repented not, for their hearts were indurate, and their eyes blinded with their own pope-holy righteousness."[83] The measure of Tyndale's commitment to Wycliffe was so great that he supported him where the attacks against Wycliffe were most severe. Tyndale rejected the accusations that the ideas of his predecessor were among the causes of the peasant revolts: "These hypocrites laid to Wycliffe's, and doyet that his doctrine caused insurrection."[84] By using the word *doctrine*, Tyndale indicates that he had comprehensive knowledge of Wycliffe's system of ideas.

One should suppose that a more detailed study of the sources Tyndale used to create his dualist philosophy will also reveal other connections, some of which might prove Continental. Here we have to address another question: If Wycliffe's influence on Tyndale is visible, how do we prove this was a dualist influence? Because of the limited scope of this study we cannot present the existing detailed evidence; we shall only say that the previous chapter clarifies the Bogomil-Cathar views of John Wycliffe.[85] As an indicative illustration, one should note that Wycliffe's well-known thesis of *Deus debet obedire diabolo*,[86] is a rather precise translation of the Bogomil view that the devil is the impious steward of this world.[87]

Naturally, as a thinker with an impressive individual presence already far beyond the initial substratum of ideas, Tyndale had his own peculiar features. Thus, although he repeatedly expressed a dualistic preference for the New Testament and although the examples in his works predominantly came from the New Testament, unlike the dualists he accepted the use of the Old Testament. Like the Bogomil-Cathar assertion that the God of the Old Testament was cruel and unjust, that that was Satan, Tyndale judged the Old Testament quite critically: "The old, cruel and fearful testament, which drew people away."[88] Respectively, he expressed a strong preference for the New Testament: "but this new and gentle testament, which calleth again, and promised mercy to all that will amend."[89] In his own interpretation Tyndale did not bring the contradictions between the two testaments to a break, but rather defined the Old Testament as a sort of antechamber to the New Testament. The Old Testament is a "covenant ... made between God and the carnal children of Abraham, and Jacob, and otherwise called Israel," while the New Testament is "a new covenant ... that Christ's blood is shed for our sins," i.e., this was a way for the spiritual elevation of man. Thus we can also see that Tyndale adopted the official doctrine of redemption,[90] while the Bogomils and Cathars did not.

The dualist theology is softened in yet another important case. Cathars, Bogomils and Lollards rejected baptism with water, asserting that true baptism was with the Holy Ghost,[91] with the Word, with Christ's passion and blood.[92] While placing baptism with the Word higher, Tyndale avoided rejection of baptism at the font and preserved its significance as preparatory to baptism with the Word: "The washing without the word helpeth not: but through the word it purifieth and cleanseth us." Of course, he did not forget to define baptism in Christ's blood as the true baptism: "The washing preacheth unto us, that we are cleansed with Christ's blood-shedding."[93] Thus he did not engage in conflict with important items in the official church tradition but introduced his own additional interpretation instead.

Regardless of his critical discussion with the Catholic Church and the perseverance with which he denied, for example, transubstantiation, Wycliffe also in other cases tended to take into account to some extent official rituals, for one can see from both his works and his conduct that his objective was to reform the institution of the church, not to bring it down. He assumed images of God could be used providing it was known they were just images and not a presence of God in the material itself: "If it is said that God and the stone are one, then this is heresy and should be denied."[94] Thus the occasion for magical devotion is taken away from the icon and it is interpreted as a symbol, which brings about contemplation of God. Such an interpretation made a contact between believers connected with the official church and those in the Lollard communities. Therefore, both Wycliffe and Tyndale, each by his own means, had the identical initiative to establish a national church with reformation material borrowed from the dualists.

Tyndale also modernized the term *perfect* which denoted the Bogomil leader. With the English the achievement of this state by the special ceremony of consolamentum becomes rather redundant, it being enough for one to devote oneself to spiritually elevating knowledge: "The principal of Scripture perfectly learned, all the rest is more easy."[95] From initiation of the elect it becomes an appeal and way for spiritual growth achievable by man. Those were the changes of the time and thinking of Tyndale — some purely dogmatic points of dualist theology were left behind to pass to the idea for a more unencumbered development of personality, of individual thinking and expression achievable by the means of education, culture, literary work and discussion. In fact that was a sort of evangelical humanism, the beginning of a Christian renaissance. One should recall here that his criticism of purgatory featured a similar aspect: purgatory was a prejudice, a mystic invention and a usury system to the enlightened, the educated with a broad view of the universe. One can even discern traits of Erasmus's *In Praise of Folly* (*Encomium moriae*) in the satirical barbs leveled at purgatory. One can also see the genetic link between Bogomil-Cathar tradition and Reformation noted by an author closer to our time. In 1879 L. P. Brockett of the American Baptist Church, who used the freshly accumulated research material on Bulgarian dualists with great insight, declared the Bogomils were forerunners of Protestantism in his brochure *The Bogomils of Bulgaria and Bosnia*.[96] Such global thinking seems difficult for a large number of modern scholars, but there are certain obvious outlines that cannot be overlooked.

Based upon the evidence, it is our conclusion that the two key translations of the Scriptures into the English language, the two momentous efforts to generate reform in the official church — that of Wycliffe in the 14th century and that of Tyndale in the 16th — were motivated by Bogomil-Cathar philosophy and were accompanied by the introduction of elements of its practice. As John Foxe beautifully put it, "over England's long night of error and superstition and soul-crushing despotism God had said 'Let there be light and there was light' with Tyndale's work."[97] The Bulgarian example of direct communion with the New Testament lay at the root of that work, of that enlightenment.

Further work on clarifying Tyndale's hidden theology will probably enrich the information presented here. It will also introduce more nuances and precision in detail. For example, one can say that although the Wycliffe-Tyndale influence is clearly visible, in certain nuances it seems they are representatives of two different trends in dualist philosophy. According to hitherto studied material, Wycliffe rather leaned toward the ideas of the Bulgarian Bogomils who had "their own church of Bulgaria, believe in and preach a good omnipotent God without beginning (or end), who created the angels and the four elements. And they say that Lucifer and his accomplices sinned in the heavens."[98] I would support this statement with Wycliffe's repeated quotation of the myth of Christ descending into hell and vanquishing it, a myth to which the Bogomils had a special predilection and which they borrowed from the *Nicodemus Gospel* included in the list of Bogomil literature. Tyndale's formulation in his *Expositions and Notes on Sundry Portions of the Holy Scriptures Together with the Practice of Prelates*, "God and devil are two contrary fathers, two contrary fountains, and two contrary causes: the one of all goodness, the other of all evil," overlaps with another tendency of dualism — that of absolute dualism preached by the Druguntia church, which reads "they believe and teach two gods, two lords without beginning or end, one good and one evil."[99] At the same time it can be seen that Tyndale obviously read the *Homily of Epiphanius*, which also describes the scene of Christ's descent into hell, although Tyndale showed a preference for another equally impressive passage there and wrote: "Christ is in thee, and thou in him, knit together inseparably."[100] This is an almost exact translation of the well-known phrase from the *Homily of Epiphanius*: "Thou art in me, as I am in thee — we are a primeval indelible face."[101]

With the exception of some 19th century authors, the idea of the dualist heresy being transferred from the Continent has received little or no attention from modern British medievalists. The philosophy and practice of the Cathars have been presented exceptionally well in Malcolm Lambert's *The Cathars*,[102] one of the best works on this subject so far, although it does not outline a connection between the European proliferation of the Cathar movement and Britain. Dualist formulas sound strange and incomprehensible to many scholars. As the excellent scholar of the Lollards James Gairdner wrote about Wycliffe's fundamental dualist thesis, "God, as he strangely put it, ought to obey the devil" (i.e., the devil rules the earthly world).[103] Some threads have been marked by an observant pioneer in this matter, W. Summers, who mentions Knyghton's information as well as one or two cases propitious for research.[104] These, however have been abandoned completely by present-day English medieval studies.

Appendix to Chapter 5:
Updating the Evaluation of Tyndale

We should like to add another observation proving the salutary efforts of the Tyndale Society to update the view of the reformer in a broader European circle. Commenting in the article "The Authorised Version the translations of the Bible by the English reformers, including Tyndale's Bible (1525)," *The Catholic Encyclopedia* noted: "That there was much good and patient work in them, none will deny; but they were marred by the perversion of many passages, due to the theological bias of the translators; and they were used on all sides to serve the cause of Protestantism."[105] One could reply that this was written a century ago and one should not be so demanding. Regrettably, this text has been placed in the online edition (www.newadvent.org/cathen/02141a.htm, (c) 1999 by Kevin Knight). It seems unacceptable for accusations of "profaned" Scriptures, rampant in such a benighted manner in the Middle Ages, to be transferred in the 21st century, particularly as the translations of the Holy Writ are imposing, sometimes tragic national causes.

Emotions aside, one should recall the self-assessment of *The Catholic Encyclopedia* regarding the alternative to Reform Catholic English translation: "and although accurate, was sadly deficient in literary form." Or add the words of Yaroslav Pelikan describing the damages done by extreme reliance on the Latin version of the Bible and unfamiliarity with the Greek: "An inability to read Byzantine Christian writers (not to mention the New Testament) with any real expertness in the original language led Thomas Aquinas astray into a dependence on misinterpretation of Eastern Christian theology, and therefore into a distortion of the differences between it and the Western church on so fundamental point of dogma as the Filioque."[106] A more fitting approach by the modern publishers of *The Catholic Encyclopedia* might be to find a way to add Pope John Paul II's 2001 apology to those persecuted by the Catholic Church with the fire and the sword.

CHAPTER 6

Bogomil-Cathar Imagery and Theology in The Vision of Piers Plowman

After having discerned how dualist concepts became an incentive for reformation, we enter literary horizons, where dualist theology gains majestic imagery. This applies to two giants of English literature, William Langland and John Milton, but a broader investigation of the subject would direct us to some other phenomena like the medieval miracle plays, which very frequently featured dualist apocryphal elements. It is assumed that William Langland's well-known poem, *The Vision of Piers Plowman*,[1] was completed around the year 1370. This multi-plane work consists of 20 chapters containing some 6,500 unrhymed verses (B-text). The poem is, in fact, a comprehensive panel of 14th century reality in Britain, a valuable source of information about public and spiritual life in that age. Its main objective is to suggest a meaning for the existence of contemporaries from a Christian point of view. Unlike ecclesiastical homilies, however, in this case problems are posed for consideration before the individual, and it is in this spirit that Langland expounds his deliberations and quests. In other words, we have a development of personal philosophy and position — a novelty in relation to medieval mass conscience. Quite a lot has been written about William Langland's poem, underscoring any number of aspects of its significance, be they historical, literary, socio-critical or religious. Two of these, however, have remained untouched. First, on many occasions *The Vision of Piers Plowman* sounds like a Bogomil-Cathar treatise in that it develops fundamental elements and images of dualist philosophy. The second lies in the context of the first, the fact being that one finds it reproduces episodes from the Bulgarian *The Legend of the Tree*, or *The Tree of the Cross*, and from other Bogomil apocrypha like *The Secret Book* of the Bogomils as central elements of meaning and composition. It is the objective of this chapter to clarify these Bogomil-Cathar motifs, for they are a case of major cultural transfer, an interaction between geographically distant cultures in the Middle Ages that has become common cultural heritage. Or, to use a contemporary French term of the sociology of culture and civilization, *interculturalité médiévale*.

To ensure that our thesis is clear and convincing we shall use the most revealing of all means of comparative analysis, direct text comparison. Then again, because of the limited scope of this chapter, we shall concentrate on the following major ideas and narrative elements in *Piers Plowman*: the fall of Lucifer and his angels; the descent of Christ into Hell and the liberation of all souls; and Christ's teaching Peter to plough and giving him a writ granting use of the land.

The dualist myth begins with the legend of Lucifer's betrayal, his desire to place himself above the Lord, which ends with the banishment of Lucifer and those with him from the heavens and their descent into the void where they created the Earth as their own conception (not without help from God, of course). The classical narration of this legend is found in *The Secret Book* of the Bogomils, and a direct comparison reveals that the story retold by William Langland is very close to the original.

The Fall of Lucifer

Piers Plowman, *Passus I, ll. 111–123*
Lucifer with legions lerned it in hevene, / And was the lovelokest to loke after Oure Lord [one] / Till he brak buxomnesse; his blisse gan he tyne, / And fel fro that felawshipe in a fendes liknesse / Into a deep derk helle to dwelle there for evere. / And mo thousandes myd hym than man kouthe nombre /

The Secret Book of the Bogomils (Carcassone text)
... et traxit cum cauda tertiam partem angelorum Dei, et projectus est de sede Dei et de vilicatione coelorum. Et descendens Sathanas in firmamentum hoc, nullam requem potuit facere sibi nec iis qui cum eo errant
[*Bogomilski knigi i legendi* (Sofia: 1925), p. 76].

103

Lopen out with Lucifer in loth-
liche forme / For thei leveden
upon hym that lyed in this
manere: / *Ponam pedemin
aquilone, et similis ero Altissimo.* /
And alle that hoped it myghte be
so, noon hevene myghte hem
holde, / But fellen out in fendes
likness [ful] nyne days togideres,
/ Til God of his goodnesse [garte
the hevene to stekie / And gan
stable it and stynte] and stonden
in quiete.

... and with his tail he dragged
away one-third of the angels of
God, and he was banished from
the throne of God and from the
overlordship of the heavens. And
Satan, descending to this firmament, was unable to find rest
either for himself or for those
who were with him

[*Monumenta bulgarica*, translation Tom Butler (Michigan
Slavic Publications, 1996), p.
193].

The reader may notice that this book more than once repeats quotations from Bogomil and dualist scripts. These recurrences are a visible
reality in different cultural monuments of the English Middle Ages. There
is yet another peculiarity: the myth of Lucifer's fall is repeated in *Piers
Plowman* at least three times, whereby the dualist thesis of Satan's overlordship on Earth becomes dominant in the poem. It is on that that the
specification of the Antichrist imposing his power in the papal institution
lies: "And thane shal Pride be Pope and prynce of Holy Chirche, / Cov-
etise and Unkyndenesse Cardinals hym to lede."[2] And the consequence
will be their power over secular authorities, for "false prophetes fele,
flatereris and gloseries / Shullen come and be curatours over kynges and
erles."[3] In other words, Langland's well-known anticlericalism is dualistic. It is in synchrony with the Cathar thesis that "since the Pope, the bishops and the Catholic priests subordinate to the Church of Rome do not
follow the holy faith and are hostile to their [the Cathars'] holy faith, they
have no power whatsoever to absolve anyone of their sins."[4] The English
Lollards were no less temperamental and closer in their imagery to Langland when they declared the pope in Rome Antichrist and all bishops,
prelates, presbyters and men of the church followers of Antichrist.[5] At the
bottom of that anticlericalism lay Bogomil criticism, which called Orthodox priests blind Pharisees and whose adepts offered a negation of the
official world order (because this world was a Devil's construction) even
more radical than Langland's: "they teach their own folk to disobey the
masters, they detest the king, they blame the boyards."[6]

Christ Descends into Hell
and Sets All Souls Free

The motif of Christ setting human souls free from hell was transferred to medieval Europe by two apocrypha, the *Gospel of Nicodemus* and the *Homily of Epiphanius*, their main distributors — particularly of the former — being dualist: Bogomils and Cathars. British historians have accepted the presence of scenes from the *Gospel of Nicodemus* in the literature and art of medieval England, *Piers Plowman* included,[7] but it seems the second aspect of the process, the fact of dualist transfer, remains outside their field of vision. By comparison in the tables we shall prove that the scene from Passus XVIII coincides quite precisely with chapters XXIV and XXVI of the *Gospel of Nicodemus* from a copy taken to Ukraine by Bulgarian Bogomils. The compiler of the excellent anthology *Apokrifi i legendi z ukrainskih rukopisiv*, the Ukrainian poet Ivan Franko, was one of the first to point out that this story spread by the Bogomils penetrated into England.[8] He was outstripped only by M. Gaster, who spoke of the same transfer in 1887, without forgetting to point out its Bogomil context or the direct relation between the *Legend of the Cross* and the *Gospel of Nicodemus*: "The legend in its simplest form is part of the apocryphal *Gospel of Nicodemus*."[9] Some would object that, albeit on the extreme periphery, this scene was mentioned by medieval Catholic authors as adopted by the Orthodox Church. In the case of the dualists, however, its means the complete destruction of hell and the liberation of all souls: "Ac alle that beth myne hole brethren, in blood and in baptisme, / Shul noght be dampned to the deeth that is withouten ende" (Passus XVIII, ll. 377–378) — while the official churches admit only the liberation of Adam and Eve (see the appendix to this chapter).

COMPLETE DESTRUCTION OF HELL
AND THE LIBERATION OF ALL SOULS

Piers Plowman, Passus XVIII	*Gospel of Nicodemus,* Chapter XXIV, XXVI:
"Dukes of this dymne place, anoon undo thise yates, / that Crist may come in, the Kynges	And the Lord stretched His hand and said: "Come unto Me all My

Christ leads the souls away from hell. Mural painting from the Boyana Church, 13th century. The Bulgarian art critic Kiril Krustev is convinced that the anonymous Boyana artist was under the influence of Bogomil ideas. The salvation of all souls is emphasized by Avel with a shepherd's stick (visible to the left), among other descendants of Adam. (Photograph: Vladimir Vitanov. Courtesy of the National Museum of History, Bulgaria.)

"The Harrowing of Hell" from the Psalter of St. Albans. As one can see here Christ saves all souls—"out of helle mennes souls," to quote *The Vision of Piers Plowman* (Passus XVIII, 1. 373). The psalter was created possibly between 1123 and 1135 at St. Alban's Abbey near London. (Psalter of St. Albans, p. 49 Dombibliothek Hildesheim HS St. God. 1. Property of the Basilika of St. Godehard Hildesheim. Used by permission.)

sone of Hevene!" [320–321].
Patriarkes and prophetes, *populus
in tenebris,* / Songen Seint
Johanes song, "*Ecce Agnus Dei!*"
[324–325]. Getest bi gile tho
that God lovede; / And I, in liknesse of a leode, that Lord am of
hevene, / Graciousliche thi gile
have quyt — to gile ayen gile! /
And as Adam and alle thorugh a
tree deyden / Adam and alle thorugh a tree shal turne to lyve; /
And gile is bigiled, and gile
fallen [356–361]. That I drynke
right ripe must, *resureccio mortuorum.* / And thane shal I come
as a kyng, crowned, with aunge-
les, / And have out of helle alle
mennes soules [372–73]. Ac to
be merciable to man thane, my
kynde is asketh, / For we beth
brethren of blood, but noght in
baptisme alle. / Ac alle that beth
myne hole brethren, in blood
and in baptisme, / Shul noght be
dampned to the deeth that is
withouten ende: / *Tibi soli pec-
cavi&* [376–79].

saints, for you have My likeness
and were sentenced to death for
the deeds of the Devil's tree. See
now that I have judged death
through the Devil's tree." And
when He said this all saints were
under the Lord's hand. And the
Lord took Adam by the hand
and said "Peace be with you and
all your children..."

And all saints kneeled before the
Lord and said as one "The Savior
of all ages has come! And the
words of the prophets and the
law have come to be. He saved
us with his life-giving cross,
came to us through His
crucifixion and saves us from
Hells' death by your power, oh
Lord"

[*Apokrifi i legendi z ukrainskih
rukopisiv.* T. II., pp. 300–301; p.
312].

At that, Christ's descent into hell and the salvation of Adam and Eve,
along with numberless others,[10] "out of helle alle mennes soules" is mentioned again in Passus XIX. There is the addition of a particularly important detail, signifying yet another element of dualist character, that is, that
after that Lucifer is chained, which is a repetition of the same scene from
The Secret Book of the Bogomils:

Piers Plowman	*The Secret Book* (Codex Carcassoniensis)
And took [Lucufer the lothly], that lord was of helle / And bond [hym] as [he is bounde], with bondes of yrene [Passus XIX, ll. 56–57].	... *et claudet Diabolum ligans eum insolubilibus vinculis fortibus.*[11] [... and he locked the Devil in powerful invincible chains].

The Bulgarian Image of Christ the Ploughman and Piers Plowman

There is only one image of Christ Ploughman in the world of apocryphal literature and that is the one in Father Jeremiah's *The Legend of the Cross*. This Old Bulgarian story from the last quarter of the 10th century features Christ teaching man to plough better, that is, in both directions, whereas until then he would go to the end of one furrow and then, instead of turning the plough again in the field, would surround it and go back to square one from where he would start on the next furrow. Naturally, this is also an image of the sowing of Christian virtues. Bulgarian popular theology thus created a new hypostasis of Christ — Christ the Ploughman — probably just as widespread in the plains at the time as Christ Pantokrator was in official church icon painting. The tetraevangelion describes the life line of the Lord's Son in the direction from earth to heaven. Christ's Passion or the road to Calvary is respected by all believers and His self-sacrifice is an unsurpassed example. The people of the plains, however, did not want Christ to leave them; they wanted to see Him among themselves, to witness His deeds in everyday life, to regard Him as a wiser brother who taught them to work and live better. According to their thinking the outcome is the descent, the return of Christ from heaven to the earth, to the people. This great and appealing image took the road to western Europe carried by the Bogomils, only to reach William Langland. What the possible ways of this transfer were we shall see a bit later.

In addition to the complete similarity of meaning and scenery in the episodes we have compared, readers cannot but notice some peculiarities of time and local custom. In Langland's case it is Grace, not Christ, who teaches Piers to plough — a process entirely metaphorical in the poem as the field of truth is ploughed, virtues are sown and the team of four oxen are the four evangelists. This difference, however is *licentia poetica*, the freedom to interpret the source apocrypha and the desire for personal expression in creativity — early tentative hits of the Renaissance in the age of Langland. Nevertheless, the links to Bogomil imagery and theology remain visible and are not lost.

CHRIST THE PLOUGHMAN

Piers Plowman, *Passus XIX, ll,
260–268*

"My prowor and plowman Piers shal ben on erthe, / And for tilie truthe a teeme shal he have." / Grace gaf Piers a teeme — four grete oxen. / That oon was luk, a large beest and a lowe chered, / And Mark, and Mathew the thriddle — mighty beestes bothe; / And joined to them oon Johan, moost gentil of alle, / The pris neet of Pires plow, passynge alle othere.

The Legend of the Tree by Father Jeremiah

One day Jesus went to Bethlehem and saw a man who was ploughing and throwing the earth on one side, going round and round the field. And the Lord saw that the day was passing [fruitlessly] and took the plough in His hands, plough three furrows, then turned the plough, gave it to the man and said: "Fare thee well, brother, plough!" [*Stara bulgarska literatura. I. Apokrifi*, p. 282].

The legend by which the land is given to Adam — to Piers Plowman in Langland's poem — is yet another fundamental Bogomil thesis that has found place in chapters 18 and 19 of the poem. Christ makes Piers his spiritual ploughman on earth. This new covenant between the Lord and the Farmer runs in contradiction with the old agreement. According to the old obligation, featured in the apocryphal *Story of Adam and Eve from the Beginning till the End*,[12] the Devil urges Adam to give him a bill (zapis) registering that he, Adam, and all his progeny will belong to him. That is because Adam has been given the right to till the land belonging to the Devil, for don't the Bogomils say that the earth is created by the Devil. The same paragraph, however, also features "but Adam knew that the Lord would descend on earth in human form and would vanquish the Devil." That Bogomil imagery was followed can also be seen in Langland's usage of the verb "register" to underscore his closeness to his source. In other words, Langland continues his dialogue with apocryphal legend. He presents the new convention by which Grace gives the land to Piers Plowman, a situation promised by the above mentioned apocryphal phrase: "but Adam knew that the Lord would descend on earth in human form and would vanquish the Devil."

CHRIST'S REGISTER

Piers Plowman, Passus XIX, ll, 260–263
"For I make Piers the Plowman my procuratour and my reve, / And register to *receyve redde quod debes.* / My prowor and my plowman Piers shal ben on erthe, / And for to tilie truthe a theeme shal he have."

Story of Adam and Eve from the Beginning till the End
And thus Adam caught the oxen and began to plough for his living. Then the Devil came, stood [before] the oxen and stopped Adam from work. And he said to Adam "Mine is the earth and the heavens and Eden are the Lord's! If you want to be mine, till the earth, but if you want to be with God — go to Eden." And Adam said "The heavens, the earth and Eden and all the universe are the Lord's." Then the Devil spake: "Thou shalt not plough if thou does not give me a writ that thou art mine." Adam then answered "He who is lord of the earth — his will be I and mine." The Devil rejoiced. But Adam knew that the Lord would descend on earth, would take human form and destroy the Devil [*Stara bulgarska literatura. I. Apokrifi,* p. 39].

One should note here that the quoted cases of borrowings from Bulgarian apocryphal literature are part of a much more comprehensive presence of Bogomil influence in the poem, but we do not have the opportunity to expound on it further here. Rather, we shall pass on to the next important issue: in what way were these fundamental Bogomil and apocryphal myths taken to England? Although such a connection might seem nearly improbable to contemporary scholars there are nevertheless 19th and 20th century authors who have noted it. As we have already mentioned, such a transfer of Bogomil apocrypha to medieval England was discussed by M. Gaster, Alexander Veselovski and Ivan Franko.

A case in point regarding results of the transfer of variants of the *Legend of the Tree* to England was that they were noted by the prominent French expert on English literature Jean Jules Jusserand, although he did not note the Bulgarian origin of the apocrypha or their dualist involvement. This he did in his *Histoire littéraire du peuple anglais*, the first volume of which was published in France in 1895, and which was rounded off to three volumes in 1909.[13] Thus, without indicating the peculiarities of the apocrypha, Jusserand nevertheless gave a remarkably comprehensive description of variants of the *Legend of the Tree*, existing in England in: *Ayenbite of Inwit or Remorse of Conscience* (London: 1886); *Legends of the Holy Rood, Symbols of the Passion and Cross poems in Old English of the XI, XIV and XV centuries* (London: 1871); *An old English Miscellany, containing a Bestiary, Kenton sermons, proverbs of Alfred and religious poems of the XIII century* (London: 1872); *The religious poems of William de Shoreham* (London: 1842) (about the Holy Sacraments, orders, deadly sins, etc.—first half of the 19th century); *Cursor mundi, the Cursor of the World* (London: 1874–1893 [seven parts compiled c. 1300]).

In other words, Jusserand perceptively identified the story typologically without going on to clarify its genesis or its dualistic characteristics. Nevertheless, this was an achievement which surpassed the efforts of his 20th century English colleagues. It is because of the same lack of time that we shall dwell here on only three cases of distinct transfer amidst the bountiful stream of manuscripts and other material that were discovered:

- *La Légende de l'Arbre de Paradis ou «bois de la croix,»* (The Legend of the Tree of Paradise or the Tree of the Cross) poème anglo-normand du XIIIe siècle et sa source latine, d'après le Ms. 66 Corpus Christi College (Cambridge: Inédit — in Zeitschrift fur Romanische Philologie, vol. 76, 1960).
- *Cursor mundi* (transferred from France and translated in Northern

England c. 1325–1330): *Cursor mundi,* ed. R. Morris. Four versions: British museum Ms Cotton Vespasian A.III; Bodlean Ms Fairfax 14; Goettingen University Library Ms. Theol. 107; Trinity College Cambridge Ms. R. 3.8. Seven parts (London: 1874/1961).
- and, above all, the famous series of 14th century ceramic tiles from the no-longer-existing church in Tring, Hertfordshire, with scenes from the apocryphal Infancy Gospel.

The above order of presentation has a significance of its own. The publication of the first manuscript provides information about the widespread presence of *The Legend* in the whole of medieval Europe, England included. *Cursor mundi* is a case of permanent popularization of the manuscript in England, while the Tring tiles represent the very scene of Christ Ploughman reproduced in Britain. Now let us consider them one by one. M. Lazar, who published *The Legend of the Tree of Paradise or the Tree of the Cross,* an Anglo-Norman poem, kept at Corpus Christi College, Cambridge, laid the stress on "the great popularity of the legend in the Middle Ages" and one that had "countless adaptations of different names in many languages."[14]

Cursor mundi is an enormous poem of some 30,000 verses, about which there are only a few British studies, none of which touches upon the problem of the manuscript's origin.[15] *Cursor mundi* comes from France (just like *The Legend of the Tree of Paradise or the Tree of the Cross*), so it is an apocryphal miscellany of second generation. It is a mixture or contamination of several dualistic texts, the compositional axle being *The Legend of the Tree.* It could be compared to the Bulgarian apocrypha *Orafione of St. John Chrysostom on How Michael the Archangel defeated Satanael,* classified by Anissava Miltenova as one "of the more general type Bogomil works intended for the general public." It was then, at the end of the 12th and the beginning of the 13th centuries, that the practice of compiling miscellanies of separate apocrypha originated in Bulgaria, in this case including parts of *The Secret Book,* the *Tiberiad Sea,* the *Dispute between Christ and the Devil,* the *Book of Enoch* and the *Apocalypse of St. John,* among others.[16]

One should, however, note that although *The Legend of the Tree* and *Cursor mundi* contain variants of the Bulgarian *Legends of the Holy Rood,* they do not feature the Christ Ploughman scene. Nevertheless this image appears in a sort of resurrection in the series of ceramic tiles from the no-longer-existent church in Tring, Hertfordshire (14th century). The series constitute episodes from the *Infancy Gospel*, but following the above mentioned practice of re-editing and mixing different apocrypha it also includes the episode in which Christ teaches the ploughman to plough correctly. In other words, an episode of *The Legend of the Tree* is incorporated in the *Infancy Gospel*. By the way, this type of mixing, incorporation and editing we call a "Bulgarian alteration" since it is one of the earliest examples registered in Europe of these peculiar types of creative freedom in unhesitant reworking of existent texts and resources. As *The Legend of the Tree* was itself created in such a way, we shall date the "Bulgarian edition" or the Bulgarian type of work with apocrypha to around the end of the 10th century. A variety of this, by the way, shall be mentioned shortly.

Now let us look at the illustrations — two scenes, of which we shall first discuss the one to the right, fig. B. (scene 28, D. 2), in which Christ teaches the ploughman the right way to plough while the latter regards Him in amazement and gratitude.

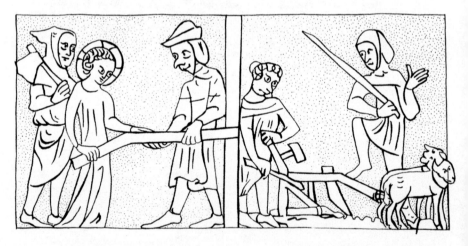

Fig. A (Scene 27)   Fig. B. (Scene 28, D. 2)

Without any doubt the scene reproduces a fundamental episode from Father Jeremiah's *The Legend of the Tree*. The text goes: "One day Jesus went to Bethlehem and saw a man who was ploughing and throwing the earth on one side, going round and round the field. And the Lord saw that the day was passing [fruitlessly] and took the plough in His hands, ploughed three furrows, then turned the plough, gave it to the man and said: "Fare thee well, brother, plough!" The eminent British medievalist M. R. James (whose 1923 depiction of the tiles is pictured here) failed to understand the contents of this scene. "In D.2 is a scene of ploughing," he wrote. "A ploughman guides the plough, which is drawn by a yoke of oxen. A man with a goad, probably the master, seems surprised."[17]

The scene on the tiles coincides with the episode in *The Legend of the Tree* even in detail. One should add here, that the ploughman really does hold a goad, the very same goad which made Father Jeremiah exclaim: "Oh, blessed tree, that the Lord took in His hands! Oh, blessed plough and blessed goad!"

Now we come to the Bulgarian correction or alteration we find in fig. A (scene 27). Here Christ, as E. Eames wrote, "straightens the beam of a plough."[18] M. R. James, whom she quoted, added that he also failed to find such an episode in *Evangelium Thomae Infantiae*[19] (or *Infancy Gospel*), and that "the scene was either altered or not understood."[20] In this way, however, without knowing it himself, the British scholar has indicated the Bulgarian alteration in this version of *Evangelium Thomae Infantiae*, which consists of the following: "in Latin is a grabatum that has to be made: here it is a plough."[21] It is true that in the traditional version of *Evangelium Thomae Infantiae*, Christ extends a plank for a simple, low-lying bed (grabatum), while in the Tring tile series Christ extends a plough beam. In other words, the idea of a plough has prevailed and been substituted for the low-lying bed (grabatum) in the traditional version of *Evangelium Thomae Infantiae* in the contamination of the *Infancy Gospel* and *The Tree of the Cross* that the Tring tiles constitute. The same Bulgarian alteration — extension of a plough beam, not of a grabatum, is found in the already familiar *Cursor mundi*,[22] as well as in the Anglo-Norman variants of the *Infancy Gospel*, published in 1985 in a monograph by Maureen Boulton. It says there that the father of Jesus, Joseph, is told to make a plough "Ço ke a charue duit aver."[23] One should note here that since all medieval manuscripts here have been registered as brought from France[24] we can also see the outline of familiar transfer of Bogomil literature, i.e., from Bulgaria to France, with the added link of England.

In conclusion, one could add to the quite apt observation of the well-known British literary historians W. L. Renwick and H. Orton, who noted that in the early Middle Ages English literature featured "three traditions, three bodies of thought and imagination articulate and inarticulate, each possessing its own appropriate matter, language, and technique: the Latin, the French, and the English."[25] But since this chapter indicates a solid transfer and influence of fundamental Bogomil motifs and manuscripts in England, we should add yet another element — the Bulgarian one. In spite of the barriers, the isolation, lack of culture and dominant dogmatism, medieval Europe nevertheless had its zones of active cross-border communication, which in many cases became incorporated and stimulated the development of national literary processes. As Dimitri Obolensky has noted, the Bogomil-Cathar cultural milieu was exactly such a case of most intensive exchange, which lay in the bed of millennial transcontinental communication between the East and the West.[26]

Appendix to Chapter 6:
Delivering the Souls

To illustrate the difference between the Cathars' position and that of the official church we shall quote two authoritative opinions on the matter — those of the Catholic and the Orthodox churches.

The Catholic viewpoint is revealed in the words of St. Thomas Aquinas (13th century). After indirect and very well mannered polemics with St. Augustine, in his capital work *Summa Theologica* (third part, question 52) he came to the conclusion that Christ gave grace — delivery from hell — only to some, at which they were released from purgatory, not hell: already cleansed sufficiently (*qui jam sufficienter purgati errant*). Aquinas yet again specifies that what is meant is selection and delivery,

and that from purgatory, not hell. Consequently, it does not follow of necessity that all were delivered from purgatory by Christ's descent into hell.[27] In other words, the conditions of delivery are complicated, it is practically very partial and that not from hell but from purgatory (the median zone the Catholic Church located between heaven and hell).

So to his own questions: Articulus V: Whether Christ descending into hell delivered the holy Fathers from thence? (*Utrum Christus descendens ad inferos Sanctos patres inde liberaverit?*); Articulus VI: Whether Christ delivered any of the lost from hell? (*Utrum Christus aliquos damnatos ab inferno liberaverit?*); Articulus VII: Whether the children who died in original sin were delivered by Christ? (*Utrum pueri qui cum originali peccato decesserant, fuerint a Christo liberati?*) Thomas Aquinas gives a negative response.

The Orthodox interpretation is rather more comprehensive. Primarily, the descent into hell in the time between the death of Christ and His Resurrection is perceived as completion of His work of redemption and a need of His human nature. The descent into hell is also regarded as bringing the blessed news (annunciation) of the Gospel to eternal darkness, thereby destroying its eternal power and "associating the entire pre–Christian world with redemption." Nevertheless, when the delivery from hell is meant, it is assumed that those were mainly "Old Testament innocents."[28]

The Bogomil-Cathar delivery is for all souls. The 13th century inquisitor Rainier Sacconi presented the Cathar thesis that "Christ descended in that Hell to help them [the souls]."[29] This is what else was put down in the records of the Inquisition in Languedoc in the 14th century—"after Christ was resurrected He descended into Hell body and soul and took out from there all human souls, be they sinners or not, with the exception of Judas Iscariot."[30]

(Some Cathar branches deny the descent into hell outright, because according to them this world created by the devil is hell. Then, for example, the birth of Christ in such a world would have the significance of a descent into hell. These dogmatic details were not so widespread and were related mainly to absolute dualism.)

One should add yet another important point. Christ also delivers all souls from hell in some early English manuscripts like the *Exeter Book*: "The exiles came crowding, trying which of them might see the victorious Son — Adam and Abraham, Isaac and Jacob, many of dauntless men, Moses and David, Isaiah and Zacharias, patriarchs, likewise too a concourse of men, a host of prophets, a throng of women and many virgins, a numberless tally people."[31] This complete salvation is a trace of Bogomils and Cathars. That is why the assumption of Renwick and Orton,[32] as well as that the poem *The Descent into Hell* from the same manuscript was compiled around the year 800, seems unconvincing, for the *Gospel of Nicodemus*, which they quote as a second possible source (and it definitely is the first) was transferred in Latin translation to western Europe not earlier than the end of the 10th or the beginning of the 11th century. The more probable specification of time would be their dating of the entire *Exeter Book* to c.

1072, when the transfer of dualist manuscripts from Bulgaria and the Balkans to western Europe began. A more precise dating of the *Exeter* manuscript should at least take into consideration the already mentioned pro-dualist delivery of all souls.

CHAPTER 7

The Spiritual Kinship *between* Paradise Lost *and* The Secret Book *of the Bogomils*

Speculation and Miltonian Self-Identification

The scope of action in Milton where man tackles evil on a cosmic or universal plane — and that from the position of fundamental Christian tenets — has made scholars use definitions like "Christian heroism."[1] This, however, is followed by a question that has been the object of much effort but that has failed to result in sufficient clarity, and that is the character of the imagery used. According to the author of the expression "Christian heroism," B. Kurth, what we have there is a Biblical epic,[2] in other words, the imagery is biblical. Alexander Shurbanov holds a similar point of view, stating that Milton sensed that old European mythologies had already been used in new European literature, that a new fund of imagery was necessary and consequently came to the choice of "a biblical theme for the new epic."[3] A more careful perusal of the material, however, gives rise to objections to those authors who define a biblical background as being fundamental for Milton. True, we have the foundations of Christian faith, complete with its great moral objectives; we have the Father, the Son, archangel Michael and the heavenly army, as well as their antagonists Satan and the rebellious angels. But it is exactly with the fall of Satan and the angels on the very first page of *Paradise Lost* that we come across plots and images absent in both the Old and the New Testament. These are borrowed from apocrypha, and apocrypha of a certain type at that, spread by medieval heretics like Bogomils, Cathars, Lollards and sometimes Waldenses.

Some of the literary critics had the idea or the intuition to relate this to the dualistic tradition, albeit without naming it directly. This happened as early as the 19th century, when S. Gurteen published *The Epic of the Fall of Man* (a comparative study on Cædmon, Dante and Milton).[4] Hugh White supported the thesis of Arthur Lovejoy propounded in an article published some fifty years ago, *Milton and the Paradox of the Fortunate Fall* (1937), and speaking of "Milton's participation in an ancient tradition which understands the Fall as *felix culpa*, an ultimately happy event, giving rise to more good than would have been without it."[5] This "ancient tradition," however, remains unexplained. Hugh White points out that although *Piers Plowman* and *Paradise Lost* are different worlds altogether, they presuppose comparison as major religious poems gauging the secrets of sin and divine love. In this case, too, White's intuition was quite correct as the two works are related by dualistic philosophy.

The *Anglo-Saxon Poetry*, compiled by S. Bradley, finds "broad similarities between parts of *Genesis* and of *Paradise Lost*,"[6] without this typologically correct assumption, however, being based on the dualistic foundations of the two works. The same relation was underscored earlier and more definitely by Marco Mincoff when he discussed the beginning of *Paradise Lost* and more specifically the fall of Satan and his angels. According to him, "it is probable that Milton knew the Cadmonic poem, a Latin translation of which had been published by Junius in 1655."[7] E. Legouis, who assumed that the friendship between Milton and Junius could have helped inspire the former, also launched a similar thesis by the old poem.[8] The poem *Genesis* is part of the *Junius XI* manuscript also known as the *Cædmon* manuscript. British colleagues date it in the 8th or 9th century, although it would seem more realistic to assume it came from the continent in the 12th century. It begins with the dualistic episode of the revolt and fall of the angels with Lucifer at their head. One could also add that the lament (of the fallen Satan from another dualistic text in the same manuscript, *Christ and Satan*) is very similar to the scene in *Paradise Lost* where Lucifer tries to raise the spirit of his fallen army.

The associations described so far seek plot similarities or precedents, which are occasional. In our time there is an energetic trend that tries to formulate the spirit of concealed philosophy in the poet. The first proponents of a more comprehensive position of heresy in Milton were Maurice Kelley, one of the most prominent Miltonian scholars of the 20th century and publisher of *De Doctrina Christiana*, and Barbara Lewalski.[9] One of the most recent publications belongs to A. Nuttall, who discovered Gnostic heresy in Milton and titled his book *The Alternative Trinity: Gnostic Heresy in Marlowe, Milton and Blake*. There one finds the assertion that "Milton's thought is quasi–Gnostic"[10] and we know that in the Middle Ages Gnosticism spread through Bogomilism and its derivative trends. The same year saw the publishing of a collection with a similar compelling title, *Milton and Heresy*, by Stephen P. Dobranski and John P. Rumrich.[11] There, according to Stephen Fallan, instead of Gnosticism Milton bore a combination of "unmistakable Armianism ... complicated by Calvinist vestiges."[12] In his review W. Walker has summed up the discussion as a question of whether Milton was a heretical theologian or it would be more correct to interpret him as an orthodox Christian.[13] Maybe the most challenging title in this regard is Neil Forsyth's *The Satanic Epic* (2002).[14]

But it might be better to substitute this intuitive quest for Milton's "invisible" heresy for the answers to two concrete questions: What are the historical sources of that heresy or nonconformity?, and what can be quoted as its direct expression? Such an approach is more successful, for it leaves behind general assumptions and builds on established facts and sociologically precise work with them. Here are two examples when the logic of general position does not lead in a sufficiently productive direction. Emil Legouis declares that Milton was the only poet who identified himself with Puritanism.[15] But why then do scholars admit they find it so difficult to gauge the true philosophy of the poet? In addition, Dobranski, Rumrich and other authors in the above-mentioned volume tend to regard Milton's theological treatise, *De Doctrina Christiana*, as an expression of his deviation from orthodoxy. The fact is, however, that it does not feature Milton's fundamental theological theses, which we find in *Areopagitica* (1644) and *Eikonoklastes* (1649). Besides, one should add that *De Doctrina Christiana* is a text discovered as late as 1823 and belongs with the *dubia*, i.e., works of dubious authorship. To this day scholars argue whether it was truly written by Milton, a discussion which was renewed in 1991. It is because of this controversy that *De Doctrina Christiana* will not be included in the evidential part of this study. True, one can find there positions Milton himself defined as common with the Protestant church,[16] as for example the denial of all who place themselves above the Holy Writ, the Scriptures being declared the sole authority: "As for me, I keep the sacred writings alone."[17]

These, however, are quite bland formulations, while in *Eikonoklastes* and *Areopagitica* Milton proclaimed the episcopal institution superfluous and proclaimed his spiritual appreciation of the Waldensian and Cathar heretical churches: "I add that many Western Churches Eminent for their Faith and good Works, and settl'd above four hundred Years ago in France, in Piemont and Bohemia, hath both taught and practis'd the same Doctrine, and not admitted of Episcopacy among them. And if we may believe what the Papists themselves have Written of these Churches, which they call Waldenses, I found in a Book Written almost four hundred Years since, and set forth in the Bohemian History, that those Churches in Piemont have held the same Doctrine and Government, since the time that Constantine with his mischievous Donations poyson'd Silvester and the whole Church."[18]

This passage shows that John Milton worked with heretical manuscripts and was familiar with the history of heretical churches from such documents. Then, although he mentioned the Waldensian church by name, he also mentioned a church in France, meaning the Cathars, as well as the Bohemian (Hussite) church. In fact, he mentioned the Waldenses from Lyons and Languedoc as the first Protestant churches[19] and therefore proclaimed a continuity between the English Reformation and the Waldenses from Lyons, while the mentioning of Languedoc can be assumed to speak of the Cathar community. Milton regarded them as having the same doctrine and practice, thus showing himself to be a historian who established at the earliest hour the link between Cathars, Waldenses and Hussites; a global historical view, which quite a few modern medievalists are still unable to adopt. This reveals a new image of Milton before us; the image of a historian with knowledge topical even today, with concrete quotations and correct conclusions one can also encounter in his assessment of Wycliffe's work.

By expressing particular respect for John Wycliffe, Milton indicated he had another important ideological resource. Incidentally, he also thus integrated in one spiritual context Cathars, Waldenses, Hussites and Wycliffe (and that means Lollards). The affinity for the reformist spirit and work of Wycliffe is expressed on several occasions. The *Areopagitica* quotes Wycliffe and Huss as authors of the first significant conflict between reform and papacy.[20] Milton placed Wycliffe at the basis of English reform, which was developing in his own time. This was a declaration of continuity, a statement that outlined the transfer inside England itself: "although indeed our Wicliff's preaching at which all the succeeding reformers more effectually lighted their tapers."[21]

Milton complemented his apology of Wycliffe by placing him in the beginning of the European Reformation, by considering that if his work had been successful on the Albion, England would have achieved international fame and recognition, would have been the center of European Reformation: "And had it not bin this obstinate perverseness of our Prelates against the divine and admirable spirit of Wiclef, to suppress him as an schismatic and innovator, perhaps neither the Bohemian Husse and Jerom, no, or the name of Luther, or Calvin had bin ever known: the glory of reforming all our neighbours had been completely ours."[22] The expression *quod erat demonstrandum* (QED) is a bit difficult to use in social sciences but in this case we can say QED, for we see Milton's self-identification with the spirit of heretical churches four centuries previously, with the ideological heritage of Wycliffe. And what a self-identification: Milton's definition of Wycliffe — "the divine and admirable spirit of Wiclef" — is one of the highest praises the poet ever gave to a compatriot of his. Therefore, the Milton-Wycliffe connection that only W. Summers mentioned categorically is actually a continuity declared by Milton himself, one which sheds light on the roots of his theology.[23]

Doctrinal Expressions

Yet another indicative proof of John Milton's emotional involvement with the work of the heretics warrants exploration. During one of the Catholic purges of Waldenses in 1655, the poet denounced that crime with a poem entitled *On the Late Massacre in Piedmont* and written in the same year:

On the Late Massacre in Piedmont

Avenge O lord thy slaughter'd saints, whose bones
Lie scatter'd on the Alpine mountains cold

> Ev'n them who kept thy truth so pure of old
> When all our fathers worshipp'd stok and stones
> Forget not: in thy book record their groans.[24]

Some experts on medieval heresies could object that the victims of the massacre in Piedmont were Waldenses and the poet should therefore be considered a friend of their church, which was not dualistic. Things take a different aspect, however, should one return to the facts. Milton had a clear idea of both the Waldenses and the dualists. He categorically approved the idea of a reformed church, common to both Cathars and Waldenses, in which the Word of God was preached in the language of the people, the Gospel was placed right in the hands of ordinary man and in which there was no place for institutions like the episcopate. In this the Cathars held priority, for they translated the New Testament into Provençal before Waldo, who borrowed the model of his organization from them. This is, so to say, the socio-reformist element common to Cathars and Waldenses, which subsequently became a sort of axis in the history of the English Reformation and designated the line of Wycliffe (and the Lollards), Tyndale, Milton and so on. In addition to that, however, Milton constantly perused dualistic writings and borrowed from their imagery with both hands, proof of which shall be provided in abundance later. In the poem about the massacre in Piedmont quoted above he used the expression "When all our fathers worshipp'd stok and stones," and that is one by which the English dualists, the Lollards, following Bogomil-Cathar theology denounced icons as "stokks and stonys."[25]

In addition, he propounded the fundamental dualistic idea quite directly: "Good and evil we know in the field of this world grow up together almost inseparably; and the knowledge of good is so involved and interwoven with the knowledge of evil, and so many cunning resemblances hardly to be discerned ... that *the knowledge of good and evil, as two twins cleaving together*, leaped forth into the world" (italics mine).[26] This formulation is in harmony with the fundamental dualistic thesis, recorded as it was by the well-known 14th century inquisitor Bernard Gui: "The Manichaean sect and heresy recognise and preach two Gods or two Fathers, one benign God and one malign God."[27] The difference is that Milton speaks of good and evil instead of God and the Devil, and here we should take in good faith the pertinent observation of C. Vaughan explaining that, in Milton's case, the religious fervor of the reformers and the Puritans was already touched by the intellectual currents of the Renaissance.[28]

In other words, the religious personification of good and evil was complemented with more abstract categories.

Nevertheless, the other theological views of the poet, which we shall quote hereafter, were not much influenced by the time, lacked such abstract complements and were presented almost as doctrinal expressions. The principal occasion for Milton to express his views was his polemic with the defenders of the Episcopal church: he defended the simple evangelical practice of the Presbyterian church. With his temperamental accusation that his opponents reproduced the vices of the Catholic Church (that although they had rejected papacy they had, in fact, embraced its practice and had distributed the power between themselves)[29] Milton actually built a comprehensive imputation against the history of deformation and repression of the Catholic Church. And that was done in the language of Cathars and Lollards — in other words, his treatises can be regarded a speech of historical retribution against the time-honored persecutor of the dualists.

The refutation of icons and the cross is a traditional dualist characteristic. Evidence of this has been recorded in the oldest documents on the Bogomils. This was what Euthymius Zigabenus wrote in his 11th century *Panoplia dogmatica*: "They also despise the holy icons and call them heathen idols, silver and gold, made by human hand."[30] The formula "made with many hands" was documented among the English Lollards at the trial in Kent in 1511–1512.[31] Milton also repeatedly attacked icons, declaring them images and idols[32] and said their veneration was a deviation from true Christian duty: "stones, and pillars and crucifixes, have now the honour and the alms due to Christ's living members."[33] To him the laudation of Christ on icons was both unacceptable and superfluous, as He was "pageanted about like a dreadful idol."[34]

It is interesting to see that here, too, Milton revealed how broad his historical culture was when he supported the iconoclastic feelings he shared with the dualists by giving as examples the actions of the iconoclastic emperors Leo III, who ruled from 717 to 741, and Constantine V Copronymus, who ruled from 741 to 775. This is an ability to draw a line of rationalism in the history of the church itself, respectively to present the veneration of images, cumbersome liturgies and complicated rites as a deviation from the early life of Christ's church, which consisted of communion with the Word (Christ) and following His example, as well as individual spiritual life following His precepts. It seems that to some degree discussion returned within the limits of official church tradition, but nevertheless expressions became quite temperamental, with Milton speaking of how those Byzantine emperors "broke all superstitious images to pieces."[35]

The trace of dualistic attitude is also visible in Milton when he speaks of the cross. The Bogomil objection to the cross is quite well known, as one can see from the following quotation from Presbyter Cosmas: "Because the Jews, crucified on it the son of God, so the cross is really offensive to God. If somebody has killed the son of the king with a cross of wood should this wood be pleasant to the king?" (p. 21).[36] One should note that English Lollards also took up this early Bogomil objection — at the proceedings in Norwich in 1430 the tailor William Hardy of Mundham gave the following explanation: "and no more worship ne reverence oweth be do to the crosee than oweth be do to the galwes whiche men be hanged on."[37] Presbyter Cosmas also pointed out that "the heretics cut down the crosses and make weapons of them."[38] Once again Milton demonstrated historical knowledge, presenting an analogy of such extremism by mentioning he knew of such "enormities" in England.[39] These, by the way, are known as moods amidst some Lollards. The information found in Milton is among the oldest found in English literature and it is confirmed by the minutes of the trials against the Lollards in Norwich published by Norman Tanner. This is what one of them says: "all ymages owyn to be destroyed and do away."[40] In his subsequent comments the poet distanced himself from the above-quoted extremes with the rationalistic objection that official pre–Reformation practice had made idols out of crucifixes. He also warned that "extreme veneration" of the cross could bring about prejudice[41] and quoted cases of fetishism of the cross in Christian tradition, for example when nails from the cross, found by Constantine and his mother Helena, were put in helmets as protective amulets or were attached to reins of mounts.[42] One can discern a certain distance from the cross in his words, as he obviously did not think Constantine and Helena had made a feat by discovering the cross, adding that if that had been so important it would have been done by the disciples of Christ themselves.[43]

We are also familiar with the Bogomil and Cathar conclusion that, with their predilection for icons and rituals, the official clergy were bearers of idolatry and that "all church fathers" were idolaters.[44] "They call the churches crossroads and the holy mass and other divine services done in the churches they treat as wasted words" (pp. 20–21).[45] These motifs have their place in Lollard texts which ridicule the rituals with wine, bread, wax, oil and incense of the Catholic Church as *vera practica necromantiae*.[46] They are repeated with a similar vocabulary in John Milton's polemic prose. He ridiculed the clergy that they dressed in "deformed and fantastic dresses, in palls and mitres, gold, gewgaws fetched from Aarons's old wardrobe" which made them neither heavenly nor spiritual.[47] The same biting phrases as "popery and idolatry" and "true heresy,"[48] characteristic of dualistic language. The same conviction of Bogomils, Cathars and Lollards that "but to the gospel each person is left voluntary, called only, as a son, by the preaching of the word."[49]

The traditional dualistic objection to baptism with water was also expressed, albeit in an implied manner: "Then the baptism changed into a kind of exorcism, and water sanctified by Christ institute, thought little enough to wash off the original spot."[50] This to some extent echoes the Bogomil-Cathar-Lollard belief that "baptism with water does not contribute to salvation in any way," for true baptism to dualists was that with the Holy Spirit, consolamentum.[51] Another case of Bogomil-Cathar influence is the expression "good men," which is found frequently in Milton's prose and which reproduces the appellation "good men," "good Christians," given to dualistic leaders, the so-called perfects. They had exceptional prestige amongst their flock for it was known that the dualistic leaders were extremely pure, dignified people and legend had it they were beloved by God.[52] Thus in the 14th century Cathar movement followers in southern France still believed in "good men" and that where there were "two good men, God stands between them."[53] The laudation of good men called *bougres* (Bulgarians) in southern France came to the point where, as it is recorded in the Doat collection (t. XXV, F° 216 v°), they by God's grace could stop lightning with books they had in Bulgaria. This information dates from 1275 and the heretic who, according to the witness Petrus Perrini de Podio Laurentia, had voiced such an opinion was an Englishwoman (Anglesiam).[54] This is the oldest positive connotation of the word *bougre*, which reached England as "bugger," already loaded with extremely negative connotations by Catholic propaganda.[55]

The Lollards defined themselves as being true to Christ and pure in an English version of the *Twelve Conclusions of the Lollards* in Anne Hudson's volume *Selections from English Wycliffite Writings*: "we pore men, tresories of Cryst and his apostlis."[56] In many preserved documents the Lollards call themselves "good men" and "true men."

Milton, too, speaks of "good men," more particularly of "good men and Saints"[57] and "thousands of good men."[58] At the same time, in order to place good men under protection, he declared: "And this all Christians ought to know, that the title of Clergy St. Peter gave to all God's people." According to Milton, the deformation had set in when "pope Higinus and the succeeding Prelates took it from them, appropriating that name to themselves and their Priests only."[59] We know that the dualists denied the existence of saints, but in this case Milton obviously resorted to dualistic mimicry, i.e., to the skill of defending heresy with a Christian precedent, with the names of the apostles of Christ presented as the first "good men." Thus he tells us that Apostle Paul "made himself servant to all,"[60] in other words, communion meant to serve people humbly. At the same time it was easy for the poet to make the radical opposition between the "good men" and episcopacy, an echo of the Cathar custom to call themselves the "good church" and the "church of Christ," and the Roman church "bad" and "mother of adultery."[61]

Several centuries later, Milton's language still applied the same style: "They are not bishops, God and all good men know they are not, they have filled this land with late confusion and violence, but a tyrannical crew and corporation of impostors, that have blinded and abused the world so long under that name."[62] Experts commenting upon Milton's prose have also noticed that he did not include bishops among the good men.[63]

Relative to the same topic, John Milton reproduced yet another dualistic theme related to the idea of "good men" as he actually explained their spiritual form. This was the idea of "internal man" quoted by Bernard Gui: "They [the Cathars] deny the future resurrection of human bodies and instead invent some spiritual bodies and an internal man; thus, they say, the future resurrection should be understood."[64] On one page of Milton's *The Reason of Church Government Urged against Prelaty* (1641), "the inner man" and the "internal man" is mentioned twice in opposition to "external man."[65] Then again, in his *Treatise of Civil Power in Ecclesiatical Causes* we find a repeated use of the term "inward man" on three pages, developed in the definition that "the inward man is nothing else but inward part of man."[66] One also encounters a description of the qualities of inward man,[67] with a calling for inward religion, as well as an explanation how Christ reaches conscience and inward man by the spiritual power with which He rules the church. Milton tried to legalize the dualistic theme of internal man by quoting the Scriptures. To both Bogomils and Cathars "internal man" called for a doctrinal specification of resurrection: that physical bodies (which will drop off like clothes) would not be resurrected but spiritual essences would return to the Good Father. It seems that Milton sensed he had placed a visible dualistic accent by using the expression that Christ deals only with the inward man[68] and safeguarded himself by adding text from the New Testament, more specifically the familiar flesh-spirituality opposition of Matthew and Paul: "Jesus replied, 'Simon son of Jonah, you are a happy man! Because it was not flesh and blood that revealed this to you but my Father in heaven" (Mt 16:17). And also, "We live in the flesh, of course, but the muscles that we fight with are not flesh" (2 Co 10:3).

One also encounters another familiar dualistic tendency: Milton lent an ear to the preference for the New Testament and the rejection of the Old Testament as the law of violence and the kingdom of Satan. The poet supported his views with examples from the New Testament and the figure of Christ, while the Old Testament was used mainly for negative examples. The above-mentioned "fantastic dresses" and "gold and gewgaws" of churchmen were taken "from Aaron's wardrobe,"[69] i.e., the founder of the Old Testament priesthood. In addition, one finds challenges to the Old Testament characteristics of God, Jehovah's face as dispenser of justice and punishment as well as denial of the "perishable rites" of the Old Testament.[70] God is presented as the Bogomil God — a Good Father with a more merciful, human and New Testament face: "God being no more a judge after the sentence of the Law, nor as it were a schoolmaster of perishable rites, but the most indulgent father governing his Church as a family of sons of their discreet age."[71] Naturally, one should also pay attention to human inconsistency, frequently found in great writers, too. Regardless of the fact that he declared a preference for the humane and gentle spirit of the New Testament, Milton supported the beheading of Charles I in the spirit of the Old Testament.

Thus far, we have presented examples of John Milton's consanguinity with the dualistic doctrine passing from direct self-definition to cases presupposing some more interpretation. Our trip to Milton's *philosophia arcana*, however, does not end here. The time has come for the most temperamental and comprehensively expressed pro-heretical theses of Milton: his polemics against the so-called "donation of Constantine," *donatio Constantini ad Sylvestrem I papam*. This is the legend according to which Constantine the Great (306–337) granted provinces, places and towns (*provincias, loca et civitates*) to Pope Sylvester I. In western Europe both the Cathars and the Waldenses rejected the idea of such a donation, for they considered it the start of corruption in the church. From a spiritual community striving after the kingdom of heaven it not only became a secular proprietor but also thus found itself secured in the earthly kingdom of Satan. It is interesting to note that *donatio Constantini* is not mentioned in the Bogomil manuscripts or the historical documents related to them. This thesis is an important complement to the history of dualism introduced by the Cathars and spread by anticlerical movements closely related to them.

In Milton one finds not one but repeated quotations of the problem, developed in one of the themes of his treatise *Of Reformation in England and the Causes that Hitherto Have Hindered It*. One should not forget the context of the then ongoing controversy between the Episcopal and the Presbyterian churches in England. For Milton, an adversary of prelatism and an adherent to the reformist idea of a "priesthood of all believers," the discussion gave him occasion to accuse his opponents from the Episcopal church of inheriting the Vatican's worst feature, ingrained corruption. On this occasion he gave in to the passion with which medieval evangelical teachings had denounced the root of that corruption — Constantine's donation. Milton declared that Christian times were spiritually unadulterated from the times of Christ until Constantine,[72] after which he described the corruption stemming from *donatio Constantini*, which meant the influx of pride and lawlessness.[73] On every subsequent mentioning of the subject Milton levied biting words against various aspects of that corruption, sometimes even to the point of a vocabulary coinciding with that of the heretics. For the two main trends in medieval heresy, the Cathars and the Waldenses, the donation in question was equal to pouring poison in the bosom of the Church: "poison has diffused in the church today."[74] The expression used by Milton was exactly the same: "since Constantine with his mischievous Donation poyson'd Silvester and the whole Church."[75]

And here we come to a culmination of European proportions: John Milton proved that the critical position against *donatio Constantini* was visible in the work of Dante (1265–1321), Petrarch (1304–1374) and Ariosto (1474–1533). We shall quote the proof he gave in full measure, for this was a case of conscious borrowing from the Italian humanists as well as one of interaction between the peaks of two cultures. By that Milton achieved two things. First, he proved that the dualistic motif of anticlerical criticism was present in works of the most outstanding figures of the

Italian pre–Renaissance and Renaissance and was therefore an important expression of European cultural history. His second visible ambition was to place himself as an heir to that trend, as its representative in England: yet another self-characteristic of Milton's "heresy."

Anticlericalism was internationalized as a condition for the complete expression of Renaissance and the new times which, according to Milton, would come when the corruption and perversion amassed in Europe's church history were revealed in full and rejected. In this sense the names of the great Italians were quoted as an example and a precedent to be followed, one that became a measure of the freedom of speech, of human choice and human thought.

To Dante — and to Petrarch to a considerable extent — criticism of the Catholic Church was a matter of personal fate. Dante's treatise *De monarchia*, in which the poet placed the supremacy of the empire (i.e. the state) above the church, was pronounced a heretical work by Pope John XXII in 1329. In turn, Petrarch received minor orders at the papal court in Avignon in 1362, communicated with the Franciscans, the order of anti-corruption leanings in the Catholic Church, and denounced that corruption in his writings. To this line Milton actually added the epic of liberation of the English language from Catholic latinization, of man's rise to free communication with the Scriptures. Milton quoted Wycliffe as the forerunner, and the time between Wycliffe's 14th century and Milton's 17th was marked by the efforts for emancipation made by the Lollards and Tyndale.

In order to support the cause he defended with the Italian example already accepted as the leading cultural horizon in Europe Milton himself translated into English the fragment from canto 19 of the *Inferno*, quoted in his work "Of the Reformation in England":

> Ah Constantine! Of how much ill cause,
> Not thy conversion, but those rich domains
> That the first wealthy pope receiv'd of thee![76]

And here is Dante's original text (lines 115–117) in Italian:

> Ahi, Constantin, di quanto mal fu matre,
> non la tua conversion, ma quella dote
> che da te presse il primo ricco patre![77]

Milton mentioned that Dante also expressed a similar position in canto 20 of the *Paradiso*,[78] as well as the objection against Constantine's mistaken move in sonnet 108 of Petrarch. There, Milton wrote, the poet spoke of the "Roman antichrist as merely bred up by Constantine," nor did he fail to mention that the same sonnet was "wiped out by the inquisitors in some editions":[79]

> Founded in chaste and humble poverty,
> 'Gainst them that rais'd thee dost thou lift thy horn,
> Impudent whore, where hast thou plac'd thy hope?
> In thy adulteres, or thy ill-got wealth?
> Another Constantine comes not in haste.[80]

An 1832 edition of Petrarch features the sonnet under number XVIII in the section entitled *Sonnets and Songs by Petrarch on Various Subjects*, the following being the respective part of the sonnet in Italian:

> Fondata in casta ed umil povertate,
> Contra tuoi fondatori alzi le corna,
> Putta sfacciata: e dov' hai posto spene?
> Negli adulteri tuoi, nelle mal nate
> Richezze tante? Or Constantin non torna:
> Ma tolga il mondo tristo, che'l sostiene.[81]

Milton also discovered similar passages in Ariosto, more precisely at the meeting between the English knight Astolfo and St. John, in canto 34:

> And, to be short, at last his guide him brings
> Into a goodly valley, where he sees
> A mighty mass of things strangely confus'd
> Things that on earth were lost, or were abus'd.

When this author read the same canto in Ariosto's poem he was unable to find verse exactly corresponding to Milton's translation. Couplet 73 does feature lines of a certain similarity,[82] but neither Milton's text nor the quotation of couplet 73 could be accepted as sufficiently obvious criticism of Vatican sins. Milton was more precise in his translation of part of couplet 80 of the same canto:

> Then pass'd he to a flowery mountain green,
> Which once smelt sweet, now stinks as odiously:
> This was that gift (if you the truth will have)
> That Constantine to good Sylvestro gave.

And here is the Italian original:

132

> Di varii fiori ad un gran monte passa,
> Ch'ebbe già buono odore, or putia forte.
> Questo era il dono (se però dir lece)
> Che Constantino al buon Silvestro fece.[83]

After he had created a uniform all–European context of anti–Catholic and anticlerical criticism, one of contact and interaction of literatures, Milton also found an opportunity to bring England to the fore. He did this by indicating that Chaucer's Ploughman in England made the same objection against Constantine's donation even before Ariosto had been born.[84] It is surprising that Milton failed to notice the preceding passage in the same couplet 80, canto 34 of Ariosto's poem, which contains traditional Bogomil-Cathar ridicule of the superfluous church services for the dead:

> Di versate minestre una gran massa
> Vede, e domanda al suo Dottor, ch'importe
> L'elemosina è (dice) che si lassa
> Alcun che fatta sia dopo la morte[85]

> And what he saw was soup spil't aplenty
> And he asked his Doctor what that meant.
> The alms someone leaves here, he responded,
> As is customary after death
> [English translation by B. Roushkova].

The ironic attitude to wakes and masses for dead souls demonstrated by the image of low quality or foul food can also be found in a work of English literature marked by dualistic influence, William Langland's *The Vision of Piers Plowman*:

> Ac hir sauce was over sour and unsavourly grounde
> In a morter, Post mortem, of many bitter peyne...[86]
> (But their sauce was too tart, four it was
> pounded into acrid mess in a mortar called Post-mortem.)[87]

This slightly breathless selection and translation of Italian quotations indicates that Milton could have done the work with an Italian friend of his during his trip to Italy. We know that he had contacts with whom he discussed Italian language and literature. For example, in a letter to Benedetto Buonmattai written in Florence on September 10, 1638, Milton shared his pleasure in enjoying the works of Dante, Petrarch and many others.[88]

Nor should one overlook yet another issue: Why did Milton, highly educated as he was and a close observer of the events and ideological life in Europe who was capable of historical comparisons dating to the iconoclastic period in Byzantium, accept Constantine's donation as a historical fact? Hadn't the Italian humanist Lorenzo Valla proved the spuriousness of this myth in his well-known treatise of 1440 titled *De falso credita et eminenta Constantini donatione declamatio* (On the False Credit Accorded to the Invented Donation of Constantine)? This work of Valla's was published for the first time in 1517 by the German humanist and critic of papism Ulrich von Hutten, and so it had become known in the circle of the enlightened. Two assumptions can be made in this case. One is that this information in some way failed to reach Milton. The other is that he followed Ariosto's example who, although probably familiar with Lorenzo Valla's work, preferred to express his criticism of corruption in the official church by using the legend of Constantine's donation as an already well-known and widespread metaphor of the problem, as an opportunity to quote Dante's criticism.[89] Petrarch also reproduced Dante's criticism[90] to some degree in his sonnet,[91] in other words Milton aptly relied on an organic line of ideas and imagery in Italian literature. The facts are beyond any doubt; what remains to be revealed are connections, relations and the personal line in these facts.

Bogomil Imagery in the Works of Milton

Beyond the theological views propounded by John Milton, the philosophy of his imagery calls for close examination. As was pointed out in the beginning of this chapter, that philosophy still remains a mystery to scholars who sense its powerful covert presence but find it difficult to explain. Marco Mincoff, for one, observed a peculiar concern in Milton's early poem *Lycidas*—"he had been disturbed by the way in which God cuts off the deserving and allowed the vicious to flourish."[92] In fact it is in this work that one can first discern feelings of the poet similar to the Bogomil-Cathar objections to the arrangements on the earthly world. According to them, this world was "an inferno, fire and ice, and evil of every kind"[93] as it was created by Satan, an unjust and cruel world. Mincoff also established a relation between the opening of *Paradise Lost* and the Old English

Genesis. As we have already mentioned, Mincoff assumed the possibility of Milton's being acquainted with the Cadmonic poem, a Latin translation of which had been published by Junius in 1655.[94] British scholars have been hesitant when dating this poem, and in speculating about its origin, but there is a fundamental historical situation that can neither be overlooked nor rewritten: The Bogomils and Cathars introduced the dualistic plot of the fall of Satan who rebelled against God to medieval Europe. Milton himself confirmed his penchant for dualistic imagery, for to the already mentioned theme, present on the very first page of *Paradise Lost*, he added Satan's interest in God's second creation according to an ancient prophesy or report in heaven. The so-called second creation was one of the main features of Bogomil myth. To add more clarity to our observations we shall directly compare fundamental dualistic texts and passages from *Paradise Lost* and *Paradise Regained*. The first comparison that follows reveals an unquestionable coincidence between the episode with Satan's fall from heaven on the first page of *Paradise Lost* and that in *The Secret Book* of the Bogomils.

VISIBLE DUALISTIC THEMES IN JOHN MILTON'S *PARADISE LOST*

Motif one: Satan's revolt against God and his fall from heaven.

Paradise Lost, Book I, The Argument:

The Serpent, or rather Satan in Serpent; who revolting from God, and drawing to his side many Legions of Angels, was by the command of God driven out of heaven with all his crew into the great Deep.[95]

Paradise Lost, Book I, verses 34–44:

... what time his Pride / Had cast him out from Heav'n, with all his Host / Of Rebel Angels, by whose aid aspiring / To set him-

The Secret Book of the Bogomils (Carcassone text):

... and with his tail he dragged away one-third of the angels of God, and he was banished from the throne of God and from the overlordship of the heavens. And Satan, descending to this firmament, was unable to find rest either for himself or for those who were with him [*Monumenta bulgarica*, trans. Tom Butler (Michigan Slavic Publications: 1996), p. 193].

135

self in Glory above his Peers, /
He trusted to have equal'd the
most High, / If he oppos'd; and
with ambitious aim / Against the
Throne and Monarchy of God?
Rais'd impiousWarr in Heav'n
and Battel proud / With vain
attempt. Him the Almighty
Power / Hurld headlong flaming
from th' Ethereal Skie / With
hideous ruin and combustion
down / To bottomless perdition.

And yet another occasion on which the same myth is mentioned, in
book VII, verses 130–133:

> Know then, that after Lucifer from Heav'n
> (So call him, brighter once amidst the Host
> Of Angels, then that Starr the Starrs among)
> Fell with his flaming Legions through the Deep
> Into his place....

The same obvious concurrence can be seen in the second table comparing the scene of the final victory over Satan from *The Secret Book* in
which he was chained in indestructible chains (*insolubilus vinculus fortibus*) and thrown in a "lake of fire" (*in lacum ignis*), and, respectively,
Satan's being hurled to dwell "in adamantine chains and penal fire" in
Book I of *Paradise Lost*.

Motif two: The chaining of Satan in Hell's lake of fire.

Paradise Lost, *Book I, verses 45–49:*	*The Secret Book* of the Bogomils (Carcassone text):
... what time his Pride Hurld headlong flaming from th' Ethereal Skie / With hideous ruine and combustion down / To bottomless perdition, here to dwell / In Adamantine Chains and penal Fire, / Who durst defie th' Omnipotent to Arms.	And then Satan and all his army shall be chained in like of fire. And the Son and His elect shall walk on the firmament, and shall imprison the Devil, locking him in chains indestructible and strong.

The third comparison shows a Bogomil myth retold by Milton, the one according to which after the creation of man part of mankind would return to the heavens to fill in the place of the fallen angels. We recalled that the second creation formula (after the Lord's) of "this visible Creation" of Satan is a familiar characteristic of dualism. *The Secret Book* says that man was created by Satan, and similar information about the said Bogomil belief was provided by Euthymius Zigabenus (12th century).[96] In our case, however, Milton chose an interpretation that was a step back from classical dualism. Milton's view of a second creation ran in harmony not with the traditional variant of *The Secret Book* (end of 11th to early 12th centuries), according to which Adam and Eve were created by Satan, but rather with the 13th century apocryphal *oratione* of St. John Chrysostom on how Michael the archangel defeated Satan.[97] Here we come to an important peculiarity of the Bulgarian Bogomil church, which constantly enhanced the role of the Father and the Son in its development. Thus, in the case of the above apocrypha, the subsequent consequence was a blending of the orthodox Christian idea of God as a creator of all creatures and all worlds. That is why the teaching of this church is called mitigated dualism, unlike the absolute dualism of the Paulicians preserving the equal positions of God and Satan. At the end of this chapter we shall return to this Bulgarian element, for it conditioned the poet's own outlook as regards the dualistic heritage. Thus we now come to the next motif.

Motif three: After the Creation of the Human Race Part of It Will Return to the Heavens to Fill in the Place of the Fallen Angels.

Paradise Lost, *Book 1, The Argument:*

To these Satan directs his Speech, comforts them with hope yet of regaining Heaven, but tells them lastly of a new World and new kind of Creature to be created, according to an ancient Prophesie or report in Heaven; for that Angels were long before this visible Creation,

Oratione of St. John Chrysostom:

And God said unto them: "Did you, my angels, see how evil Satan fled and lured away many angels; I created them with the Holy Spirit and saw them as my celestial army but he seduced them and took them to the darkness outside. I shall create them again and men shall be elected to do My will, be they apostles, was the opinion of many ancient Fathers.

Paradise Lost, Book VII, verses 151–160:

Already done, to have dispeopl'd Heav'n / My damage fondly deem'd, I can repair / That detriment, if such it be to lose / Self-lost, and in a moment will create / Another World, out of one man a Race / Of men innumerable, there to dwell, / Not here, till by degrees of merit rais'd They open to themselves at length the way / Up hither, under long obedience tri'd, / And Earth be chang'd to Heav'n, & Heav'n to Earth, / One Kingdom, Joy and Union without end.

prophets or martyrs, and they shall be like angels to Me. And my army of angels shall exceed a hundredfold the angels who fell from heaven" [Bulgarskata literatura i knizhnina prez XIII vek, p. 151].

At the same time, the poet's preference for some elements of Bogomil theology does not preclude obvious cases of lexical similarity between Milton and traditional dualistic theology. Thus, although the poet returned to the orthodox idea of God as the author of all things created, we can see how the expression "this visible Creation" (*Paradise Lost*, Book I, The Argument) repeats for a moment the fundamental Bogomil-Cathar thesis that "all other things visible were created by the devil who fell from the heavens."[98] It is interesting to note, as it has been quoted in the right column above, that Dante also paid attention to this dualistic myth in his *Il Convivio*.[99] The reader should bear in mind that exactly because they passed from theological canon to literature, Bogomil-Cathar writings developed many nuances, which could be in doctrinal contradiction but remain united by the impressive beauty of their imagery, the poetics of wisdom, compassion and moral endeavor. Thus Milton, too, freely borrowed ideas and concepts not from one, say *The Secret Book*, but from different dualistic apocrypha. Although he endowed Satan with the modern skill of building machines, the next episode actually reproduces the battle of Michael with Satan in the already mentioned *oratione* of St. John Chrysostom (and possibly from *The Tiberiad Sea*, which contains the same motif), with Michael coming out victorious with God's intervention. Milton created his own variant of the counterattack against the devil as a triumphant march of the Messiah, i.e., Christ.

Motif four: Michael, sent forth by God, defeats the Devil in a dramatic battle.

Paradise Lost, Book VI, The Argument:

Raphael continues to relate how Michael and Gabriel were sent forth to battel against Satan and his Angels. The first Fight describ'd: Satan and his Powers retire under Night: He calls a Councel, invents devilish Engines, which in the second dayes Fight put Michael and his Angels to some disorder; But, they at length pulling up Mountains overwhelm'd both the force and Machins of Satan: Yet the Tumult not so ending, God on the third day sends Messiah his Son, for whom he had reserv'd the glory of that Victory: Hee in the Power of his Father coming to the place, and causing all his Legions to stand still on either side, with his Chariot and Thunder driving into the midst of his Enemies, pursues them unable to resist towards the wall of eaven; which opening, they leap down with horrour and

Apocryphal oratione of St. John Chrysostom:

After Gabriel fails to sum up courage to fight with Satan the Lord forgave Gabriel and again said unto Michael: "You were first in the kingdom of Adam, who proceedeth from me, and it is thine today to go down to that vile antichrist and take from him the heavenly mantle, the crown and the sceptre of angelic orders, which he stole from Me. And divest him of his beauty and glory so that his servants see who the Father is" [*Bulgarskata literatura i knizhnina prez XIII vek*, p. 151].

The Tiberiad Sea:

And God sent Michael to Satan. And Michael went but was scorched by Satan and returned to God and said "I did what You sent me to do but the fire of Satan fell unto me." ... And Michael came and struck Satan with the sceptre and threw him down with all his army. And

confusion into the place of punishment prepar'd for them in the
Deep: Messiah returns with triumph to his Father.

they fell three days and three
nights like drops of rain [*Stara
bulgarska literatura. I. Apokrifi*,
p. 32].

The Tiberiad Sea also includes the particularly important dualistic
story according to which Satan allows Adam to plough the earth, which
belongs to the Devil, under the condition that Adam and his offspring
would go to hell after their death. Or, as the apocrypha explains, "the
Devil received and sent to Hell both the godly and the sinners."[100] This
accretion is made to enable us to bring to the fore a Bogomil association
which is implied in *Paradise Regained*: after the injustice of the Devil taking all human souls in bondage and locking them in hell before the coming of Christ has been done, there comes the understandably noble gesture
of Christ (an episode in the *Epiphanius Homily* and the *Gospel of Nicodemus*) who goes down to hell to free the imprisoned. The following fundamental Bogomil-Cathar motifs are outlined in *Paradise Regained*: Satan
and the rebel angels are driven from heaven; the Devil, enraged by yet
another spiritual feat performed by Christ, his fast, flies to the desert to
tempt Him; a description of the Devil as the lord and master of this world;
the Devil threatens Christ; Christ descends into hell and sets the souls
imprisoned there free; the victory of Christ over the Devil in the two versions of hanging him head down from the clouds and being trodden down.
All of these, with the exception of the beautiful myth of the human souls
being set free from hell by Christ, are contained in some brief form in the
well-known apocryphal *Dispute between Christ and the Devil*.[101] In other
words, the apocrypha can be defined as the core of ideas and imagery in
Paradise Regained, and there is also some similarity in composition. Donka
Petkanova assumes that the *Dispute* was generated in dualistic circles.[102]
Milton himself indicated the apocryphal literature he used in *Paradise
Regained* with the words that he would laud feats of Christ that were "in
secret done" and "unrecorded left through many an age."[103] In fact, the
texts on Christ being tempted by the Devil in the New Testament cover
only 11 lines in Matthew (4:1–11) and 13 lines in Luke (4:1–13) but they
nevertheless do not contain the episodes in *Paradise Regained*. Volume has
also been added in relation to the apocryphal source of the *Dispute*, which
consists of several pages while the poem contains more than 2,000 verses.

To add conviction to such an assertion we shall again resort to direct comparison between passages in *Paradise Regained* and the dualistic apocrypha. Once again we come to the episode of Satan being driven from heaven with which the dualistic mythology begins and which we repeatedly encountered in *Paradise Lost*. This practically divides the world into two: the realm of God in the heavens and that of the Devil on earth.[104]

VISIBLE DUALISTIC THEMES IN JOHN MILTON'S *PARADISE REGAINED*

Motif one: Satan is cast from heaven.

Paradise Regained,[105] Book I, verses 356–361:

Is true, am that spirit unfortunate / Who, leagued with millions more in rash revolt / Kept no my happy station, but was driven / With them from the bliss to the bottomless deep...

Paradise Regained, Book II, verse 150:

Belial, the dissolutest spirit that fell...

Paradise Regained, Book IV, verses 602–608:

The Son of God, with godlike force endued Against the attempter of thy Father's throne And thief of Paradise, him long of old Thou didst debel, and down from heaven cast With all his army; now thou hast avenged Supplanted Adam, and, by vanquishing Temptation, has lost Paradise.

The Secret Book, or Interrogatio Johannis (Carcassone text):

... and with his tail he dragged away one-third of the angels of God, and he was banished from the throne of God and from the overlordship of the heavens. And Satan, descending to this firmament, was unable to find rest either for himself or for those who were with him [*Monumenta bulgarica*, p. 193].

The next episode in *Paradise Regained*, given here as motif two, is an inception of all subsequent action, just as it is in the apocryphal *Dispute*.

Motif two: Enraged by the fasting of Christ the devil flies to the desert to tempt Him.

Paradise Regained, Book II, verses 241–244:	*Dispute between Christ and the Devil*:
Then to the desert takes with these his flight / Where still, from shade to shade, the Son of God, / after forty days' fasting, had remained, / Now hungering first, and to himself thus said...	And the Lord came to the mountain and said unto his disciples "now let us fast 40 days!" and Christ began to fast with his disciples to overcome the devil in dispute. And when he heard of Christ's fast the devil was enraged and stood before Him in his anger [*Stara bulgarska literatura. I. Apokrifi*, p. 173].

Tempting Christ with the earthly pictures and visions of this world, the Devil feels like a lord, the "master of this world," as the Bogomils used to say. Once again we have obvious lexical proximity with Milton calling him the "supreme of earth" and the Cathars, according to Bernard Gui, the *princeps hujus mundi*.

Motif three: The devil described as the master of the world.

Paradise Regained, Book I, verses 99–100:	*Synodicon of Boril*:
Ere in the head of nations he appear, / Their king, their leader, and supreme of earth.	And thrice accursed those who claim that the Devil is the autocrat of this world [1211].
	Manuel de l'inquisiteur, p. 10:
	... they call him Evil God, God of this world and Prince of this world [1322].

The envy and open malice of the Devil in the *Dispute* are developed in a more rhetorical manner in *Paradise Regained*, but this is one and the same threat of the evil one to use his earthly power against Christ.

Motif four: The Devil threatens Christ.

Paradise Regained, Book IV, verses 386–388:

Sorrows and labours, opposition, hate, / Attends thee; scorns, reproaches, injuries, / Violences and stripes, and, lastly, cruel death...

Dispute:

And the devil said: "If I do not prevail over thee I shall not be equal to the Lord. And I made me a nest in the heart of Caiaphas, the Jew to make them torture you, crucify you and bring about your death" [*Stara bulgarska literatura. I. Apokrifi*, p. 175].

The humanity and completeness of Christ's victory are expressed by the great gesture in which the gates of hell are destroyed and the human souls set free. This scene was borrowed from the *Gospel of Nicodemus* spread by Bogomils and Cathars.

Motif five: Christ descends into hell and sets the souls imprisoned there free.

Paradise Regained, Book I, verses 153–155:

All his [Christ] vast force, and drive him back to hell / Winning by conquest what the first man lost / By fallacy surprised.

Gospel of Nicodemus:

And the Lord said with hand extended: "Come unto Me all My saints, for you have My likeness and were sentenced to death for the deeds of the Devil's tree" [*Apokrifi i legendi z ukrainskih rukopisiv.* T. II., p. 300].

The note on which the *Dispute* and *Paradise Regained* end draws an exceptionally impressive, irreversible victory over the Devil. The unequivocal tone of the *Dispute* was probably the reason why Milton chose to base himself on the apocrypha which begins with Christ promising to defeat the Devil with the words "And the Lord said 'I have come to erase thee from the face of the earth'" and ends with another promise of His to deal once and for all with the enemy of man at a place called Chise — "And there, oh devil, shall I destroy you!"

Motif six: Christ finally defeats the devil by casting him from heaven, hanging him from the clouds or treading him underfoot.

Paradise Regained, Book IV, verses 618–621:

But thou, infernal serpent, shalt not long / Rule in the clouds; like an autumnal star, / Or lightning, thou shalt fall from heaven, trod down / Under his feet ... [of Jesus Christ]

Dispute:

And when Peter said that the Lord ordered the cloud to descend from the sky like lightning, to tie the devil and hang him down amidst the heavens [*Stara bulgarska literatura. I. Apokrifi*, p. 174].

... for Jesus Christ hath hung our master in the heavenly clouds [ibidem, p. 175].

Thus the two Bogomil myths, 1) of Satan's revolt and his respective casting from heaven and 2) of the final victory of Christ over the devil described in detail, seem to leap forth as a global frame of the two poems, this being particularly obvious in *Paradise Regained*. And inside that frame there is an abundance of images and interpretations borrowed from a whole set of dualistic apocrypha. In other words, dualistic imagery is the principal structure and it is that which determines the stream of thoughts and ideas. Nowhere else in world literature has Bogomil-Cathar philosophy enjoyed such comprehensive — and obviously magnificent — reproduction, not even in that of Bulgaria, even though the teaching was born in Bulgaria.

If we sum up the apocryphal material used we could say that images, fragments and sometimes vocabulary from *The Secret Book*, the *Dispute between Christ and the Devil*, *Gospel of Nicodemus*, the *Oratione of St. John Chrysostom*[106] and possibly the *Tiberiad Sea*[107] can be discerned in the two poems. This author has so far failed to encounter a scholar to have remarked on this peculiarity or to have mentioned the presence of apocryphal influences in these two great poems. With the exception of some cases when they were mentioned in passing by scholars such as Marco Mincoff or Emile Legouis, medieval apocrypha are absent from the analyses of Milton experts. What we have at best are attempts at vague definitions. Emile Legouis called *Paradise Lost* the most Hebraic of great English poems,[108] obviously because he failed to discern the apocryphal material. True, apocrypha frequently include Hebraic motifs, but after all, starting with *The Secret Book* and ending with the *Dispute*, all dualistic apocrypha, whose influence is revealed in this chapter, retold a prehistory stemming not from the Old but from the New Testament. There the figure of Christ is a leading one in terms of expectation, appearance, accomplishment and final victory.

This is where we should comment on an opinion shared by some of the Miltonian scholars. According to Emile Legouis, in spite of himself Milton was in deep sympathy with Satan, the great rebel of Heaven and enemy of God,[109] but it seems that things are a bit more complicated. Should one look carefully at *Paradise Lost* one would see that this epic poem was not completed, and it is even difficult to say to what extent the planned plot was fulfilled. This incompleteness or deficiency[110] was probably due to the fact that the poet may have overestimated his powers, for he fell short of both the time and energy to cover more comprehensively the panorama of the universal battle between God and Satan. And when he realized that his lifespan was running short, that his human and poetic potential was restricted, he decided to present the final victory of Christ over the devil in an unquestionable way. That was why he wrote *Paradise Regained* relying on a time-honored formula — an apocrypha presenting precisely the defeat of the enemy of God and man.

Although he expressed himself in the medieval style of the apocrypha, Milton laid the stress not so much on the divine as on the human nature of Christ, thus allowing man not only to bow before Christ's passion but to take up directly, to follow the example of His battle and overcome the demon on his own.[111] Albeit in a much more succinct form than in *Paradise Lost*, the poet carried out his personal covenant, which was a double victory of Christ and of man over the devil.

The victory of man is in some respects a modern solution, for it represents spiritual struggle, a struggle not of power, but of character. In this struggle Satan tries to denigrate light, Christ and man and to lead him astray with temptations such as today's consumer society offers in abundance. The answer is practically imperative: spiritual elevation is the destiny of Christ and man who follows the road of emulation of the Son. This can neither be eroded nor misled. Thus man is given the meaning of his existence against the backdrop of the entire universe.

Naturally, the specifics of the genre have registered their influence. Even formally *Paradise Regained* strives after connection with the Gospel, with the devil and the demons being driven in the herd of swine, just as in the New Testament parable. There is also dogmatic intonation. The rigorist characteristics of the Christian apocrypha *A Dispute between Christ and the Devil*, chosen as the direct model of *Paradise Regained*, resound for example in the surprising denigration of antiquity as a "temptation." The same Milton who bore a love of ancient Greek literature repeatedly expressed in his essays and with a presence of its own in the numerous gods and heroes of antiquity in *Paradise Lost*, reached the point in *Paradise Regained* where, obsessed with the idea of complete supremacy of Christ as the "light from above, from fountain regained,"[112] he disqualified that culture as "but dreams / Conjectures, Fancies, built on nothing firm."[113] Thus the poet paid certain due to his vacillation among genres because of his human failure to harmonize the beauty of ancient sensitivity and Christian feelings. When he chose poetic pathos with complete freedom of imagination and artistic temperament he seemed to fall a bit short of the Christian finality he would have wanted to see in his work. When he related categorically the triumph of Christ it turned out he had taken up the objections of many Christian theoreticians against the "pagan" Greek antiquity. The presentation of Christ's victory over the devil in Milton's poem and the apocryphal *Dispute* was a task exceeding classical Christian teaching, for such a victory is not described but expected through the New Testament. The task Milton set before himself was suprahuman; it was a task of the Divine Plan.

Dante was a bit more merciful towards Greek and Roman antiquity by placing their personages in purgatory and giving Virgil the freedom to be a guide in the journey between the worlds. This heritage of unresolved contradiction between Christ as a noble ideal but one that imposes a strict, icon-like type of conduct, and the increasing freedom of human enterprise from the Renaissance onwards was carried over time right to the literature of the 20th century. What is probably its most original solution can be found in the plays of the writer and thinker Stefan Gechev titled

The Case of the Disappearance of the Body of Jesus of Nazareth[114] and *Barabbas' Calvary.*[115] In both of these Christ is actually absent from the stage — He is called upon as a memory, as an idea to enable the remaining mortal protagonists to carry out their idea of Christ with the complete freedom of the best they carry and can find in themselves.

17th Century Waldensian Translocations

Where could Milton's association with apocrypha have come from? The Puritans, the main ideological trend in the English bourgeois revolution, are known to have sympathized with the Waldenses, the last surviving continental heresy. The 17th century saw the translocation of Waldensian literature from the valleys of Piedmont to England. One of the earliest comments on the significance of that translocation was made by the prominent 19th century Russian scholar of the Cathar movement Nikolai Osokin: "When the persecution of Waldenses was renewed in the 17th century and they felt threatened by extermination the most important manuscripts were transported to England — and Cromwell — who was then considered to be the head and protector of Protestantism, or *capo et protettore* to quote Venetian relations. They have been kept at the library of Cambridge since 1658. These are numerous pieces of theological, edifying, historical, ritualistic or *purely poetic character*" (italics mine).[116] The same author has added the information, important for us, that the said literature was included in the following publications: Jean Paul Perrin, *Histoire des Vaudois* and *Histoire des Chrestiens albigeois* (Genève: 1618) and J. Léger, *Histoire des Eglises Evangéliques des vallées de Piémont* (Leiden: 1669). According to Osokin, Jean Perrin made no distinction between Cathars and Waldenses,[117] which indicates that Waldensian and Cathar literature already constituted a mixed fund.

Anne Brenon, a contemporary scholar of note of the Cathar movement, has made several publications confirming this information since the 1970s. She quoted the evidence of Jean Léger, a pastor in the valley of Lucerne and moderator of the Piedmont valley churches, that he personally gave six manuscripts "into the hands of Mr. Morland, special commissioner of milord Oliver Cromwell, Protector of Great Britain."[118]

In turn, Samuel Morland presented the manuscripts to the university in Cambridge and published in London the *History of Evangelical Churches in Piedmont* in 1658. Another group of texts in 12 volumes, collected by the erudite archbishop of Armagh, James Ussher (1581–1656), arrived in a similar albeit slightly more roundabout way in Dublin and finally Trinity College. It is assumed that he bought all or at least eight of them from a French jurisconsult, Perrin being the starting point. After Ussher's death his library, including the above-mentioned collection, was added to that of Trinity College. According to Anne Brenon, Waldensian manuscript collections usually contain biblical texts and liturgical sermons, moral and theological treatises.[119] She has provided a rather more comprehensive description of the manuscripts in Dublin in another paper, published in 1973, in which she pointed out that MS Du10, which probably dates from the end of the 14th century, "is not Waldensian but Cathar and contains only two treatises."[120] In fact, she leads us on to the important discovery of the Belgian philologist Théo Venckeleer of 1960–1961,[121] who made a detailed study of the manuscript previously known as A.6.10 and today as MS 269, which has conditionally been accepted to have been copied from an unknown original around 1375–1376. According to Théo Venckeleer, the said manuscript A.6.10. in the Dublin collection of Waldensian manuscripts was a "Cathar document"[122] of French Provençal origin, the first part presenting the basic tenets of the Cathar church and the second being a gloss of the principal Cathar prayer Pater Noster. As we cannot quote them all here we shall dwell on the following basic points:

1. The main Bogomil sacrament, baptism with the Holy Spirit, is described in the first part of the manuscript: "lo saint baptism sperital, ço es lo enposament de las mans, per lo cal es donat lo Saint Sperit."[123]
2. The well-known Bogomil-Cathar view on the expression "panem nostrum supersubstantialem" in Pater Noster is quoted in the second part of the manuscript as "suprasubstantial bread," i.e., spiritual food intended not for the body but for the human soul. As even Euthymius Zigabenus wrote, the Bogomils "say that Jesus fed them with the Word."[124] With John Wycliffe the same thing is underscored very strongly as the reformer translated "panem nostrum supersubstantialem" as "oure breed ouer othir substaunce"[125] in English and explained that daily bread should be understood as spiritual, that this is a divine precept.[126] By the way, such a translation is closer to the Greek original "ton arton hemon ton epiousion" than the daily bread in the Authorized edi-

tion and, widely adopted in Catholic services, the "panem nostrum quo-tidianum" from Luke in the Vulgate. This is so because *epiousion* means "suprasubstantial," without the dualistic stress on word as spiritual bread being incorporated in the Orthodox one. The nonmaterial aspect has also been brought to the fore in an unquestionable manner in the Dublin manuscript, but in this case it is the love of Jesus Christ not the word that is the spiritual bread: "ço es lo sobre substantial, ço es la la carita; car la carita per ço es apela pan sobre sustancial car es sobre totas las aotras sustancias."[127]

3. In the gloss the Pater Noster ends with the expression "for thine is the kingdom and the virtue and the glory" (quoniam tuum est regnum et virtus et gloria). This expression is absent from the Vulgate as well as from the King James Bible, but it is present in the Greek text of the Orthodox Bible: "dioti sou einai he basileia kai he diunamis kai he doksa eis tous aionas." For Théo Venckeleer this is a sure sign of Greek origin.[128] And this Greek trace — as Nikolai Osokin assumed nearly 150 years ago and as Ch. Schmidt confidently stated before him — is a sign that the Cathars borrowed the Pater Noster from the Cyrillo-Metho-dian version (on the basis of the Greek Orthodox Bible), which the Bogomils took West.[129]

In addition to the evidence of the Cathar character of the manuscript quoted here, it turned out that this was not an isolated phenomenon. Théo Venckeleer accorded it a key position in Cathar literature, considering it the third authentic Cathar manuscript after *Le rituel provençal* (published by Cunitz for the first time in 1852 and again by L. Clédat in 1887) and the *Liber de Duobus Principiis*, published by R. P. A. Dondaine in 1939. The unquestionable Cathar spirit is also confirmed by the fact that, according to Venckeleer, chapters 1 and 2 of the Dublin manuscript almost coincide textually with *Le rituel provençal* (ff. 237ra-vb, resp. 329ra-vb).[130] The documents we have quoted allow the conclusion that the 17th century witnessed repeated heretical transfers containing Cathar texts to England. How this "fine example of heretical syncretism,"[131] to use the apt definition of Anne Brenon, actually occurred is a question answered even by Niko-lai Osokin. He noted that after the Cathars were subdued in the beginning of the 13th century the Waldenses were joined by all sects of purely evangelical teaching.[132] According to Anne Brenon herself, regardless of the controversies between Cathars and Waldenses, the Cathar euchologion was adopted in the said set of Waldensian literature, for the treatise on the church of God it contains has a purely evangelical intonation, one that was shared by those pre–Reformation movements. Leo Seifert, a scholar of the first third of the 20th century, wrote about the conviction of later heretics (meaning the Hussites and the Bohemian Brethren) that Wycliffe originated from the Waldenses, under which name they understood the whole group of sects based on dualism.[133]

We shall expand the review of Waldensian literature with obvious Cathar faith admixtures by mentioning two earlier cases, respectively dating from the 12th and the 14th centuries. The first was indicated by Jean Duvernoy when he wrote that dualistic opinions on creation and a negation of purgatory were noticed at a disputation between Catholic clerics and Waldenses in southern France (chaired, by the way, by the English priest Raimond of Daventry).[134] The second case harks from north Italy. The records of a trial held in 1387–1388 note that the defendants were Waldenses, poor men of Lyons and other heretics, *fraticelli*. It is exactly the documents of that trial, however, that on several occasions feature fundamental dualistic theses[135] and, what is more, information that Italian Cathars communicated with "Bogoleni" (Bogomils) of the Ecclesia Sclavoniae, the Bosnian Bogomil church related in terms of ideas to the Bulgarian one.[136]

Conclusion

In conclusion, two final questions warrant consideration — whether even more detailed specification of Milton's dualistic views is possible; and why the case of Milton's affiliation to the philosophy of dualism remains unrevealed to this day, just as the genetic link between the Lollards and continental heresies remains unknown to British medievalists. In answer to the first question, we can try to specify for which trend of dualism he had a preference. Which of the two main dualistic churches transferred to western Europe did he choose as his source: the church of absolute dualism, for which the Good and the Bad God were equal without beginning or end, or the Bulgarian church of moderated dualism, according to which the Good God would after all prevail and Satan would be shamed and conquered? The *Areopagitica* features the following assertion: "Good and evil we know in the field of this world grow up together almost inseparably; and the knowledge of good is so involved and interwoven with the knowledge of evil, and so many cunning resemblances hardly to be discerned ... that *the knowledge of good and evil, as two twins cleaving together,* leaped forth into the world"(italics mine).[137] It seems that we are faced with a definition of absolute dualism, but Milton did not leave it to remain all-powerful. He found that the painfully potent power of evil on earth was temporary, to become a test for virtue in which virtue would learn to discern good from evil by itself and, on the basis of that bitter experience, would no longer let itself be misled or deceived. As Milton further on explained, in that way Adam's fall meant to know good by evil.[138] This interpretation of his is an answer to the hypothesis of Arthur Lovejoy and Hugh White of the *felix culpa,* of the fall with a supreme meaning. It is in this spirit, but against the backdrop of modern historical experience, that Stefan Gechev updated the meaning of Bogomil philosophy as an idea of whether mankind could leave evil at all: "But I think that there is something very important with Bulgarian Bogomilism as the Bogomils asked a question crucial to mankind, i.e. could there be God without there being a devil. In other words, could there be good without there being evil?"[139] This is a dramatic question left to us, for we enter into many conflicts in the new millennium while having sufficient knowledge and means to avoid them. Theoretically man is now stronger than evil and is familiar with its faces and temptations from past experience. Therefore man has to make his choice of good on his own and thus prove himself as a power of goodness.

Milton's painfully achieved optimism is in harmony with the reasoning of the Bulgarian Bogomil church, for we see the ultimate victory of Christ over the devil categorically stated in *Paradise Regained.* It rings closely to both the Bogomil apocrypha model of the poem the *Dispute between Christ and the Devil,* and to information from records of the Inquisition regarding "the beliefs of the Cathars from Bagnolo and Concorreggio, who received their faith from Sclavonia, i.e. Bosnia" (which adopted the Bulgarian Bogomil church): "These others from Bulgaria believe in one omnipotent God without beginning."[140] Then we have grounds to note that Milton not only sympathized with the theology of the Bulgarian Bogomil church but also gauged the tendency towards internal evolution in it — the hope that the Good God would prevail. By the way, this essentially monotheistic position converges with another important intention of Milton's. Like Wycliffe and Tyndale he did not set himself the task of creating a separate dualistic zone in English society but tried to carry out a radical reform in the English church with the spiritual material and the evangelical example of the dualists. It seems that the same reasons, i.e., a necessary compromise with widely established orthodox beliefs, made Milton acknowledge the Blessed Virgin's immaculate conception and declare John the Baptist the forerunner of Christ at whose hands He was baptized, just as the gospels say. Now let us recall that the dualists allotted John the Baptist a place among the Devil's entourage in the Old Testament. And another example: while Bogomils, Cathars and Lollards denied the saints and acknowledged only Jesus Christ and the Father, the saints in book 6 of *Paradise Lost* fight the devil as champions of Christ.[141] Milton's desire to preserve the reformed church as a national institution and to complete the reformation in it is also quite obvious in his polemics with the adherents of the Episcopal church, not to mention the fact that he considered the church necessary for the establishment of the republic, of civic society. That was why he also considered the prospects of its unification in spite of his polemic opinions.

On the other hand, when church controversy entered political life, Milton, who was a Puritan of exceptional note involved directly in Cromwell's politics, discarded the spirit of peace and the dualist philosophy of nonviolence, and became a fervent advocate of the dictator. The subject of episcopacy is a priori encumbered with political connotations, as the king is "defender of the faith" (*defensor fidei*) by right and episcopacy is respectively a support of the monarch. This type of attack against the episcopate was reflected in a popular image of Cromwell in those times, depicting him with a sword in one hand and the Bible in the other, a case in which Milton definitely was no dualist but rather an aggressive politician, a new element when the explosion of political passion took him beyond Bogomil thought and lifestyle.

Milton's affiliation to Bogomil theology consequently found itself preserved in another way, transformed as it was by him into poetics. In terms of a period in life this corresponded with his complete exclusion from politics after the Restoration; in other words, a return from politics to poetry and dualistic philosophy. Some would object to this, quoting the numerous battles and clashes of force in *Paradise Lost*. These, however, are no blood battles but raging emotions, which gradually raise man above the kingdom and the temptations of Satan, which call upon a spiritual feat, an appeal resounding with repeated insistence in *Paradise Regained*. Therefore I think one could make such a summary in advance as it would allow a more precise understanding of the exceptionally varied Miltonian life and world. By the political sign of Puritanism Milton left the New Testament world of Bogomils, Cathars and Lollards and returned to the Old Testament practice that was history then and is history today. Later, after his political downfall, he raised Bogomil theology to the firmament of poetry, which is a world of spiritual evolution and of beauty, maybe close to the heavens of the good Father where the dualists dreamed of returning.

Now we have to answer the second question: why did such an engagement of Milton's with basic tenets of dualistic theology in the frequently lexical coincidence of images and expressions with dualistic texts remain unrevealed for nearly 250 years? As time will probably provide the comprehensive answer, here we shall just outline two visible peculiarities.

The first is that both in the 20th century and today, English medieval and heresy studies adopt the axiom that the island remained untouched by the major medieval heresies on the continent.

One of the reasons for that is that the English heretics, the Lollards with whom Wycliffe was associated, concealed their continental origin very carefully to avoid large-scale persecution like the destructive internal crusades Pope Innocent III organized in Provence, France, in the beginning of the 13th century. Such skillful concealment of identity and history did not allow the Catholic Church in England to gauge what its opponents actually were and whose spirit they were bringing to the island. Even today we find the following thesis in the *Catholic Encyclopedia*: "The few heretics who were heard of were all foreigners and they seem to have found no following in the country.... It is to these social and religious distempers that we must look for the causes of the Peasant Revolt and the Lollard movement ... just as Lollardy is the only heresy which flourished in medieval England."[142] This is an erroneous assertion for at least two reasons. First of all, it is impossible that the Lollards, who constituted widespread and influential communities in the 14th century, who sent a petition to Parliament in 1395 and had their own schools and literature, did not previously undergo a period of inception and growth in order to achieve the various dimensions of all that varied activity. In other words, judging by the familiar rates by which a culture developed in the Middle Ages, as the Lollards were a most active factor in social life at the end of the 14th century such a culmination should have been preceded by at least two centuries of development.

Besides, the term Lollard is of proven continental origin, as the *Encyclopædia Britannica* states.[143] In the 19th century authors such as Nikolai Osokin and Jean Jusserand wrote about English relations with continental heresies, but their studies — particularly Osokin's — remain beyond the field of vision of our British colleagues. It seems that the problem which hinders their communication with major authors such as Nikolai Osokin or Lev Karsavin is a linguistic one. Or maybe sometimes one should speak of a certain dose of conservatism, for the excellent bibliography of Krastina Gecheva on Bogomilism,[144] where she has quoted works containing proof of Lollard continental origin and the dualistic character of their teaching, a book published in 1997, has not been mentioned in any of the recent English publications to the best of my knowledge.

That Milton's dualistic philosophy was not gauged may also be due to the fact that most of his scholars see the politician but overlook the theologian in his essays. Milton's writings pay due to the political passions of the period, and in terms of style they constitute publicist pieces — sometimes, as Milton aficionados have noted to their chagrin, reaching the point of crude attacks on opponents. These essays are not only political pamphlets, however, for half or at least one-third of them contain theological disputation.

To underestimate the theological aspect is an inadequate and unproductive approach. Thus the *Cambridge History of English and American Literature* finds that Milton's prose is not an easy subject to study, that it has been repeatedly overlooked — at least in the general reviews of his work.[145] What this history offers, however, is no alternative, as his essays are practically analyzed only in terms of style to reach the conclusion that, with the exception of some passages, this prose was below the poet's own level.[146] Neither their ideological dimensions have been mentioned nor their significance as expressing one of the most energetic positions of the Reformation.[147] In this respect older English publications register more interest in Milton's treatises. In his preface to Milton's 1659 essay *Considerations Touching the Likeliest Means to Remove the Hirelings out of the Church* J. John wrote in 1883: "Few readers perhaps expect the rare display of learning and logic which they will find in this treatise."[148]

This study has no claim to being comprehensive, for it is a beginning which explains principles of Milton's philosophy and imagery, a formidable task which necessitates further intensive work. Fascinating problems continue to sprout in the field of research as a forgotten reality begins to speak, wanting to be reborn. Since the poet used apocrypha and other dualistic literature so abundantly, what are those sources? Although he expressed affiliation to the work of the Waldensian and Cathar churches or to the heretical John Wycliffe, Milton did not name his direct sources. Historically amassed dust or the cautious withholding of truths that could be used against the ongoing reform — these are questions that could be considered, especially after additional facts are found.

One should also take a closer look at Milton's correspondence or his associates. He shared some of his meetings and contacts of anticlerical pathos. Thus in 1638 he visited the aged Galileo in Italy[149] and paid attention to his meetings with Jean Diodati (1576–1649), a noted Protestant theologian who made a new translation of the Bible in Italian and published the treatise *De fictitio Pontificiorum Purgatorio* (1619), which rejected the idea of purgatory. Milton should have left a trace somewhere, be it in letters or in memoirs of his peers and friends. A letter of Milton's to Emeric Bigot mentions the Cotton MSS, the first part of which contains the dualistic *Dialogue between Salomon and Saturn*, as well as a fragment of the *Gospel of Nicodemus* used by the dualists.[150] In other words, those were older dualistic sources possibly on English territory since the 12th century. At that, the letter is dated March 24, 1658, during the period in which the already blind poet was probably in the atmosphere of his great work, *Paradise Lost.*

Naturally, the scarcity of details about Milton's direct contacts with heretical literature does not invalidate the arguments presented here in favor of his dualism. Dualism acquires the significance of a flight in the heavens. It turns out that the grandest trips in different worlds, man's most encompassing view of the universe and human elevation to a general view of God's deeds were achieved through poetics borrowed from dualism. Dante's *Divina Commedia* relied on it in its construction of the worlds and Milton's epic, dedicated to the universal struggle between good and evil, is full of its imagery and theogony. This super-scope was also noticed by J. Goodridge, who wrote that Dante's *Divina Commedia*, Milton's *Paradise Lost* and William Langland's *Piers Plowman* worked with the widest of all themes, "the meaning of man's life on earth in relation to his ultimate destiny. Like Milton, Langland seeks to 'justify the ways of God to men.'"[151] *Piers Plowman* acquired this scope from dualistic poetics, for this poem also has the aspect of a Bogomil-Cathar treatise.

What are the similarities and the differences between the poetics of Dante and those of Milton? Above all, Dante was not a dualist. He was carried away by a struggle with the Church on principle. With his treatise *De Monarchia* he wanted the Church to be subordinate to the state. He was familiar with dualistic apocrypha like *Visio Paoli*, from which he borrowed the idea of the descent into the underworld and the trip there. Milton embraced *The Secret Book* of the Bogomils and other fundamental apocrypha of theirs, an embrace of dual meaning in the sense that on the one hand he borrowed the universal scope, and on the other he shared the finalist views of the Bulgarian dualists that were harbingers of defeat for the devil and his demons. Naturally, in *Paradise Lost* the poet updated their views with the culture and the humanistic leanings of the 17th century. Spatially speaking, Dante took the drama of the underworld, i.e., the antechamber of catharsis and redemption, for it is in the *Inferno* that he is most powerful. Milton took the entire universe in order to give Christ the final victory in *Paradise Regained*, a victory of the Son that man is destined to repeat. In other words, the English poet succeeded in compiling a positive epic of Christian humanism. The works of Dante and Milton seem to persuade us that the picture of the universe in literature can be achieved most successfully through a dualistic prism.

And now a modern aspect: In the great work of *Paradise Lost* Bogomil philosophy and imagery have found a happier reproduction than in Bulgarian literature itself. This is the most convincing possible example of cultural interaction or *interculturalité*, to use the French term. Besides such a statement, however, there are things that remain unsaid. What does this mean — that ideas have some law of their own of materializing regardless of the place of their genesis? Or vice versa — that their more comprehensive materialization elsewhere predicts a new, more impressive one on their own cultural and historical soil? In any case, with the material development of mankind that should leave us free for more spiritual occupations we are embarking upon times of interaction, when the spiritual wealth of the world is revealed not only as accessible to all, but also as a result of processes of shared creation and as a prospect to renew the most sublime meanings, the still resourceful aspects of the same processes.

BLAKE AND BEYOND: THE NEED FOR
FURTHER EXPLORATION*

We documented that since the 12th century the presence of dualist apocrypha in England is clearly denoted, right until the 17th (in the works of John Milton), and that there was an infusion of a potent cultural and philosophical trends in English culture, trends which were founded on the dualist Bogomil-Cathar heresy. The Lollards with their iconography, the reformers John Wycliffe and William Tyndale, the poet William Langland, the apocryphal volume *Cursor mundi*, as well as the Anglo-Norman variants of *The Legend of the Tree of the Cross* and *Les enfaunces de Jesus Christ*, are all profoundly keen to the word in John Milton's great poems *Paradise Lost* and *Paradise Regained*. They all converge within this time span, in a rich blend of ideas and strongly perceptible imagery and cognitive concepts.

We are faced with a chain of dualist events, works and outstanding individuals who frequently reach the highest pinnacles of English culture. At this moment it is important to glance forward, facing new surprises in the field of our scholarly exploits. We have entered in a very engaging domain, where explaining one event immediately leads to discovering another. These links are marked by their own temper; they are revelations with an impressive connectivity. As usual, history outdoes fiction. Now we encounter a new episode in the process of the transfer of dualist philosophy to England. This time the action takes place in the 18th century and involves a most interesting personality: Johan Heinrich Fussli, born to an artist's family in Zurich, Switzerland, in 1741.

In England he was known as Fuseli or Fussly. Under his father's guidance he tried to become a preacher, but after a confrontation with a powerful magistrate moved to London, where he earned his living as a translator and, after seven years of study in Italy, as a painter. As an artist he won European fame and attracted the interest of Goethe, and also became a close friend of Blake. Currently Fuseli is considered as precursory to the symbolists and even the surrealists. He died in 1825 after serving as a professor of painting at the Royal Academy in London. Fuseli created 200

I would like to thank the art scholar and expert Ivan Valtchev, adjunct professor at NYU, for his insight and help in shedding more light on the connections between Blake, Fuseli and the Reformation.

paintings, many of which reside in the best European museums, and the Tate Gallery in London has an entire collection of his oeuvre.

Why are we focusing on this man? Because his deeds lead to answers of a recently pressed question by A. Nuttall: What is so particular about the philosophy of William Blake? While labeling generally his universe as a "Gnostic heresy," Nuttall asks: "By what means could have Blake known of Gnosticism?"[152] However, we see in the poet's philosophy a discernible trace of the dualist heresy, and now we introduce an initial answer to the evolution of his thinking. Of course the poet had a number of other influences. Blake mentioned the Swedish mystic Swedenborg six times in *The Marriage of Heaven and Hell.* Still, the imported dualist features which we intend to reveal are also present in this work.

While claiming that John Milton depicted Satan with a greater craft, William Blake emphasized the dualist fabric by a specific mention of the fundamental Bogomil-Cathar myth about expelling Lucifer from heaven. "And the original Archangel or possessor of the command of the heavenly host, is call'd the Devil or Satan and his children are call'd Sin & Death."[153] Additional facts will support and enrich our forthcoming conclusion.

For example, William Blake creates a particular image of Jesus — as *The Good Farmer* (1780–85), "where Jesus advises people how to sow, plough and reap the wheat from which they will produce bread."[154] The prevailing interpretation till now was that this group of seven sketched images "all appear to illustrate the Parable of the Wheat and the Tares from St. Matthew's Gospel." But their imagery and sense seem to be much closer to the apocrypha *Infancy Gospel*, beloved by Bogomils and Cathars, and the author Rumyana Hristova quite correctly associates the series with "ancient unofficial religious doctrines."

We would like to emphasize William Blake's direct takes from the Bogomils' apocrypha. The book's cover displays an etching by the painter, known by a popular title: "Michael Binding Satan" (circa 1802). This image's full title, given personally by Blake, is *He Cast Him into the Bottomless Pit, and Shut Him Up.* The subject strikingly corresponds to the Bogomils' 13th century apocrypha the *Oratione of St. John Crysostom on how Michael the Archangel defeated Satan.*

This scene also parallels obviously the finale of the most famous Bogomil apocrypha — *The Secret Book* (11th century). The Carcassone version of *The Secret Book* predicts that Christ "will lock the Devil in chains indestructible and strong" (clauded Diabolum ligans insolubilibis vinculis fortibus).

And now we can point to the likely agent of conveyance, the medium of transference. It also happened that Blake's personal and highly valued friend Henry Fuseli had a close relative, the Swiss theologian Johann Conrad Füssli (Fuessli). During 1761, in Bern, Switzerland, Füssli published two most unusual theses — *Dissertatio de fanaticis seculo XI in Italia detectis* and *Dissertatio de fanaticis seculo XII in Anglia repertis*. These dissertations were written in Latin. The second thesis discussed the migration and the infusion of the heresies of the Middle Ages — the Waldensians, Albigenses, and the Publicans in England, during the twelfth century. In addition Johann Conrad Füssli published three volumes of bibliography in German about Middle Ages heresies.[155] The author described his work as an impartial (unparteishe) history of the Middle Age church and heresies. Now we can state with greater certainty that this established scholarly authority on Bogomil-Cathar infusion in England almost directly influenced Blake and led him to absorbing to a considerable degree the heretics' philosophy. The Swiss-English painter Henry Fuseli, who drew his knowledge of heresy from his Swiss relative, theologian Johann Conrad Füssli, was a motivated transmitter of the Bogomil-Cathar philosophy in England during the 18th century and in particular to his friend William Blake. The spiritual friendship of Henry Fuseli and William Blake supported the idea of a dualist doctrine. This is heightened by the fact that Henry Fuseli expressed and nursed intense spiritual interest in the greatest dualist epic of John Milton, *Paradise Lost*. In fact Fuseli created forty illustrations for the poem, and he named his gallery in London after Milton. He also painted John Milton "When a Youth."[156]

Seeing the spiritual incentive of Fuseli, we may expect that such a faithful, academically and scholarly documented emissary of the Bogomil-Cathar morphism would have been in close communion with the prominent intellectuals in Switzerland, England and Germany. This would be a new testimony to the latest generation of Bogomil-Cathar hermeticism, revived in England by the Central European artist. All these findings and events call for continued further research. Before us, a book published in 1879 by the American Baptist historian Dr. L.P. Brocket declared a vital connection between the Bogomil-Cathar teachings and the Reformation-spawned Protestants. The book title speaks more strongly than any comments: *The Bogomils of Bulgaria and Bosnia (The Early Protestants of the East) — An Attempt to Restore Some Lost Leaves of Protestant History*.[157] This unprecedented documentation of a vital bond between the Middle Ages

Balkan Bogomils and the late 1800s American Protestants, noted by a prominent Baptist historian, deserves the greatest attention possible. He is the first American to our knowledge to link the medieval heretics to the solid ground of the New World's uncompromising Protestants, relieved from the cults of Mary and the saints and solely worshiping Christ.

Chapter Notes

Preface

1. Kr. Gecheva, *Bogomilstvoto: Bibliografia*, with titles in the original language (Sofia: 1997).

Introduction

1. *Encyclopaedia Britannica*, vol. 14 (1970), p. 256.

2. Ign. von Döllinger, *Dokumente vornemlich zur Geschihte der Valdesier und Katharer* (München: 1890), p. 381.

3. Ibidem.

4. M. Lambert, *Medieval Heresy: Popular Movements from the Gregorian Reform to the Reformation,* 3rd ed. (Oxford: 2002), p. 200.

5. Murdock's translation of Mosheim's *Ecclesiastical History from the Birth of Our Saviour to the Eighteenth Century*, book 3, part 2, ch. 2 (Boston and London: 1802), p. 393.

6. Ibidem, p. 381.

7. H. Ch. Lea, *A History of the Inquisistion of the Middle Ages*, vol. 2 (London: 1888), p. 368.

8. Ign. von Döllinger, op. cit., p. 408.

9. Ibidem, p. 410.

10. Ibidem, p. 410.

11. *Annae Comnenae porphyrogenitae caesarissae Alexias* (Venice: Ex typographia Bartholomae Javarina, 1724), p. 384. See *The Alexiad of the Princess Anna Comnena* (London: 1918), reprinted in *Documentary History of Eastern Europe* (New York: 1970), p. 8: "A Bogomil looks gloomy and is cov-

ered up to the nose and walks with a stoop and *mutters*, but within he is an uncontrollable wolf" (italics mine).

12. I. Franko, "Peredmova," in *Apokrifi i legendi z ukrainskih rukopisiv*, vol. 2 (L'viv, 1899).

13. H. Osokin, *Istoriya al'bigoytsev i ih vremeni* (Moskva: 2000 [1st ed. Kazan: 1869]).

14. M. Gaster, *Ilchester Lectures on Greeko-Slavonic Literature and its Relation to theFolklore of Europe During the Middle Ages* (London: 1887).

15. Here we once again fall upon a circle of contradictions — adopting the thesis of the British roots of the Lollards, the *Catholic Encyclopedia* quotes a European origin (this time in Flanders) of their name: The name was derived by contemporaries from *lollium*, a tare, but it was used in Flanders early in the fourteenth century in the sense of "hypocrite," and the phrase "Lollardi seu Deum laudantes" (1309) points to a derivation from *lollen*, to sing softly (cf. Eng. *lull*) (*The Catholic Encyclopedia*, vol. 9 [Robert Appleton Company, 1910], p. 333).

16. D. Daniell, *William Tyndale: A Biography* (New Haven and London: Yale University Press, 2001), p. 2.

17. "It is agreed on all hands that the English of the *Authorised Version* is, in essentials, that of Tyndale." *The Cambridge History of English and American Literature in 18 volumes,* 1907–1921, vol. 4, p. 48.

18. D. Obolensky, *The Bogomils: A Study in Balkan Neo-Manichaeism* (London: Cambridge University Press, 1948), p. vii.

19. Such an opinion has already been voiced by V. Zaytsev, *Bogomil'skoe dvizhenie i obstestvennaya zhizn' Severnoy Italii epohi Duecento* (Minsk: 1967).

Chapter 1

1. S. Runciman, *The Medieval Manichee: A Study of Christian Dualist Heresy* (Cambridge: Cambridge University Press, 1947), p. 122.

2. M. Loos, *Dualist Heresy in the Middle Ages* (Academia-Prague, 1974), p. 117.

3. A. Veselovski, *Solomon i Kitovras* (Saint Petersburg: 1872); M. Gaster, *Ilchester Lectures on Greeko-Slavonic Literature and Its Relation to the Folklore of Europe During the Middle Ages* (London: 1887).

4. D. Obolensky, *The Bogomils: A Study in Balkan Neomanichaeism* (Cambridge: Cambridge University Press, 1948), pp. 273–274.

5. A. Baugh (with K. Malone), "The Middle English Period (1100–1500)," in *A Literary History of England*, vol. 1 (London: 1967).

6. One of the sessions of the Commons received the name "the Lollard Parliament." G. G. Coulton, *The Medieval Panorama* (Cambridge: 1949), p. 490.

7. *Encyclopaedia Britannica*, vol. 14, 1970, p. 256.

8. Du Cange, *Glossarium mediae et infimae latinitatis*, vol. 5, p. 134.

9. L. Moreri, *Dictionnaire historique ou mélange curieux de l'histoire sacrée et profane*, vol. 5 (1740), p. 213.

10. *Encyclopédie des sciences religieuses*, publ. sous la direction de F. Lichtenberger, vol. 8 (Paris: 1880), p. 347. Both Moreri and Lichtenberger quote the popular etymology of the appellation "Lollard" as derived from the name of the heresy leader Walter Lollard, burnt in Cologne in 1323. It is possible that Lichtenberger got his note from Moreri. Another piece of interesting but unchecked information is given by Moreri: a Lollard called Basnage who had preached in Piemont had later immigrated with his followers to England.

11. Norman Tanner, ed., *Heresy Trials in the Diocese of Norwich, 1428–31*, Camden Fourth Series, vol. 20 (London: 1977), mentions some episodic connections of English Lollards with the continent. Johannes Fynche de Colchester admits to have been in connection with Laurence Tyler, a Dutchman (p. 185); another defendant speaks of a book that "came recently from the oversee lands" (iam nuper venit de partibus ultramarinis ad istas partes, p. 75).

12. M. D. Lambert, *Medieval Heresy: Popular Movements from Bogomil to Hus* (London: 1977), p. 269.

13. I would like to thank Dr. Lydia Denkova and Dr. Boyka Sokolova for their help with the Latin and Middle English texts.

14. *Bogomilstvoto v Balgaria, Vizantya i Zapadna Evropa v izvori*, Sastav. D. Angelov, B. Primov, G. Batakliev (Sofia: 1967).

15. "...diabolos qui ceciderunt cum Lucifero di celo, qui quidem cum cadendo in terram intrarunt in ymagines stantes in ecclesiis, et eisdem continue habiturunt adhuc habitant latinantes." Tanner, ed., *Heresy Trials*, p. 49. The heretic Margeria mixtes up the fall of Lucifer with another belief of the Bogomils mentioned by Zigabenus — that the devils dwell in the churches and about the icons made in their honor.

16. "Magnum regem dicunt nunc esse diabolum, ut mundi principem." Euthymii Zigabeni, "Panoplia dogmatica," in *Patrologia Graeca*, vol. 130, § 40.

17. "Quod Deus debet obedire diabolo." John Wycliffe, "XXIV Conclusiones damnatae Londoniis in synodo," in *Shirley, Fasciculi Zizaniorum*, p. 278.

18. "Baptismum nostrum Joannis baptismum esse dicunt, per aquam enim fieri, suum vero Christi, per Spiritum enim fieri, ut ipsis videtur." Zigabenus, § 16.

19. Tanner, ed., *Heresy Trials*, p. 121.

20. "Solam precationem appellant quam Dominus tradidit in Evangeliis, id est, Pater noster." Zigabenus, § 19.

21. Tanner, ed., *Heresy Trials*, p. 81.

22. Kozma Presviter, "Beseda protiv bogomilite," p. 54.

23. Tanner, ed., *Heresy Trials*, p. 147.

24. "Item quod omnis confessio soli Deo est facienda, et non alteri sacerdoti." Tanner, ed., *Heresy Trials*, p. 131.

25. "Item dicunt, non esse purgato-

rium." F. Rački, "Prilozi za povjest bosanskih patarena," *Starine* 1 (1869): 139. Also in *Bogomilstvoto v Bulgaria*, p. 221. On this subject see also "A Neglected Byzantine Notice on Bogomils" by Ivan Duychev in his book *Prouchvania varhu srednovekovnata balgarskia istoria i kultura* (Sofia: 1981). Dujčev discovers this notice in a polemical treatise published in London in 1624, also published in Constantinople in 1627. The dualists explained the negation of purgatory in this way: this world is the kingdom of Satanael, so this world is a place of suffering, a purgatory, even a hell in itself ("Item dicunt, in hoc mundo infernum esse, i.e. hic esse ignem et frigus et omnem malum, et non est alius infernus, nec fuit, nec erit," as found in Salve Burce, "Supra stella" in *Dokumente vornehmlich zur Geschichte der-Valdesier und Katharer*, Döllinger [München: 1890], p. 327). So that existential aim of the adept is to free himself, to cut relations with this world so he can return to the Father in Heaven.

26. "At qui sint ejusmodi, eos negant mori, sed tanquam in somno transmutari, et sine ullo labore coenosum hoc carnis in dumentum exuere, atque immortalem ac Divinam Christi stolam induere, idemque corpus et formam eamdem induere, et praeeuntibus angelis et apostolis in Patris regnune admitti, corpus autem, in cinerem pilveremque dissolve, numquam amplius surrecturum." Zigabenus, § 23.

27. "Item quod Ricardus Belward docuit istum quod iste mundus est locus purgatorii, et omnis anima quamcito egressa fuerit de corpore statim sine medio transit ad celum sive ad infernum et adeo frustra fiunt oraciones vel misse dicte vel facte pro defunctis." Depositions of John Burell, servant of Thomas Mone, in Tanner, ed., *Heresy Trials*, p. 74.

28. Prezviter, "Beseda protiv bogomilite," p. 51.

29. Tanner, ed., *Heresy Trials*, p. 141.

30. "Neque per Hierosolymam, inquit juraveris, quonam civitas est magni regis. Magnum regum dicunt nunc esse diabolum, ut mundi principem." Zigabenus, § 40.

31. "Item dicunt quod non sit licitum alicui defendere se ita, quod invasor possit laedi. Item dicunt quod nula potestas terrena possit uti gladio materiali in vindictam malefactorum." "Errores haereticorum Catharorum," in Döllinger, op. cit., p. 323.

32. Tanner, ed., *Heresy Trials*, p. 142.

33. "Quod homicidium per bellum vel praetensam legem justitiae pro temporal; causa sine spirituali revelatione, est expresse contraria Novo Testamento; quod quidem est lex gratiae et plena misercordiarum." "Sequntur Conclusiones Lollardorum in quidam libello porrectae pleno parlamento regni Angliae, regnante illustrissimo principe Rege Ricardo secundo, anno ejus circiter XVIII." Walter W. Shirley, ed., *Fascicui Zizaniorum* (London: 1858), p. 366.

34. "Nostram antem Ecclesiam Herodem interpretatuntur, quae Verbum apud eos natum conetur occidere." Zigabenus, § 28.

35. Tanner, ed., *Heresy Trials*, p. 57.

36. Prezviter, "Beseda protiv bogomilite," p. 50.

37. "Item quod omnes ecclesie materiales sunt nisi synagoge, ac modicum vel nichil deberent haberi in reve rencia quia Deus exaudit preces orantis in campo tam bene sicut preces orantis in tali synagoga." Depositions of John Godesell, parchemyn-maker, in Tanner, ed., *Heresy Trials*, p. 61.

38. Prezviter, "Beseda protiv bogomilite," p. 35.

39. Tanner, ed., *Heresy Trials*, p. 57.

40. Prezviter, "Beseda protiv bogomilite," p. 34.

41. Tanner, ed., *Heresy Trials*, p. 154.

42. "Venerandas enim imagines aspernantur et idola gentium appellant, argentumque et aurum et opera manuum hominum." Zigabenus, § 11; "...quomodo beatorum Patrum reliquiis inhaerent daemones." Zigabenus, § 12.

43. "...quod nullus honor est exhibendus aliquibus ymaginibus sculptis in ecclesiis per manus hominum." Depositiones of Johannes Burrel, in Tanner, ed., *Heresy Trials*, p. 73.

44. "Item quod relique sanctorum scilicet carnem et ossa hominis mortui, non debent a populo venerari." Depositiones of John Skylly of Flixton, in Tanner, ed., *Heresy Trials*, p. 53.

45. Prezviter, "Beseda protiv bogomilite," p. 40.

46. "Item quod nullus honor exhibendus aliquibus ymaginibus crucifixi, Beate Marie vel alicuius alterius sanctis." Tanner, ed., *Heresy Trials*, p. 108.

47. "Item quod si episcopus vel sacerdos existat in peccato mortali: non ordinant, conficit, nec baptizat." Shirley, *Fasciculi Zizaniorum*, p. 278.

48. "Item quod quilibet homo existens in vera caritate est sacerdos Dei et quod nullus sacerdos habet maiorem potestatem at ministranda aliqua sacramenta in Ecclesia quam habet aliquis laicus non ordinatus." Tanner, ed., *Heresy Trials*, p. 52.

49. R. Nelli, *Le phénomène cathare (perspectives philosophiques et morales)* (Toulouse: 1988), pp. 32, 39.

50. J. Thomson, *The Later Lollards 1414–1520* (Oxford University Press, 1965), p. 248.

51. Lambert, *Medieval Heresy*, p. 240.

52. Ibidem, p. 242.

53. M. A. Deanesly, *The Lollard Bible (and Other Medieval Versions)* (Cambridge: 1920/1966).

54. Prezviter, "Beseda protiv bogomilite," p. 49.

55. Shirley, *Fasciculi Zizaniorum*, p. 362.

56. Tanner, ed., *Heresy Trials*, p. 20.

57. The German authors quoted by I. Franko are of special interest: R. Reischshen, *Die Pseudo-Evangelien von Jesu und Marias Kindheit in der romanischen und germanischen Literatur* (Halle: 1879); R. P. Wülker, *Das Evangelium Nicodemi in der Abendländischen Literatur* (Padeborn: 1872); C. Horstman, *Altenglische Legenden* (Padeborn und Heilbron, 1878).

58. M. A. Aston, "Lollardy and Sedition 1381–1431," *Past and Present*, Apr. 1960, p. 15.

59. Lambert, *Medieval Heresy*, p. 268.

60. Ibidem, p. 63.

61. Tanner, ed., *Heresy Trials*, p. 111.

62. Ibidem, pp. 115–116.

63. Ibidem, p. 57.

64. D. Angelov, *Balgarinat v Srednovekovieto. Svetogled, ideologia, dushevnost* (Varna: 1985), p. 28.

65. V. Yagich, *Istoriya serbohorvatskoy literatury* (Kazan: 1879), p. 96.

66. Tanner, ed., *Heresy Trials*, p. 69, 73, 100.

67. Ibidem, p. 93.

68. Ibidem, p. 48.

69. Ibidem, p. 69, 73, 100.

70. Lambert, *Medieval Heresy*, p. 257, 240.

71. A. Hudson, "Some Aspects of Lollard Book Production," in *Schism, Heresy and Religious Protest*, Studies in Church History 9 (Cambridge: 1972).

72. Deanesly, *The Lollard Bible* p. vii.

73. J. Thomson, *The Later Lollards*, p. 242.

74. Deanesly, *The Lollard Bible*, p. 363.

75. Gaster, *Ilchester Lectures*, p. 49.

76. A. Galahov, *Istoriya russkoy slovesnosti — drevnoy i novoy. I.* (SPB, 1880), p. 198.

77. Gaster, *Ilchester Lectures*, pp. 25–26.

78. Thomson, *The Later Lollards*, p. 101.

79. Ibidem.

80. As Beguins he understands the Franciscan Fratres Minores, followers of Pierre-Jean Olieu (Petrus Johannis Olivi).

81. B. Gui, *Manuel de l'inquisiteur*, ed. and trans. G. Mollet, vol. 1 (Paris: 1926), p. 26.

82. Ibidem, p. 62. See also the appendix.

83. Ibidem, p. 142.

84. Tanner, ed., *Heresy Trials*, p. 73.

85. Lambert, *Medieval Heresy*, p. 240.

86. *Patrologia Graeca*, vol. 104, col. 55.

87. A serious initial effort in this direction is M. Deanesly's. Her study of biblical translations of the Lollards begins with the information from the Dialogue by Sir Thomas More. Deanesly, *The Lollard Bible*, pp. 2–6. The same title is included as an appendix in vol. 5 of J. Gairdner, *Lollardy and Reformation in England*.

88. Thomson, *The Later Lollards*, p. 253.

89. Deanesly, *The Lollard Bible*, p. 42.

90. C. Schmidt, *Histoire et doctrine de la secte des Cathares ou Albigeois*, vol. 2 (Paris, Geneva: 1849), p. 271.

91. Y. Ivanov, *Bogomilski knigi i legendi* (Sofia: 1925), p. 111.

Chapter 2

1. *The Oxford English Dictionary*, vol. I (Oxford: Clarendon Press, 1933), p. 1160.

The dictionary provides another, less studied historical meaning of the word "bugger": usurer. It suggests that the heretics dealt in money-lending because the money provided their independence from the feudal power and hierarchy.

2. *The Oxford Dictionary of English Etymology*, ed. by C. T. Onions (1966), p. 124.

3. *Webster's Third International Dictionary* (Massachussets: 1961), p. 291.

4. Indeed this process of self-emerging attributing of new word meanings begins by the end of the sixteenth century. For example, the verb *rabougrir* appeared in French in 1600 and the verb *abougrir* was introduced, even earlier, in 1564, describing an ill growing plant, waning due to drought and inclement conditions. These verbs could be applied to the condition of people. The context is clear — the French have witnessed that the Cathar heresy, persecuted by the internal crusades and the Papal inquisition, has declined and became an example of wilting. Next the word *bougre* gains a new meaning indicating a *chetif* (weak), *faible* (feeble) person. The reflective derivative verb *se rabourgrir* appears in 1690 according to *Le Robert, Dictionnaire de la langue francaise*, vol. 7 (Paris: 1985), p. 985. Similar is the interpretation of the *Grand Larousse encyclopédique*, vol. 7 (Paris: 1963), p. 974: "arrêter le développment normal"— translated as "to stop, halt a normal development." The meaning of the same word in Provençal dialect is close: "to suppress or smear a person" (*Lou trésor doú felibrige — Dictionnaire Provençal-Français*, vol. 1 [Paris: 1932], p. 40).

5. Gaster, M., op. cit., p. 78. To appreciate the contribution of Faber and Gaster in clarifying this problem we should mention the fact that in the *Etymological Dictionary of the English language*, published by W. S. Keat in 1879–1882, Oxford, the word "bugger" is missing.

6. *OED* vol. 1, pp. 1019, 1160.

7. *Funk & Wagnalls New Standard Dictionary of the English Language* (New York, London: 1933), p. 341.

8. E. Partridge, *A Short Etymological Dictionary of Modem English* (London: 1959/1966), p. 63.

9. R. Nelli has explained the relatively late negative connotation of the word "bougre": "In the beginning [the 13th century] the troubadours did not lend a negative meaning when they mentioned the name 'bougre' as, for example, in the *Song of the Crusade against the Albigensians*. It was only later that the word acquired a disparaging connotation and became a term of abuse in the mouths of those who persecuted 'the Bulgarian heresy'— Catharism" (quoted in Vl. Topencharov, *Dve jaravi — edin plamak* [Sofia: 1982], p. 174).

10. This slander spread over a considerable territory. Borislav Primov has noted the existence of the word "buzzerone" in Italian with the meaning of "homosexual" or "sodomite," and the participle "buzerans" in Hungarian which means "a man sexually involved with another man." According to B. Primov, both the latter and the verb "buzeral," meaning "to trouble," "to pester," have come to the Hungarian from the Italian through German of Serbo-Croatian mediation. B. Primov, *Bugrite: Kniga za pop Bogomil i negovite posledovateli* (Sofia: 1970), pp. 305–306. To corroborate this link we shall mention that A. Prati indicates that the Italian term for sodomite "buggerone" originates from the word *Bulgari* (Bulgarians)—"that had turned to Manicheans and therefore [were] suspected in sodomy sins." *Vocabulario etimologico italiano* (Torino: 1951), p. 180. D. Oliveri in his dictionary *Dizionario etimologico italiano, concordato coi dealetti, le lingue straniere e la topoonomastica* (Milano: 1953), p. 106, indicates that the "Bulgarians were accused in sodomy practices as adherents to the patarene heresy." D. Oliveri draws similarity to the contamination of the French word *bougre* with the meaning of a sodomite pervert. B. Primov's observation is confirmed by Du Cange, who points out that the Spanish word "bujaran" is loaded with the same negative meaning — "masculorum concubitor," i.e. "one who lives with a man" (*Glossarium mediae et infimae latinitatis*, vol. 1, p. 772). Although it has acquired a pejorative content, this term creates a trace which outlines the large geographical territory of "Bulgarian," that is, Bogomil, influence.

11. The noted Russian historian and

philosopher quotes the opinion of more sincere Catholic chroniclers. One of them characterized the Patarene Diotesalva as "respected, with honest conduct and dignified bearing" (aspectu venerabilem, honestum incessu et exteriori habitu). Karsavin also quotes another chronicler: "They say that the heretics are virtuous and accomplish miracles" (Dicebant quod heretici faciebant virtutes et miracula). L. Karsavin," Ocherki religioznoy zhizni v Italii XII–XIII vekov (St. Petersburg: 1912), p. 54. See also the appendix to this chapter.

12. J. L. Seifert, Die Weltrevolutionäre: Von Bogomil über Hus zu Lenin (Zürich-Leipzig-Wien: Amalthea-Verlag, 1931), pp. 52, 111. The Czech dictionaries give a rather different meaning of "flamendr," i.e., "vagrant," but etymologists point out that it primarily entered the Czech through the German as signifying a "merchant from Flanders." V. Machek, Etymologický slovník jazyka českého (Prague: 1971), p. 146. As many historians have pointed out, it was the merchants who were among the main propagators of the Cathar heresy in Europe. One should also mention that, quoting C. S. Faber, M. Gaster also mentioned how the name Vaudois (Waldensian) was loaded with the meaning of "sorcerer." Gaster, op. cit, p. 78.

13. S. Runciman, The Medieval Manichee: A Study of Christian Dualist Heresy (Cambridge University Press, 1947), p. 122.

14. Runciman, ibidem. Milan Loos, in Dualist Heresy in the Middle Ages (Akademia-Prague: 1974), pp. 117, 125, quotes a barely studied case of probable Cathar heresy in England, mentioned in Guilberti Foliot Epistola CCL (Ad Rogerium Wigorniesem episcopum) Patrologia Latina 190, col. 935–936: "we hear of these weavers who recently entered [our] diocese...." (Quod super his textoribus sentiamus, qui vestra nuper ingressi diocesim....) It was a typical Bogomil-Cathar detail that they preached in the popular tongue: "Who preach and spread in the vernacular concepts of heretical spirit" (Qui corde conceptas haereses in vulgus spargendo praedicant).

15. Runciman, Medieval Manichee, p. 123.

16. C. Schmidt, Histoire de la doctrine de la secte des cathares ou albigeois, vol. 2 (Paris and Geneva: 1849), p. 280. Schmidt quotes Muratori as the first historian to deduct the direct Cathar-Paulician link (Antquit. ital. med. Oevi. V, 83). He also quoted the authoritative opinion of Mosheim that the Cathars were Paulicians who, coming from Bulgaria and Thrace, spread their doctrine in Italy and the rest of the West (Institut. hist. eccl., 379), p. 261.

17. Du Cange, op. cit., vol. 6, p. 412, says about the "Publicani": "that is how our Manichaeans are called."

18. Concilium Lateranse III, cap. XXVII, "De hereticis," Mansi, vol. 22, col. 232.

19. F. Niel, Albigeois et Cathares (Paris: Presses Universitaires de France, 1959), p. 59.

20. B. Primov, "Balgarskoto narodno ime v Zapadna Evropa vav vrazka s bogomilite," in Izv. Inst. Balg. Ist. 6 (1956). Always correct to the smallest detail, Ch. Schmidt does not forget to recall the exact phonetic way of producing "Poblicans": paulikiavoı or paulikavoı was pronounced by the Greeks as "Pawlikani," from which the French can spontaneously produce the form of "Poblicans." This last, by the way, is the Old French pronunciation of "Pauliciens."

21. D. Obolensky, relying on P. Šafarik and N. Filipov, also located the Dragovitsa church (Ecclesia Dugunthiae) in or around Plovdiv, near the Dragovitsa River. Thus he had reason to question the claim of Fr. Rački (later adopted by Dr. Dragojlović and others) that the Dragovitsa church was located in Macedonia. D. Obolensky, The Bogomils: A Study in Balkan Neo-manichaeism (Cambridge: 1948), pp. 158–169.

22. B. Gui, Manuel de l'inquisiteur, vol. 1 (Paris: 1926), p. 24: "quod ipsi tenent locum apostolorum ... cum tamen ipsi sint boni homines et boni christiani, sicut pharisei persequebantur Christum et apostolos ejus."

23. Scriptorum veterum (quorum pars magna nunc primum e MSS. Codibus in lucem arodit) qui Ecclesiae Rom: Errores & Abusus detegunt & damnant necessitatem qui Reformationis urgent (London: 1690).

24. *Scriptorum veterum*, pp. 46, 49.
25. N. Osokin, *Istoriya Al'bigoytsev do konchiny papy Innokentiya 3* (Kazan: 1869), p. 204.
26. Prezviter, "Beseda protiv bogomilite," p. 31.
27. Döllinger, op. cit., p. 54: "Dicunt enim omnes, scilicet Catheri, quod in matrimonio temporali est fornicatio, dicenda malum Deum istum, Diabolum istud ordinasse."
28. B. Gui, *Manuel de l'inquisiteur,* vol. 1, p. 18: "et per totum anum residium diebus jejunant in pane et aqua in quolibet septimana.... Item, non tangunt aliquam mulierem."
29. Döllinger, op. cit., p. 54: "Item dicunt; jungere se cum uxore sua aut con matre aut con filia aut on alia uxore unum et idem peccatum esse, quantum est Deo, sed qantum est mundum, scandalum est."
30. R. Sacconi, "Summa de Catharis," in *Archivum Fratrum Praedicatorum* 44 (Rome: 1974), p. 45: "multi credentes eorum tam uiri quam mulieres non tient magis accedere ad sororem suam et fratrem — etc."
31. J. Duvernoy, "L'acception: 'haereticus' (iretge)," in *The Concept of Heresy in the Middle Ages,* vol. 1 (Paris–La Haye: 1976–77).
32. J. Duvernoy, *Le Régistre d'inquisition de Jacques Fournier 1318–1325,* vol. 1 (Toulouse: 1965), p. 437.
33. Duvernoy, *Le Régistre d'inquisition de Jacques Fournier,* vol. 3, p. 335.
34. Ibidem, p. 307.
35. R. Abels and E. Harrison, "The Participation of Women in Languedocian Catharism," in *Medieval Studies* 41 (1979), p. 245.
36. J. L. Seifert, *Die Weltrevolutionäre,* p. 45.
37. Prezviter, "Beseda protiv bogomilite," p. 74.

Chapter 3

1. "Interrogatio Johannis (*The Secret Book* of the Bogomils)," in *Bogomilski knigi i legendi*, Ivanov, p. 78.

2. Fr. Rački, "Prilozi za povest bosankih patarena" *Starine* 1 (1869), p. 318.
3. Prezviter, "Beseda protiv bogomilite," p. 54.
4. D. Angelov, *Bogomilstvoto* (Sofia: 1982), p. 257.
5. "Prostranno zhitie na Teodosiy Tarnovski ot patriarh Kalist," in *Stara bulgarska literatura,* vol. 4, *Zhivotopisni tvorbi* (Sofia: 1986), pp. 452–453.
6. St. Lazarov, *Prouchvania varhu kulturata na bogomili i katari: teatar, muzika (aftoreferat na disertatsiya)* (Sofia: 1989), p. 4.
7. "Hodene na Bogoroditsa po makite," in *Stara bulgarska literatura,* vol. 1, *Apokrifi,* p. 247, or the "Descent of the Holy Virgin." It is interesting to quote Moses Gaster: "*The Descent of Christ to Hell* itself gave rise to a remarkable imitation, *The Descent of the Holy Virgin,* and it is easy to imagine the influence it would have on the popular fancy, especially as it was from the beginning regarded as the clue to the mysterious life after death, and therefore gave an opportunity to entering into all possible torments, while the original Gospel only spoke of a place of wailing and gnashing of teeth." Gaster, *Ilchester Lectures,* p. 52. One has to pay attention to a theological subtlety. The anonymous Orthodox author of the *Descent of the Holy Virgin* has his way to discuss with the dualist: he puts them in the inferno because they refused to preach the name of Our Lady, as they negated the material nature of the Christ's body. This detail reveals *The Descent of the Holy Virgin* as a remake-reply against the Bogomils.
8. J. Guiraud, *Cartulaire de Notre Dame de Prouille, précédé d'étude sur l'Abigéisme languedocien au XIIe et XIIIe siècles,* vols. 1–2 (Paris: 1907).
9. G. Koch, "Frauenfrage und Ketzertum in Mittelalter," in *Forschungen zur mittealterlichen Geshihte* 9 (Berlin, 1962). Quoting according to Abels and Harrison, "The Participation of Women in the Languedocien Catharism," in *Medieval Studies,* vol. 41 (Toronto).
10. R. Nelli, *La vie quotidienne des Cathares au Languedoc au XIIIe siècle* (Paris: 1969).
11. Ladurie E. Le Roy, *Montaillou, vil-*

lage occitan de 1294 à 1324 (Paris: 1975/ 1982), pp. 383–385.

12. Abels and Harrison, "The Participation of Women in the Languedocien Catharism."

13. A. Brenon, *Les Femmes Cathares* (Paris: 1992).

14. Abels and Harrison, op. cit, p. 226.

15. Ibidem, p. 225.

16. A. Brenon, op. cit., p. 215. Brenon, as Guiraud did before her, enumerates the Cathar institutions: house for the neophytes, hospital/asylum, craftsman's workshop, shelter (p. 215).

17. Abels and Harrison, op. cit., p. 217: "Because of poverty, the minor nobility turned to the heretical convents to place their unmarried daughters and widow female relations." The authors mention also the education role of such establishments: "Cathar convents occasionally functioned as seminaries for daughters of the rural nobility" (p. 232).

18. R. Nelli, *La vie quotidienne des Cathares du Languedoc au XIIIe siècle*, pp. 106–107.

19. Abels and Harrison, op. cit., pp. 22–229.

20. Le Roy Ladurie, *Montaillou, village occitan de 1294 à 1324*, pp. 383–385.

21. E. Long, "Feminism and cultural studies," in *Critical perspectives on media and society,* ed. R. Avery and D. Eason, p. 117 (New York, London: 1991).

22. The troubadours knew well the name of Roland. See Peire Vidal of Toulouse, who says: "My audacity is equal in this of Roland and Olivier, while in art of love I am equal to Berart de Mondesdidier's art of love," in J. Robaud, *Les Troubadours*, a bilingual anthology (Paris: 1971), p. 220. But in the troubadour's poetry the image of Roland was displaced by the admiration of the beloved lady.

23. R. Manselli, "Dolore e morte ella esperienza religiosa catara," in Todi, *Presso di l'Academia Tudertina* (1967), p. 258.

24. Pierre de Corbian, "Prière à la Vierge," in *Anthologie des troubadours XIIme–XIIIme siècles* (édition refondue) (Paris: 1974), p. 367. Pierre de Corbian shares practically the same heretical view that is criticized in the "Descent of the Holy Virgin."

25. *Anthologie des troubadours XIIme–*

XIIme siècles, p. 198. J. Roubaud in his anthology *Les Troubadours* qoutes the names of some other women poets like Avalais de Porcaraiques, Na Castelloza, Clara d'Anduse, and Bieris de Romans, plus one anonymous poetess.

26. A. Jeanroy, introduction to *Anthologie des troubadours*, p. 29.

27. Guillaume de Tudèle, *La Chanson de la Croisade Albigeoise: Cansos de la Crozada,* ed. and trans. Eugene Martin-Chabot, vol. 5 (Paris: 1976), p. 165.

28. R. Nelli, op. cit., p. 108.

29. J. de Voragine, *La légende dorée,* trans from the Latin by T. de Wyzewa (Paris: 1920), pp. 402–403.

30. J. Guitton, *Le Christ équartelé: crises et conciles dans l'église* (Paris: 1963), p. 196.

31. See chapter 1.

32. *Heresy Trials in the Diocese of Norwich, 1428–31,* ed. Norman Tanner, Camden Fourth Series, vol. 20 (London: 1977), p. 147.

33. Ibidem, p. 26.

34. J. Fines, "Heresy Trials in the diocese of Coventry and Lichifield, 1511–12," *Journal of Ecclesiastical History* 14 (1963): 161–162.

35. Ibidem, p. 162.

36. E. Long, "Feminism and Cultural Studies," *Cultural Perspectives on Media and Society,* ed. R.K. Avery and D. Eason (New York: The Guilford Press, 1991), p. 120.

37. Lambert, *Medieval Heresy*, p. 249.

38. J. Fines, op. cit., p. 165. These words seem to be a euphemism when John Foxe gives the information that in 1542 Thomas Bernard and James Morden were burned because "the one teaching the Lord' Prayer in English, and the other for keeping the Epistle of St. James translated into English." See W. H. Summers, *The Lollards of Chiltern Hills* (London: 1906), p. 97.

39. J. Fines, op. cit., p. 162.

40. Ibidem, p. 166.

41. B. Millet and J. Wogan-Browne, eds., *Medieval English Prose for Women* (Oxford: 1990), p. xv.

42. Ibidem, p. 109. A precise quotation is more expressive here: "...we should look from the vision of hell to the joy of heaven, feel fear from the one, love towards the other...." The text also includes three allegories of the type used in the *Le Roman de*

la Rose, and that is an indication of the influence of French medieval literature. Fear relates about the inferno whereas Reason, helped by the Prudence and Fortitude in God, describes paradise.

43. M. Gaster gives information how the apocryha reached England: "Roger of Hovedene gives this *Letter from Heaven* in his Chronicle under the year 1201 and says that it had been brought in this to England by Abbot Eustachius of Flays. The Letter was directly copied thence by Roger of Wendower into his own Chronicle. An Anglo-Saxon translation is said to be in existence at Corpus Christi College in Oxford" (op. cit., p. 67).

44. Millet and Wogan-Browne, eds., *Medieval English Prose for Women,* p. xiv.

45. Ibidem, p. xxiii.

46. Ibidem, p. xvi.

47. A. Jeanroy, op. cit., p. 16.

48. See for example J. A. Cuddon, *Dictionary of Literary Terms and Literary Theory* (London: 1977/1991), pp. 1007–1008: "The troubadours (who composed in langue d'oc) had a very considerable influence on Dante and Petrarch, and indeed on the whole development of the lyric (q.v.), especially love lyric in Europe."

49. Prezviter Cosmas, "Beseda protiv bogomilite," p. 54.

50. J. Gouillard, *Quatre procès de mystiques à Byzance,* vol. 4, *Les évêques "bogomiles"de Cappadoce* (Paris: Institut des études Byzantines, 1978), p. 74.

51. "Errores Manichaeorum: Confessio Raymundi Valsiera de Ax," in *Beiträge zur Sectengeschichte des Mittelalters,* vol. 2, *Dokumente vornehmlich zur Geschichte der Valdesier und Katharer,* by Ign. v. Döllinger (München: 1890), p. 165.

52. Tanner, ed., *Heresy Trials,* p. 142.

53. Ibidem, p. 67.

54. Ibidem, p. 147.

55. M. Aston, *Lollards and Reformers: Images and Literacy in Late Medieval Religion* (The Humbledon Press, 1984), pp. 62, 69.

Chapter 4

1. *Kirilo-Metodievska entsiclopediya,* vol. 1 (Sofia: 1985), pp. 631–632.

2. Deanesly, *The Lollard Bible,* p. vii.

3. *Cambridge History of English and American Literature in 18 volumes (1907–1921),* vol. 2, *End of the Middle Ages,* pp. 29–30.

4. V. Hotchkiss, "Outlawed English," in *Formatting the Word of God,* ed. V. Hotchkiss and Ch. Ryrie (Dallas: 1998), p. 65.

5. *The Cambridge History of English and American Literature,* vol. 2, p. 30. H. Hargreaves also shares the opinion on the difficulties involved in reconstructing "the history of Wycliffe's Bible," in "The Marginal Glosses to the Wycliffite New Testament," *Studia Neophilologica* (Upsalla) 33 (1961): p. 300.

6. *Wycliffite Manuscript, The New Testament, England, 1400–1450,* ed. by Bridwell Library (Dallas), on CD (Oakland, CA: Octavo, 1999).

7. *The Holy Bible, containing the Old and New Testament with the apocryphal books, in the earliest English versions made from the Latin Vulgate by John Wycliffe and his followers,* ed. J. Forshall and Fr. Madden, vol. 4 (Oxford: 1850). Although this edition was not used in our case, this author does not underestimate its value. It is a great publishing achievement, with an excellent introduction and analysis that is topical even today.

8. Literature on the subject quotes as such: *New Testament, translated out of the Latin Vulgate by John Wyclif,* about 1378, ed. by John Lewis (London: 1731); *New Testament translated from the Latin, in the year 1380 by John Wiclif, D. D. To which are prefixed Memoirs of the Life, Opinions, and Writings of Dr. Wiclif, and an Historical Account of the Saxon and English Versions of Scriptures, previous to opening of the fifteenth century,* 4to (London: 1810); *New Testament, The earlier version,* by Lea Wilson, 4to (London: 1848); *MS Bodley 959 Genesis-Baruch 3.20 in Earlier Version of the Wycliffite Bible,* ed. C. Linderg (Stockholm Studies in English, 6, 1959; 8, 1961; 10, 1963; 13, 1965; 20, 1969).

9. *The Holy Bible, made from the Latin Vulgate by John Wyccliffe and his followers,* vol. IV, p. 18.

10. Ivanov, J., *Bogomilski knigi i legendi,*

p. 113. The same fact is quoted in *Slovník jazyka staroslovnskeho: Lexicon linguae palaeslovenicae*, vol. 2, p. 322.

11. Ign. von Döllinger, *Dokumente vornehmlich zur Geschichte der Valdesier und Katharer herausgegeben*, vol. 2 (München: 1890), p. 38: "...dicendo in oratione Pater Noster: panem nostrum supersubstantialem." This case was also quoted by Y. Ivanov.

12. One should mention here that there are only a few good interpretations of Bogomil and Cathar theology, including Raicho Karolev's 19th century work, those of H. Puech and A. Vaillant, as well as Edina Bozoki, among others. In the case of Bulgaria, the cause was the fact that, after 1944, research of the Bogomil movement fell under Marxist interpretation, with their teaching seen above all as a social movement. In the West, powerful Catholic influence was a barrier to studies of the finer peculiarities of dualistic philosophy. There is not a single study in this sense in Great Britain.

13. H. Vaillant and A. Puech, *Le traité contre les Bogomiles de Cosmas le Prêtre* (Paris: 1945), p. 245.

14. *Patrologia Graeca*, 130, col. 1313.

15. N. Osokin, *Istoriya al'bigotsev do konchiny papy Innokentiya III*, vol. 1 (Kazan: 1869), p. 214.

16. J. Giuraud, *Cartulaire de Notre Dame de Prouilles, précédé d'une étude sur l'Albigéisme languédocien au XIIe et XIIIe siècles*, vols. 1–2 (Paris: 1907), p. CXXII.

17. Schmidt, *Histoire et doctrine*, vol. 2, p. 117.

18. Ibidem.

19. "Confessio Magistri John Wycliff," in Shirley, *Fasciculi Zizaniorum*, p. 120.

20. *Patrologia Graeca*, 130, col. 1313.

21. Seifert, *Die Weltrevolutionare*.

22. J. Wycliffe, *Summa in theologia: De civili domino* (London: 1825), p. 373.

23. H.E. Fosdick, ed., *Great Voices of the Reformation* (New York: Random House, 1952), p. 27.

24. II. Yoan-Pavel, *Kiril i Metodiy: Blagovestie i ekumenizam* (Sofia: 1996), p. 55.

25. Deanesly, *The Lollard Bible*, p. vii.

26. F. Robinson, "Commentary," in

Wycliffite Manuscript, The New Testament, England, 1400–1450, ed. by Bridwell Library (Oakland, CA: Octavo Corporation, 1999), p. 3.

27. Ibidem, p. 3.

28. *Oxford English Dictionary*, vol. 1 (1989), p. 241.

29. Ibidem.

30. *Oxford English Dictionary*, vol. 1 (1989), p. 178.

31. Ibidem.

32. This was how the inquisitor Bernard Gui recorded that fundamental Cathar tenet: "...who instead of baptism in water invent another baptism, which they call baptism in the Holy Spirit (consolamentum)" (confingentes loco baptismi facti in aqua baptismum alium spiritualem, que vocant onsolamentum Spiritus sancti) (*Manuel de l'inquisiteur*, p. 12). As to the view of the Lollards, cappelanus Robertus Cavell wrote the following in his confession: "That the sacrament of Baptem doon in water in fourme custumed of Churche ys litell to be pondred for as muche as whan a child cometh to yeres of discrecion and receyvyth Christis lawe and hys commaundments he ys sufficiently baptized and so he may be saved withowtyn ony other baptism." Depositions of Ricardus Crace, skinner, de Beccles, in Tanner, ed., *Heresy Trials*, p. 121.

33. "Ingressus fratris Kynyngham Carmelitae contra Wicclyf," in *Fasciculi Zizaniorum*, ed. Shirley, p. 5.

34. "XXIV Conclusiones Wycclyf damnatae Londoniis in synodo," in *Fasculi Zizaniorum*, ed. *Shirley*, p. 279. A similar statement is also made on p. 264: "sicut Graecos."

35. Wycliffe, *Summa in theologia*, p. 99.

36. F. Hearnshow, *Some Great Political Idealists of the Christian Era* (London, Bombay, Sydney: n.d.), 44–45.

37. F. Robinson, "Commentary," in *Wycliffite Manuscript*, p. 4.

38. P. Lavrov, *Materialy po istorii vozniknoveniya drevneshey slavyanskoy pismennosti* (Leningrad: 1930), p. VII.

39. Ibidem.

40. B. Hamilton, "Wisdom from the East: the Reception by the Cathars of Eastern Dualist Texts," in *Heresy and Literacy* (Cambridge: 1994/1996), p. 51. In his arti-

cle on the Lyonnaise Ritual, Yordan Ivanov wrote that this peculiarity contained the Bogomil-Cathar (one could say the Greek) version of the Lord's Prayer. Ivanov, *Bogomilski knigi i legendi,* p. 112.

41. Tr. Krastanov, A. M. Totomanova, and I. Dobrev, *Vatikanski palimpsest* (Sofia: 1997), p. 101.

42. Shirley, *Fasciculi Zizaniorum,* p. 190.

43. A. Hudson, "'Laicus literatus': The Paradox of Lollardy," in *Heresy and Literacy, 1000–1530* (Cambridge: 1994/1996).

44. Walter Brut's beliefs principally coincide with the dualist views: "The eucharist was primarily a memorial, papal pretensions to powers of absolution, along pontiff's claims to temporalities, demonstrated his identity with antichrist, war and legal execution were against Christian insistence on charity, oaths were illegal.... the just layman, more outrageously to his readers, the just laywoman was a priest.... he [Brut] wonders why canon law and the fathers quoted there so often base themselves on the Old Testament shadow of the Law and not on the light of Christ gospel." Ibidem, pp. 224–225.

45. Ibidem, p. 223.

46. Ibidem, p. 228.

47. A. Sanders, *The Short Oxford History of English Literature,* p. 191.

48. Ibidem.

49. "Prose and Poetry: Sir Thomas North to Michael Drayton," in *Cambridge History of English and American Literature in 18 Volumes,* vol. 4, p. 48.

50. Sanders, *Short Oxford History,* p. 51.

51. *Encyclopaedia Britannica,* vol. 3, 1970, p. 584.

52. Ibidem, p. 583.

53. Sanders, *Short Oxford History,* p. 50.

Chapter 5

1. D. Daniell, *William Tyndale: A Biography* (New Haven, London: Yale University Press, 2001), p. 2.

2. Ibidem.

3. According to R. Vaughan, Chaucer adopted many of Wycliffe's doctrines. R. Vaughan, *The Life and the Opinions of John*

de Wycliffe, D. D., vol. 2 (London: 1831), p. 437; see also vol. 1, p. 137.

4. H. Workman, *The Dawn of the Reformation,* vol. 4, *The Age of Wyclif* (London: 1901), p. 203.

5. D. Obolensky, *The Bogomils: A Study in Balkan Neo-Manichaeism* (Cambridge: 1948), p. VII.

6. D. Daniell, *William Tyndale,* p. 161.

7. *Expositions and Notes on Sundry Portions of the Holy Scriptures Together with the Practice of Prelates by William Tyndale, Martyr 1536* (Cambridge: 1849), p. 190.

8. *Christian Dualist Heresies in the Byzantine World c. 650–c. 1405,* translated and annotated by Janet Hamilton and Bernard Hamilton (Manchester: Manchester University Press, 1998), p. 100.

9. "De duobus autem principiis ad honorem patris sanctissimi, volui inchoare." *Livre des deux principes,* introduction, critique, traduction, notes and index by Christine Thouzhellier (Paris: 1973), p. 160.

10. G. Byron, *Complete Poetical Works* (Oxford: 1970), pp. 536, 537.

11. Prezviter, "Beseda protiv bogomilite," p. 49.

12. *Doctrinal Treatises and Introduction to Different Portions of the Holy Scriptures by William Tyndale, Martyr, 1536* (Cambridge University Press, 1848), p. 47.

13. Prezviter, "Beseda protiv bogomilite," p. 31.

14. W. Tyndale, *An Exposition upon the V, VI, VII Chapters of Matthew* (Antwerp: 1533), p. 57.

15. "bene tamen se vocabant boni christiani, boni homines et sancti." Ign. v. Döllinger, *Dokumente vornehmlich zur Geschichte der Valdesier und Katharer herausgegeben,* vol. 2 (München: 1890), p. 195.

16. W. Tyndale, *The Obedience of a Christian Man* (London: 2001), p. 118.

17. Ibidem, pp. 113, 129.

18. *Doctrinal Treatises and Introduction to Different Portions of the Holy Scriptures by William Tyndale, Martyr, 1536* (Cambridge University Press, 1848), p. 27.

19. In Bulgarian: *Balgarski bogomilski i apokrifni predstavi v angliyskata srednovekovna kultura (Obrazat na Hristos Orach v poemata na William Langland "Vi-*

denieto na Petar Oracha"). (Sofia: 2001). See chapter 1.

20. In comparison we suggest the expression "quod heretici vestiti essent Spiritus Sanctus," from Döllinger, *Dokumente vornehmlich zur Geschichte der Valdesier und Katharer herausgegeben,* vol. 2, p. 195, and Tyndale's expression in *The Obedience of a Christian Man* (London: 2001), p. 113.

21. *Christian Dualist Heresies,* p. 161. Greek text: "legoiusin hoi asebeis, hoti hagios oute estin oute ofeilei legesthai, alla hagios ies estin ho Theos." G. Ficker, *Die Phundagiagiten* (Leipzig: 1908), p. 76.

22. Tyndale, *Obedience,* p. 145.

23. Tyndale, *The Parable of the Wicked Mammon* (Antwerp: 1528), p. 66.

24. Tyndale, *Obedience,* p. 142.

25. Prezviter, "Beseda protiv bogomilite," p. 33.

26. Tyndale, *Obedience,* p. 143.

27. Ibidem, p. 145.

28. Prezviter, "Beseda protiv bogomilite," pp. 50, 36.

29. Tyndale, *Obedience,* p. 110.

30. Ibidem, p. 139.

31. *Christian Dualist Heresies,* p. 161.

32. Tyndale, *Obedience,* p. 111.

33. "Priest is to say an elder." Tyndale, *Obedience,* p. 197.

34. "Dicunt etiam haeretici: quod homo vadit ad confessionem, jam compunctus est et contritus pro peccatis suis et statim Deus dimissit ei peccata sua." Döllinger, *Dokumente vornehmlich zur Geschichte der Valdesier und Katharer herausgegeben,* p. 282.

35. "Quod oraciones non sunt effundende ad sanctos sed ad solum Deum, qui solus audit orantes." N. Tanner, ed., *Kent Heresy Proceedings 1511–12* (Kent Archeological Society: 1997), p. 2.

36. Tyndale, *Obedience,* p. 111.

37. "Haec confession fit publice praelato tenenti librum evangeliorum super caput eius; reliqui dexteram apponunt cum orationibus." In Döllinger, *Dokumente vornehmlich zur Geschichte der Valdesier und Katharer herausgegeben,* p. 295.

38. W. Tyndale, *An Exposition upon the V, VI, VII Chapters of Matthew* (Antwerp: 1533), p. 477.

39. M. Aston, *Lollards and the Reformers: Images and Literacy in Late Medieval Religion* (London: 1984), p. 49.

40. *Christian Dualist Heresies,* p. 159. Greek text: "ten giunaika aiutoiu kateleipen poiesas aiuten pseudabadian." In G. Ficker, *Die Phundagiagiten* (Leipzig: 1908), p. 66.

41. Aston, *Lollards and the Reformers,* p. 49.

42. Tanner, ed., *Heresy Trials,* p. 57. And also: "every good man and good woman is a prest." Ibidem, p. 147.

43. Döllinger, *Dokumente vornehmlich zur Geschichte der Valdesier und Katharer herausgegeben,* p. 165.

44. W. Tyndale, *Practice of Prelates,* p. 284.

45. W. Tyndale, *Expositions and Notes on Sundry Portions of the Holy Scriptures together with the Practice of Prelates by William Tyndale, Martyr 1536* (Cambridge, 1849), pp. 221–222.

46. W. Tyndale, *Doctrinal Treatises and Introduction to Different Portions of the Holy Scriptures by William Tyndale, Martyr, 1536* (Cambridge University Press, 1848), p. 373.

47. Ibidem, p. 363.

48. *Christian Dualist Heresies,* p. 202. The original reads: "oinov men kaloiusi neon ten didaskalian eaiuton." Ficker, *Die Phundagiagiten,* p. 109.

49. Tyndale, *Doctrinal Treatises,* p. 379.

50. Prezviter, "Beseda protiv bogomilite," p. 34.

51. "Dicentes quod non sit ibi corpus Christi, quia si esset ita magnum sicut unus maximus mons, jam christiani comedissent totum: item, quod illa hostia nascitur de palea et quod transit per caudas equorum vel equarum, videlicet quando farina purgatory per sedatium; item, quod mittitur in latrinam ventris et emitter per turpissimum locum, quod non posset fieri, ut aiunt, si esset ibi Deus." Gui, *Manuel de l'inquisiteur,* p. 26.

52. Tyndale, *Expositions and Notes,* p. 215.

53. *Treatise against the Bogomils,* p. 50.

54. *Christian Dualist Heresies,* p. 195. The original reads: "Eroden de noosi ten kat' hemas ekklesian, peiromenen anelein ton par' aiutois gennetenta logov tes aleteias." "Euthymii Zigabeni de haeresi bogomilorum narratio," in *Phundagiagiten,* by G. Ficker, p. 103.

55. "appellant matrem fornicationum, Babilonem magnam, meretricem et basilicam dyaboli et Sathane synagogam." Gui, *Manuel de l'inquisiteur*, p. 10.

56. "papa est Antechristus et caput draconis de quo fit mencio in sacra Scriptura, et quod episcope et ecclesiam prelati sunt corpus draconis, et quod fratres mendicantes sunt cauda draconis, episcope ac alii ecclesiarum prelati sunt discipuli Antechristi." In Tanner, ed., *Heresy Trials*, p. 61.

57. Tyndale, *Parable of Wicked Mammon*, p. 106.

58. *Christian Dualist Heresies*, p. 199. Greek text: "Siu de otan proseiuhe fasin eiselthe eis eis to tamieion soiu, tamieion legoiusi tov noiuv." In *Phundagiagiten*, by G. Ficker, p. 107.

59. Tyndale, *Expositions and Notes*, p. 79.

60. Tyndale, *The Independent Works of William Tyndale*, p. 100.

61. Tyndale, *Expositions and Notes*, p. 298.

62. Tyndale, *Obedience*, p. 144.

63. Tyndale, *Expositions and Notes*, p. 243, p. 244.

64. Tyndale, *Obedience*, p. 119.

65. Ibidem, pp. 119–120. And also: "They compel us to hire friars, monks, nuns, canons, and priests, and to buy their abominable merits, and to hire the saints that are dead to pray for us." Ibidem, p. 142.

66. "Norwicensem episcopum, et eius ministros, qui sunt membra diaboli, ante istud tempus nisi papa transmisset ad istas partes illas falsas indulgencias ... que indulgencia induxit populum simplicem ad ydolatriam maledictam." Tanner, ed., *Heresy Trials*, p. 46. And here is Robert Harryson's position: "Robert said of indulgences and pardons to be of noon effecte nor profit." Tanner, N., ed., *Kent Heresy Proceedings*, p. 4.

67. "Item dicunt, non esse purgatorium." Fr. Rački, "Prilozi za povjest bosanskih patarena," *Starine* (University of Zagreb) 1 (1869): 139.

68. "...non est purgatorium nec infernos nisi in hoc mundo." Döllinger, *Dokumente vornehmlich zur Geschichte der Valdesier und Katharer herausgegeben*, p. 267.

69. Tanner, ed., *Kent Heresy Proceedings*, p. 46.

70. Tyndale, *Obedience*, p. 91.

71. Ibidem, p. 100.

72. "Purgatorim negant ... omnia suffragia ecclesiae subsannant, dicentes quod oblations ad altare pro defunctis bonae sint, scil. ad pascendu sacerdotes ut eo lautius comedant at luxuriasius vivant." (Incipit *Summa de haeresibus*). In Döllinger, *Dokumente vornehmlich zur Geschichte der Valdesier und Katharer herausgegeben*, p. 298.

73. Tyndale, *Obedience*, p. 155.

74. Ibidem, p. 154.

75. Ibidem, p. 90.

76. Tyndale, *An Exposition upon the V,VI, VII Chapters of Matthew*, p. 104.

77. "Albigenses haeretici veneruunt in Angliam, quorum aliqui comburebantur vivi," as well as the English version: "Mony of the heretikes Albigense, commyn into Ynglonde, were brente in lyfe." In *Chronicon Henrici Knighton vel Cnitthon Monachi Leycestrensis*, ed. J. R. Lumby, D. D., vol. 1 (London: 1889), pp. 190, 191.

78. W. H. Summers, *The Lollards of Chiltern Hills: Glimpses of English Dissent in the Middle Ages* (London: 1906), p. 28: "The Reformation of the sixteenth century was the inevitable resultant of series of forces which had been at work a century and half before in the life and teachings of John Wycliffe, for six years the rector of Buckinghamshire."

79. G. Nauert, Jr., editor's preface to "Lollard Themes in the Reformation Theology of William Tyndale," in *Sixteenth Century Essays and Studies*, vol. 6 (1986), p. 11.

80. Daniell, *William Tyndale*, pp. 31, 94.

81. "Almost half a dozen times Tyndale likewise invoked the name of Wyclif always in a positive reference." D. D. Smeeton, "Lollard Themes in the Reformation Theology of William Tyndale," in *Sixteenth Century Essays and Studies*, vol. 6 (1986), p. 75.

82. Ibidem, p. 34. Note: The term "Wycliffite literature" denotes texts created in the circle of Wycliffe's followers and disciples.

83. Tyndale, *Doctrinal Treatises*, p. 458.

84. Ibidem, p. 224.
85. See chapter 4.
86. "XXIV conclusions Wycclyf damnatae Londoniis in synodo," in *Fasciculi Zizaniorum*, ed. Shirley, p. 278.
87. Prezviter, "Beseda protiv bogomilite," p. 43.
88. Tyndale, *Doctrinal Treatises*, p. 364.
89. Ibidem, p. 455.
90. "...all good things are thine already purchased by Christ's blood." Tyndale, *Wicked Mammon*, p. 64. Or: "Christ's blood only putteth away all the sin that ever was." Ibidem, p. 72.
91. "infunditur gracia Spiritus Sancti..." Tanner, ed., *Heresy Trials*, p. 95.
92. "baptized in the blood of Crist..." Ibidem, p. 146.
93. Tyndale, *Obedience*, p. 109.
94. "Est, ita quod sit sensus quod deus et lapis penitus et omnino sunt unum et idem, tunc est sensus hereticus..." Wyclif, J. *Miscellanea Philosophica*, vol. 2 (London: 1905), p. 104.
95. Tyndale, *Doctrinal Treatises*, p. 27. And also: "...a good and learned man." Tyndale, *Obedience*, p. 118.
96. L. P. Brockett, *The Bogomils of Bulgaria and Bosnia: The Early Protestants of the East: An Attempt to Restore Some Lost Leaves of Protestant History* (Philadelphia: 1879).
97. *Foxe's Christian Martyrs of the World* (Westwood, New Jersey: 1985), p. 358.
98. "...qui habent ordinem suum de Bulgaria, credunt i predicant tantum unum bonum deum omnipotentem sine principio, qui creavit angelos et IIIIor elementa. Et dicunt quod Lucifer et complices sui peccaverunt in celo." A. Dondaine, "Hiérarchie cathare en Italie," in *Archivum fratrum Praedicatorum* XIX (Rome: 1949), p. 310.
99. "...qui habent ordinem suum de drugonthia, credunt et predicant duos deos sive sine principio et sine fine, unum bonum et alterum malum penitus." Ibidem, p. 309.
100. Tyndale, *Doctrinal Treatises*, p. 79.
101. Greek text: "Siu gar en emoi kago ev soi, en kai adiairetov iuparhomen prosopon." "L'Homélie d'Epiphane sur l'ensevelissement du Christ (édition par A. Vaillant)," in *Radovi Staroslavenskog instituta* (Zagreb: 1958), p. 77.

102. M. Lambert, *The Cathars* (Oxford and Malden, Mass.: Blackwell, 1998).
103. Gairdner, *Lollardy and Reformation in England*, vol. 1, p. 14.
104. W. Summers, *Our Lollard Ancestors* (London: 1904), p. 26. See also W. Summers, *The Lollards of Chiltern Hills: Glimpses of English Dissent in the Middle Ages* (London: 1906), p. 9.
105. *The Catholic Encyclopedia*, vol. 2 (Robert Appleton Company, 1907), p. 141.
106. Y. Pelikan, with Valerie R. Hotchkiss and David Price, *The Reformation of the Bible: The Bible of the Reformation* (New Haven and London: Yale University Press; Dallas: Bridwell Library, Southern Methodist University, 1996), p. 7.

Chapter 6

1. W. Langland, *The Vision of Piers Plowman: A Complete Edition of the B-text* (London, Melbourne, Toronto, New York: 1978). A critical edition of the B-text based on Trinity Colledge Cambridge MS B.15.17 with selected variant readings, an introduction, glosses, and textual and literary commentary by A. V. C. Schmidt.
2. Ibidem, p. 242; passus XIX, ll. 224–225.
3. Ibidem; passus XIX, ll. 222–223.
4. "Sed papa, episcope, sacerdotes catholici vel ecclesiae Romanae, quia non tenebant sanctam fidem et errant inimici fidei eorum, non habebant potestatem aliquam absolvendi aliquem a peccatis." Döllinger, *Dokumente vornehmlich zur Geschichte der Valdesier und Katharer herausgegeben*, pp. 194–195.
5. This is what we read in the confession of Johannes Reve de Becles at the well-known Norwich trial (1428–1431): "Item quod papa Romanus est Antechristus.... Item quod omnes episcopi, prelati et presbiteri et viri ecclesiastici sunt discipuli Antechristi." Tanner, ed., *Heresy Trials*, p. 108.
6. Prezviter, "Beseda protiv bogomilite," pp. 37, 51.
7. In the notes to passus XVIII of *The Vision of Piers Plowman*, Schmidt makes reference to the Gospel of Nicodemus (pp. 350–352). We find more detailed notes by

J. F. Goodridge; cf. p. 308 of W. Langland's edition, *Piers the Plougman Translated into Modern English,* with an introduction by J. F. Goodridge (New York: 1959/1977). But they pertain to separate details without interpreting the philosophy underlying the Gospel of Nicodemus and its perception by Langland.

8. Franko, *Apokrifi i legendi z ukrainskih rukopisiv,* vol. 2 (L'viv, 1899), p. VII.

9. Gaster, *Ilchester Lectures,* p. 35.

10. Langland, *The Vision of Piers Plowman,* passus XIX, ll. 53–58: "And tho was the conquerour called out of quyke and dede, / For yaf Adam and Eve and othere mo blisse / that longe hadde yleyen before as Luciferis cherles."

11. Ivanov, *Bogomilski knigi i legendi,* p. 86.

12. As Donka Petkanova has clarified, the origin of the apocrypha indicates the *Book of Jubilees* was written sometime between 140 and 100 BC. There is an independent version in Greek literature or else it is part of *The Apocalypsis of Moses.* The Bulgarian translation was made around the 10th century, the motif of Adam's writ being absent from the Greek version, in other words making it a Bulgarian Bogomil addition. *Stara bulgarska literatura,* vol. 1, *Apokrifi,* p. 348.

13. The bibliographic reference this author made indicates the following edition of the same story in English, the translation belonging to Jusserand himself: *A Literary History of the English People: From the Origins to the End of the Middle Ages,* 3rd ed. (New York: 1926). In our case, we have used the Russian edition of 1898: *Istoriya angliyskago naroda v ego literature* (St. Petersburg: 1898).

14. M. Lazar, "La Légende de 'l'Arbre de Paradis' ou 'bois de la croix': poème anglonormand du XIIIe siècle et sa source latine, d'après le Ms.66. Corpus Christi College, Cambridge (Inédit)," in *Zeitschrift für Romanishe Philologie* 76 (1960): 34.

15. The only more serious, albeit rather short analysis we have found belongs to Cl. Tomson, "Later Transition English I: Legendaries and Chroniclers," in *Cambridge History of English Literature,* vol. 2, ch. 14 (Cambridge University Press, 1933).

16. A. Miltenova, "Belezhki," in *Balgarskata literatura i knizhnina prez XIII* (Sofia: 1987), p. 251.

17. M. R. James, "Rare Medieval Tiles and Their Story with a Note by R. L. Hobson," *The Burlington Magazine for Connoisseurs* (London) 42 (Jan.–June 1923): 34.

18. E. Eames, *Medieval Lead-glazed Earthenware Tiles in the Department of Medieval and Later Antiquities, British Museum; Text and Catalogue* (London: British Museum Publications, 1980), p. 58.

19. K. Tischendorf, *Evangelia apocrypha* (Leipzig: 1852).

20. James, "Rare Medieval Tiles," p. 34.

21. Ibidem.

22. *Cursor mundi,* ll. 12387–12414.

23. M. Boulton, ed., *Les enfaunces de Jesu Christ* (London: Anglo-Norman Text Society, 1985), p. 73.

24. Judging by the sgraffito used in the Tring tiles, E. Eames assumed they were made in France. *Medieval Lead-glazed Earthenware Tiles,* p. 23.

25. W. Renwick and H. Orton, *The Beginnings of English Literature to Skelton 1509,* vol. 1 (London: 1939/1952), p. 33.

26. D. Obolensky, *The Bogomils: A Study in Balkan Neo-Manichaeism* (Cambridge University Press, 1948), p. VII.

27. "...et ideo non oportet, quod per descensum Christi ad inferos omnes fuerint a purgatorio liberati." Thomae Aquinatis, *Summa Theologica,* pars tertia, quaestio LII, articulus VIII (Rome: Ex Typographia Forzani et S. MDCCCXCIV), p. 448.

28. *Pravoslavnayabogoslovskaya entsiklopedia ili bogoslovskiy slovar,'* vol. 1 (Petrograd: 1900), p. 821.

29. "...et ad hunc infernum descendit Christus, ut auxiliaretur eis." Sacconi, "Summa de Catharis," p. 57.

30. "...postquam Christus resurrexerat, descendit ad inferos in corpore et anima, ed de inde extraxit animas omnium hominum, tam peccatorum, quae ibie errant, excepta animae Judae Scariot...." Döllinger, *Dokumente vornehmlich zur Geschichte der Valdesier und Katharer herausgegeben,* pp. 193–194.

31. *Anglo-Saxon Poetry: An Anthology of Old English poems in Prose Translation,* with an Introduction and Headnotes by S. A. J.

Bradley (London, Melbourne, Toronto: 1982), p. 393.

32. Renwick and Orton, *Beginnings of English Literature*, p. 198.

Chapter 7

1. B. Kurth, *Milton and Christian Heroism* (Berkeley and Los Angeles: 1959).

2. Ibidem, p. 9.

3. A. Shurbanov, "Svetotvorchestvoto na Milton," in *Izgubeniya ray* (Sofia: 1981), p. 29.

4. S. H. Gurteen, *The Epic of the Fall of Man: A Comparative Study on Caedmon, Dante and Milton* (New York: 1896).

5. H. White, "Langland, Milton and Felix Culpa," *The Review of English Studies* 45, no. 179 (1994): 336.

6. *Anglo-Saxon Poetry*, p. 12.

7. M. Mincoff, *A History of English Literature*, part 1, *From the Beginnings to 1700* (Sofia: 1970), pp. 528–529.

8. E. Legouis, *A History of English Literature*, vol. 1, *The Middle Ages and the Renaissance*, Modern Times by L. Cazamian, revised ed. (London: 1957), p. 40.

9. Referential quotation: *Studies in English Literature* 32 (Winter 1992), articles by Barbara Lewalski, Christopher Hill, Maurice Kelley.

10. A. Nuttall, *The Alternative Trinity: Gnostic Heresy in Marlowe, Milton and Blake* (Oxford: 1998), p. 127.

11. Stephen P. Dobranski and John P. Rumrich, eds., *Milton and Heresy* (New York: Cambridge University Press, 1998).

12. Ibidem, pp. 4, 14.

13. W. Walker, "Review of Stephen P. Dobranski and John P. Rumrich, eds., Milton and Heresy," *Early Modern Literary Studies* 7, no. 1, Special Issue 8 (May 2001).

14. N. Forsyth, *The Satanic Epic* (Princeton University Press, 2002).

15. Legouis, *A History of English Literature*, p. 567.

16. J. Milton, *Latin Writings: A Selection*, ed. J.K. Hale. Medieval & Renaissance Texts & Studies, vol. 191 (Tempe, AZ: Van Gorcum, 1998), p. 216: "cum universa Protestantium ecclesia." English version: "A Treatise of Christian Doctrine Completed from the Holy Scriptures Alone," in *The Prose Works of John Milton*, vol. 5 (London: 1883).

17. "De me, libris tantummodo sacris adhaeresco...." Milton, *Latin Writings*, p. 217.

18. J. Milton, *Eikonoklastes in Answer to a Book Intitul'd Eikonbasilike the Portracture of His Sacred Majesty King Charles the First in His Solitudes and Sufferings* (Amsterdam: 1690), p. 136.

19. "The Tenure of Kings and Magistrates." *Prose Works of John Milton*, vol. 2, p. 27.

20. "...for about that time Wiclef and Husse growing terrible, were they who first drove the Papal court in a stricter policy of prohibition." *Areopagitica: A Speech of Mr. John Milton for the Liberty of Vnlicenc'd Printing, to the Parliament of England* (London: 1644), p. 7.

21. "Of the Reformation in England and the Causes That Hitherto Have Hindered It: In Two Books," in *Areopagitica and Other Prose Works of John Milton* (London, New York, Toronto: 1927), p. 58.

22. *Areopagitica*, p. 31. Naturally, he recognised the influence of European reformers in England: "We have looked so long upon the blaze that Zuinglius and Calvin hat beaconed up to us, that we are stark blind." Ibidem.

23. W. Summers, *Our Lollard Ancestors*, p. 29. Compared to Summers, the other assumptions this author has encountered were much more hesitant. In 1977 A. L. Rowse mentioned a possible Wyclifitte influence in his book titled *Milton the Puritan: Portrait of a Mind* (London: Macmillan, 1977).

24. J. Milton, "On the Late Massacre in Piedmont," in *Selected Shorter Poems and Prose* (London, New York: 1988/9).

25. An expression recorded on August 8, 1511, at the trial of the Lollards in Kent. Tanner, ed., *Kent Heresy Proceedings*, p. 85. On the basis of factological material presented in chapter 1, I consider the connection between Bogomils, Cathars and Lollards sufficiently well outlined.

26. *Areopagitica and Other Prose Works by John Milton* (London, New York: 1927), p. 13.

27. "Manicheorum itaque secta et heresies et ejus devii sectatores duos Deos aut duos Dominos asserunt and fatentur, benignum Deum videlicet et malignum..." Gui, *Manuel de l'inquisiteur*, p. 10.

28. C. Vaughan, Introduction to *Areopagitica and Other Prose Works by John Milton*, p. XIII.

29. This historical aspect was noted by John Toland, who saw its beginnings even in the time of Henry VIII. It was also confirmed by the publisher of Milton's prose, J. John, in 1883–1884. "Editor's preliminary remarks," in *The Prose Works of John Milton*, vol. 2 (London: 1883), p. 363.

30. "Euthymii Zigabeni de haeresi bogomilorum narratio," in *Die Phundagiagiten*, ed. G. Ficker, p. 97.

31. Tanner, ed., *Kent Heresy Proceedings*, p. 85.

32. "Of the Reformation in England," in *Areopagitica and Other Prose Works of John Milton* (London, New York, Toronto: 1927), p. 91.

33. Ibidem, p. 66.

34. Ibidem, p. 57.

35. Milton, *Eikonoklastes*, p. 135.

36. Prezviter, "Beseda protiv bogomilite," p. 34.

37. Tanner, ed., *Heresy Trials*, p. 154.

38. Prezviter, "Beseda protiv bogomilite," p. 33.

39. Milton, *Eikonoklastes*, p. 153.

40. Tanner, ed., *Heresy Trials*, p. 86.

41. Milton, "Of the Reformation in England," p. 69.

42. Ibidem.

43. Ibidem.

44. "Euthymii Zigabeni de haeresi bogomilorum narratio," p. 99.

45. Prezviter, "Beseda protiv bogomilite," p. 50.

46. Shirley, *Fasciculi Zizaniorum,* p. 362. English version: "þat exorcismis and halwinge made in þe chirche of wyn, bred and wax, water, and oyle and encens..." A. Hudson, *Selections from English Wycliffite Writings* (London, New York, Melbourne: Cambridge University Press, 1978), p. 25.

47. Milton, "Of the Reformation in England," p. 56.

48. J. Milton, "A Treatise of Civil Power in Ecclesiastical Causes," in *Milton's Prose* (Oxford, London, New York, Toronto: 1925/1949), p. 426.

49. Ibidem, p. 439.

50. Milton, "Of the Reformation in England," p. 57.

51. "...dicunt, quod baptismus aquae nihil facit ad salvationem." Döllinger, *Dokumente vornehmlich zur Geschichte der Valdesier und Katharer herausgegeben*, p. 322.

52. "Patarini, qui se dicunt bonos homines et sine peccato." Döllinger, *Dokumente vornehmlich zur Geschichte der Valdesier und Katharer herausgegeben*, p. 376.

53. Ibidem, p. 241. Confessio Guillelmi Bavili de Monte Alione: "Sibila credidit haeriticos esse bonos homines in eo quod faciebant multas abstinentias et quod non accipiebant aliquid de alieno nec reddebant malum pro malo et quia etiam servebant castitatem"; p. 250: "qui bonos homines in domos suas recipiebant, quia ubicunque duo de bonis hominibus errant, in medio eorum erat Deus."

54. "...quod audivit Anglesiam, uxorem quondam Petri Raterii, que fuit combusta propter heresim, dicentem quod heretici habebant quondam librum quem respiciebant quando videbant tale tempus, et hoc in Bulgaria." J. Duvernoy, "Météorologie et Bulgarie," *Bulgarian Historical Review* 1–2 (2003): 255.

55. On this matter see chapter 1. Nikolai Osokin correctly pointed out that the Albigensians were subject to the same type of maligning that "the first Christians also fell victim to." Osokin, *Istoriya al'bigoytsev*, p. 170.

56. Hudson, *Selections from English Wycliffite Writings*, p. 24.

57. "The Reason of Church Government Urged against Prelaty," in *Milton's Prose*, p. 108.

58. Ibidem, p. 97.

59. Ibidem, p. 127.

60. Milton, "A Treatise of Civil Power in Ecclesiastical Causes," p. 439.

61. "Item duas, confingunt esse ecclesias, unam benignam, quam dicunt esse secta suam, eamque asserunt Ihesu Christi; aliam vero ecclesiam vocant malignam, quod dicunt esse Romanam ecclesiam... appellant matrem fornicationem." Gui, *Manuel de l'inquisiteur*, p. 10

62. Milton, "Of the Reformation in England," p. 62.

63. "As for the bishops, many of whom he denies not have been good men." C. Vaughan, introduction to Milton, "Of the Reformation in England," p. 54.

64. "Item, resurrectionem corporum humanorum futuram negant, loco ejus configentes quedam spiritualia corpora et quedam interiorem hominem, in quibus et qualibus dicunt resurrectionem futuram esse intelligendam." Gui, *Manuel de l'inquisiteur,* vol. 1, p. 14. Nikolai Osokin also speaks of "internal man" as a familiar Cathars one.

65. Milton, "The Reason of Church Government," p. 126.

66. Milton, "A Treatise of Civil Power," pp. 427–29.

67. Ibidem, p. 428: "...flow of faculties of the inward man ... inward religion."

68. Milton, "A Treatise of Civil Power," p. 429.

69. Milton, "Of the Reformation in England," p. 56.

70. Milton, "The Reason of Church Government," p. 126.

71. Ibidem.

72. In actual fact there was no such donation. Constantine, who paid a lot of attention to the theocratic reconstruction of the empire, tried to mobilize all regions to that end, including by giving quite a number of rights to the Christian church. Thus it enjoyed equal privileges with the pagan temples and its clerics were exempt from taxes; a special form of liberating slaves through the church was introduced and it was permitted to receive donations from believers and to inherit property. This last fact evolved into a legend about which some clerics from the Catholic Church created a false document in the 8th or the 9th century, one that is placed in the collection of the so-called False Decretals.

73. Milton, "Of the Reformation in England," p. 68.

74. "hodie diffusum est venenum in ecclesia Dei." Döllinger, *Dokumente vornehmlich zur Geschichte der Valdesier und Katharer herausgegeben,* p. 356.

75. Milton, *Eikonoklastes,* p. 136.

76. Milton, "Of the Reformation in England," p. 71.

77. Dante, *La Divina Commedia,* ed. G. Einaudi (1954), p. 122.

78. Ibidem, p. 588:

(55) L'altro che segue, con le leggi e meco,

(56) sotto buona intenzion che fe'mal frutto

(57) per cedere al pastor si fece greco....

79. Milton, "Of the Reformation in England," p. 71.

80. Ibidem.

81. *Le Rime del Petrarca,* vol. 2 (Florence: 1832), p. 327. According to the commentary to this edition, the last sentence, particularly the expression "Or Constantin non torna," was an obscure passage (passo oscuro), p. 327. The same commentary stated that pessimism stemmed from the fact that Constantine did not return to take back the ill-spent wealth. Milton, however, did not hold back from giving his own, quite free translation in the form of "Another Constantine comes not in haste."

82. L. Ariosto, *Orlando furioso* (Firenze: 1957), p. 469:

Da l'Apostolo santo fu condutto
In un vallon fra due montagne istretto,
Ove mirabilmente era ridutto,
Ciò che si o per nostro diffeto,
O per colpa di tempo o di Fortuna....

83. Ibidem, p. 470.

84. Milton, "Of the Reformation in England," p. 72.

85. Ariosto, *Orlando furioso,* p. 470.

86. W. Langland, *The Vision of Piers Plowman,* ed. A. V. C. Schmidt (London, Melbourne and Toronto: 1978), passus XIII, 1.44. One finds a Lollard theological objection on principle against memorial services in the twelve conclusions of the Lollards of 1395: "the special prayers for the dead in our church ... are a false foundation for charity" (speciales orationas pro animabus mortuorum factae in ecclesia nostra ... est falsum fundamentum eleemosynae). Shirley, *Fasciculi Zizaniorum,* p. 363.

87. Modern English version: W. Langland, *Piers the Ploughman* (Penguin Books: 1966), p. 152.

88. "I sometimes retire with avidity and

delight to feast on Dante, Petrarch, and many others." "To Benedetto Buonmattai," *The Prose Works of John Milton*, vol. 3 (London: 1883), p. 497.

89. Such an assumption is expressed in the commentary on verse 80 of canto 34 in *Orlando furioso*, p. 470.

90. A small correction is in order here: this edition quotes the source "anti-donation" statement of Dante's as being in *Paradiso*, canto 19, line 115. There is no such thing there, however, the one meant probably being *Paradiso*, canto 20, line 56: "sotto buona intenzion che fe' mal frutto."

91. Petrarch, *Sonetti e canzoni di Francesco Petrarca*, in *Le Rime del Petrarca*, vol. 2 (Florence, 1832), p. 327.

92. M. Mincoff, *A History of English Literature*, part 1, *From the Beginning to 1700* (Sofia: 1970), p. 522.

93. "...in hoc mundum inferno esse, i.e. hic esse ignim et frigum et omne malum." Döllinger, "Das Buch Supra Stella von Salvus Burche zu Piacenza aus dem J.1235 (Florenz) über Cathari, Albanenses et Concorricii," *Dokumente vornehmlich zur Geschichte der Valdesier und Katharer herausgegeben*, p. 58.

94. Mincoff, *A History of English Literature*, part 1, *From the Beginning to 1700*, pp. 528–529.

95. The quotations from *Paradise Lost* are after *The Poetical Works of John Milton* (London, New York, Toronto: Oxford University Press, 1958).

96. G. Ficker, ed., *Die Phundagiagiten*, p. 98.

97. "Slovo na Yoan Zlatoust za tova kak Mihail pobedi Satanail," in *Balgarskata literatura i knizhnina prez XIII vek* (Sofia: 1987), p. 156. A publication of this text under the title "Slovo za lazhlivia antichrist, bezbozhnia Satanail, kak go pleni archangel Mihail, voevoda na vsichki angeli" was previously made by Donka Petkanova, *Stara bulgarska literatura*, vol. 1, *Apokrifi* (Sofia: 1982), pp. 41–48.

98. "...et omnia alia visibilia a diabolo, qui cecidit de coelo, erant creata et facta." "Processus contra Valdenses, Pauperes de Lugduno, aliosque haereticos, Fraticellos, etc.," in Döllinger, *Dokumente vornehmlich*

zur Geschichte der Valdesier und Katharer herausgegeben, p. 266.

99. Dante, "Il Convivio," in *Dantis Alagherii Opera Omnia 2* (Leipzig: 1921), pp. 113–114: "Dico che di tutti questi ordini si perdereno alquanti tosto che furono create forse in numero della decima parte, alla quale restaurare fu l'umana natura poi creata."

100. *Stara bulgarska literatura*, vol .1, *Apokrifi*, p. 34.

101. "Prenie na antihrist s Gospoda nash Isus Hristos" in *Stara bulgarska literature*, vol. 1, *Apokrifi*, pp. 173–175.

102. Ibidem, p. 380.

103. *Paradise Regained*, book I, verses 14–17:
...to tell deeds
Above heroic, though in secret done,
And unrecorded left through many an age,
Worthy to have no remained so long unsung.

104. The contemporary scholar René Weis has given an example of such a definition of the essence of Cathar belief when he wrote, "These were known as Cathars, and they believed that the devil was co-eternal with God and that the material world and the flesh were his evil creation." *The Yellow Cross: The Story of the Last Cathars' Rebellion against the Inquisition 1290–1329* (New York: 2002), p. XXI.

105. The quotations after J. Milton, *Complete English Poems, Of Education, Areopagitica* (London: 1909/1990).

106. It is about this apocrypha that Anissava Miltenova has made the following important observation: "There is no known Greek source of this apocrypha so far. This gives us grounds to assume that the oratione dedicated to Michael's victory over Satan was an original Bulgarian work, the chronology of which is determined by the already existent spread Bogomil apocrypha used in its compilation: *The Secret Book, The Tiberiad Sea, A Dispute between Christ and the Devil*, the *Book of Enoch* and the *Revelation*, among others. It is assumed that the compilation of this apocrypha can be dated in the end of the 12th or the 13th century." *Balgarskata literatura i knizhnina prez XIII vek*, p. 251. This scholar has out-

lined a set of Bogomil literature which obviously traveled in time and space and reached Milton at one point.

107. *Stara bulgarska literature*, vol. 1, *Apokrifi*, p. 380.

108. Legouis, *A History of English Literature*, p. 580.

109. Ibidem, p. 581.

110. Such incompleteness was discerned by Kurth, *Milton and Christian Heroism*, p. 7: "The Fall should be viewed as the beginning of a larger action rather than the end of a tragedy."

111. His intention was discerned by an excellent French expert on English literature, Jean Jules Jusserand, who wrote that with his resistance to the demon Christ saved the mankind woman had brought down by giving in to the snake. J. Jusserand, *Histoire abrégée de la littérature anglaise* (Paris: 1896), p. 153.

112. Milton, *Paradise Regained*, book IV, verse 289.

113. Ibidem, verses 291–292.

114. St. Gechev, *Golgotata na Varava: Piesi* (Sofia: 1999). Presented in Columbia Arts Center, Washington, 1994. Reviewed in *The Washington Times*, June 1, 1994, and in *The Washington Post*, June 6 and 16, 1994.

115. Ibidem.

116. Osokin, *Istoriya al'bigoytsev*, p. 183.

117. Ibidem, p. 815.

118. A. Brenon, *Localisation des manuscripts vaudois*, Centro studi piemontesi (Torino: 1978), p. 196.

119. A. Jolliot, "Les communautés vaudoises des Hautes Vallées alpines aux XVe et XVIe siècles," in *Fédération historique du Languédoc méditerranéen et du Roussillon, XLIVe Congrès*, Privas, 2–23 May 1971 (Montpellier: Université Paul Valéry, 1972), p. 189.

120. A. Jolliot, "Les livres des Vaudois. Catalogue," *Ecole pratiques des hautes études. Ve section — sciences religieuses, Annuaire*, Tomes LXXX–LXXXI. Extraits du fascicule 2, p. 71.

121. T. Venckeleer, "Un recueil cathare: le manuscrit A.6.10 de Dublin. Une apologie," *Revue Belge de Philologie et d'Histoire* 38 (1960): 815–834; "Une Glose sur le Pater," *Revue Belge de Philologie et d'Histoire* 39 (1961), pp. 759–762.

122. T. Venckeleer, "Un recueil cathare," p. 816.

123. Ibidem, p. 829. In comparison we shall quote the same ritual described by Salve Burce in his anti-heretical treatise *Supra stella* (1235): "Dicunt Albanenses et Concorricii, quod homines per impositionem manuum accipiunt Spiritum sanctum et fiunt salvi." Döllinger, *Dokumente vornehmlich zur Geschichte der Valdesier und Katharer herausgegeben*, p. 61.

124. "...hoti evebromatisen aiutois ho Isous logov." G. Ficker, *Die Phundagiagiten* (Leipzig: 1908), p. 110.

125. *The Holy Bible, Made from Latin Vulgate by John Wyccliffe and his Followers*, vol. 4 (Oxford: 1850), p. 18.

126. "Restat igitur ut panem cotidianum accipiamus spiritualem, precepta scilicet divina, que cotidie oportet meditari et operari." J. Wyclif, *Opus Evangelicum*, vols. 1 and 2 (London: 1895), p. 285.

127. Venckeleer, "Une Glose sur le Pater," p. 774.

128. Ibidem, p. 760.

129. Osokin, *Istoriya al'bigoytsev*, p. 143. Also in Schmidt, *Histoire et doctrine*, vol. 2, p. 271.

130. Venckeleer, "Une Glose sur le Pater," p. 833.

131. A. Brenon, *Les archipels cathares. Dissidence chrétienne dans l'Europe médievale* (Cahors: 2000), p. 109.

132. N. Osokin, *Istoriya al'bigoytsev*, p. 183.

133. L. Seifert, *Svetovnite revolyutsioneri: ot pop Bogomil do Lenin* (Sofia: 1994), p. 50. Original title: *Die Weltrevolutionäre: Von Bogomil über Hus zu Lenine* (Vienna: 1931).

134. J. Duvernoy, "Les origines du movement Vaudois," in *Heresis* vols. 13, 14 (1990), p. 184.

135. "Processus contra Valdenses, Pauperes de Lugduno, aliosque haereticos, Fraticellos etc.": "Et docuerunt primo, quod deberet credere, quod Deus non creavit seu fecit aliquam rem visibilem, sed mundus iste et omnia alia visibilia a diabolo qui cecidit de coelo, errant create et facta." Döllinger, *Dokumente vornehmlich zur Geschichte der Valdesier und Katharer herausgegeben*, p. 266.

136. Ibidem, p. 255: "veniendo succes-

sive de loco Machiarum versus Bogolenum..., loco Bogoleni, ... dicti Sclavoni."

137. *Areopagitica and Other Prose Works of John Milton* (London, New York: 1927), p. 13.

138. Ibidem.

139. Interview in the *Novo Slovo* newspaper, Sofia, November 26, 1994.

140. "Quidam alii de Bulgaria credunt tantum unum Deum omnipotentum sine principio" Döllinger, *Dokumente vornehmlich zur Geschichte der Valdesier und Katharer herausgegeben*, p. 612. This information could be dated around the middle or the end of the 13th century for it mentions heretical communities in northern Italy described in *Summa Fratris Raynerii de Ordine Fratrum Predicatorum de Catharis et Leonistis seu Pauperibus de Lugduno* (1250).

141. *Paradise Lost*, book VI, verses 45–46:
"Gabriel, lead forth to Battel these my Sons
Invincible, lead forth my armed Saints..."

142. *Catholic Encyclopedia,* vol. 9 (Robert Appleton: 1910), p. 333.

143. *Encyclopaedia Britannica*, vol. 14, 1970, p. 256.

144. Kr. Gecheva, *Bogomilstvoto: Bibliografiya* (Sofia: 1997).

145. *The Cambridge History of English and American Literature in 18 Volumes* (1907–21), vol. 7, *Cavalier and Puritan*, V. Milton, p. 56.

146. Ibidem, p. 67.

147. It is in a similar way that the *Cambridge History* presents William Tyndale — primarily as a theological pamphleteer. *The Cambridge History of English and American Literature*, vol. 3, 2, "Reformation Literature in England," p. 32. Further on the analysis leaves out the definition theological and lays the stress on the pamphlet, the word itself being mentioned on another two occasions in the same chapter. At one point the author even heaves a sigh of relief: "It is a relief to turn from the pamphlets to Tindale's Biblical translation" (ibidem, p. 33). This relief, however, means that further analysis has been given up, for the works described as pamphlets are in fact

important theological treatises with which Tyndale motivated his translation and explained some of its peculiarities. This theology has neither been recognised nor analysed.

148. J. John, "Preface to 'Considerations Touching the Likeliest Means to Remove the Hirelings out of the Church where is also Discoursed of Tithes, Church Fees, and Churche Revenues; whether any Maintenance of Ministers Can Be Settled by Law...,'" in *The Prose Works of John Milton,* vol. 3 (London: 1883), p. 1.

149. "...I found and visited the famous Galileo, grown old a prisoner to the Inquisition, for thinking in astronomy otherwise than the Franciscan and Dominican licensers thought." *Areopagitica and Other Prose Works of John Milton* (London, Toronto, New York: 1927), p. 25.

150. J. Milton, "To the accomplished Emeric Bigot," in *The Prose Works of John Milton*, vol. 3 (London: 1883), p. 513.

151. J. Goodridge, introduction to *Piers the Plougman,* by W. Langland (London: 1959/1977), p. 11.

152. A. Nuttall, *The Alternative Trinity: Gnostic Heresy in Marlowe, Milton, and Blake* (Oxford: 1998), p. 200. This scholar associates the eccentricity of Blake's behavior with the Begards, but does not elaborate on a specific conceptual connection (p. 194).

153. *The Complete Writings of William Blake, with All the Variant Readings*, ed. Geoffrey Keynes (London, New York: 1957), p. 150. An abridged version of this topic we see in plate 24: "Note: This Angel, who is now become a Devil..." "A Memorable Fancy," p. 158.

154. R. Hristova, *The Influence of Ancient Unofficial Religious Doctrines on William Blake's Art and Writings,* paper presented on 34th annual conference of British Society for Eighteenth-Century Studies (BSECS), 6–8 January 2005, St. Hugh's College, Oxford.

155. Blake praised his friendship with Fuseli with the following words: "The only man that e'er I knew / who did not make me almost spew." Also it is well known that Fuseli stimulated Blake's creative environment.

156. J. K. Füssly, *Neue und unparteische Kirchen und Ketzerhistorien der mittler Zeit,* vols. 1–3 (Frankfurt am Main etc.: 1770–1774). Quoted according to the bibilography: Kr. Gecheva, *Bogomilstvoto: Bibliografiya* (Sofia: 1997), p. 36.

157. The French title is longer and sounds more romantic: "Milton adolescent, contemplé par une dame italienne."

158. L. P. Brockett, *The Bogomils of Bulgaria and Bosnia: The Early Protestants of the East* (Philadelphia: American Baptist Publication Society, 1879).

Bibliography

Primary Works

CYRILLIC (TRANSLITERATED)

Angelov, B., and M. Genov, eds. *Stara bulgarska literature (IX–XVIII vek)*. Sofia: 1922.
"Anonimen katarski tractat." In *Rakopisite na katarite*. Sofia: 1999.
Apokrifi i legendi z ukrainskih rukopisiv. Ed. I. Franko. Vol. 2. Lviv: 1899.
Bogomilstvoto v Bulgaria, Vizantiya i Zapadna Evropa v izvori. Ed. D. Angelov, B. Primov, G. Batakliev. Sofia: 1967.
Bulgarskata literatura i knizhnina prez XIII vek. Ed. and with notes by Iv. Bozhilov and St. Kozhuharov. Sofia: 1987.
Cesarius of Heisterbach. *Dialog na chudesata*. Sofia: 1999.
Dante, A. *Bozhestvena komedia*. Trans. Iv. Ivanov and L. Lyubenov. Sofia: 1975.
Genov, M. *Antologiya na starobulgarskata literatura*. Sofia: 1947.
"Hodene na Bogoroditsa po makite." In *Stara bulgarska literature*, vol. 1, *Apokrifi*. Sofia: 1982.
Ivanov, Y. *Bogomilski knigi i legendi*. Sofia: 1925.
"Katarski trebnik (XIII vek)." In *Bogomilski knigi i legendi*, trans. Yordan Ivanov. Sofia: 1925.
"Legenda o bratstve." In *Pamyatniki starinnoy ruskoy literatury (Skazaniya, legendy, skazki i pritchi)*, trans. and notes N. Kostomarova. Vol. 1. St. Petersburg: 1860.
Milton, J. *Izgubeniat ray*. Trans. Al. Shurbanov. Sofia: 1981.
"Nikodimovo evangelie." In *Apokrifi i legendi z ukrainskih rukopisiv*, vol. 2. Lviv: 1899.
Ohridski, Kl. "Slovo za Pasha." In *Stara bulgarska literature*, vol. 2, *Oratorska prosa*. Sofia: 1982.
Pamyatniki otrechennoy ruskoy literatury, sobrany i izdany N. Tihonravovym. Vol. 1. St. Petersburg: 1860.
"Patriarh Teofilakt do Petar, tsar na bulgarite." In *Stara bulgarska literature*, vol. 2, *Oratorska prosa*. Sofia: 1982.
Peev, Peyo D. *Povest za krastnoto darvo — svoden variant v Prezviter Eremiya*. Disertation. Shumen-Sofia: 1990.
"Pismo na Evtimiy ot Akmoniya (XI vek)." In *Bogomilstvoto v Bulgaria, Vizantiya i Zapadna Evropa v izvori*, ed. D. Angelov, B. Primov, G.Batakliev. Sofia: 1967.
"Pismo na ierusalimskiya monah Atanasiy do Panka." In *Stara bulgarska literature (IX–XVIII vek)*, ed. B. Angelov and M. Genov. Sofia: 1922.

"Pohvalno slovo za Moysey, za splitaneto na darvo ot ela, kedar i kiparis — variant na Povest za krastnoto darvo." In *Novi prilozi za literature bibkijskih apokrifa*, V. Jagich. *Starine V.* Zagreb: 1873.

"Polemichno sachinenie srestu bosnenskite bogomili." In *Bogomilstvoto v Bulgaria, Vizantiya i Zapadna Evropa v izvori*, ed. D. Angelov, B. Primov, G. Batakliev. Sofia: 1967.

Popruzhenko, B. *Sinodik tsaria Borila.* Sofia: 1928.

"Povest za krastnoto darvo." In *Stara bulgarska literature.* vol. 1, *Apokrifi.* Sofia: 1982.

"Prenie na antihrist s Gospoda nash Isus Hristos." In *Stara bulgarska literature,* vol. 1, *Apokrifi.* Sofia: 1982.

Presviter Kozma. "Beseda protiv bogomilite." In *Stara bulgarska literature,* vol. 2, *Oratorska prosa.* Sofia: 1982.

"Prostranno zhitie na Teodosiy Tarnovski ot patriarh Kalist." In *Stara bulgarska literature,* vol. 4, *Zhivotopisni tvorbi.* Sofia: 1986.

Raynov, N. "Satanailovo tsarstvo: Bogomilski apokrif." In *Sachinenia v 5 toma,* vol. 2. Sofia: 1990.

"Sinodik na tsar Boril." In *Darjava i tsarkva prez XIII vek.* Sofia: 1999.

"Skazanie za krastnoto darvo (Rkp v Sbornik N 925 na Solov. Manastir v Kazanskata duhovna akademiya)." In *Stara bulgarska literatura (IX–XVIII vek).* Sofia: 1922.

"Slovo za Adam i Eva ot nachaloto do svarsheka." In *Stara bulgarska literature,* vol. 1, *Apokrifi.* Sofia: 1982.

"Slovo za lazhlivia antichrist, bezbozhnia Satanail, kak go pleni archangel Mihail, voevoda na vsichki angeli." In *Stara bulgarska literature,* vol. 1, *Apokrifi,* ed. and notes by Donka Petkanova. Sofia: 1982.

"Slovo na Yoan Zlatoust za tova kak Mihail pobedi Satanail." In *Bulgarskata literatura i knizhnina prez XIII vek.* Sofia: 1987.

Snegat zelenina sanuva (Antologia na provansalskata lirika). Podbral i prevel ot provansalski Simeon Hadzhikosev. Sofia: 1990.

Speranskiy, M. *Slavyankiya apokrificheskiya evangeliya (obstiy obzor).* Moskva: 1895.

"Videnie na svetia apostol Pavel, koyto beshe vaznesen ot angel na tretoto nebe." In *Stara bulgarska literature,* vol. 1, *Apokrifi.* Sofia: 1982.

Zigavin, E. "Dogmatichesko vseorazhie." In *Bogomilstvoto v Bulgaria, Vizantiya i Zapadna Evropa v izvori.* Sofia: 1967.

OTHER PRIMARY SOURCES

Anglo-Saxon Poetry: An Anthology of Old English Poems in Prose Translation. With introduction and headnotes by S. A. J. Bradley. London, Melbourne, Toronto: 1982.

Annae Comnenae porphyrogenitae caesarissae Alexias. Venice: Ex typographia Bartholomae Javarina, 1724.

Ariosto, L. *Orlando furioso.* Florence: Samsoni, 1957.

Blake, W. *The Complete Writings (with All the Variant Readings).* Ed. Geoffrey Keynes. London, New York: 1957.

Borenius, T., and E. W. Tristram. *English Medieval Paintings.* Ed. Pantheon. Casa editrice Firenze; The Pegassus Press. Paris: 1927.

Boulton, M. *Anglo-Norman Texts: Les enfaunces de Jesu Christ.* London : Anglo-Norman Text Society, 1985.

Bozoki, E. *Le livre secret des Cathares: Interrogatio Iohannis, apocryphe d'origine bogomile.* Beauchesne, Paris: 1980.

"Das Buch Supra Stella von Stella von Salvus Burche zu Piacenza aus dem J.1235 (Florenz) über Cathari, Albanenses et Concorricii." In *Dokumente vornehmlich zur Geschichte der Valdesier und Katharer herausgegeben*, by Ign. v. Döllinger. Vol 2. Munich: 1890.

Byron, G. "Cain (Mystery)." In *Complete poetical works*. Oxford: 1970.

La Chanson de la Croisade Albigeoise (Canzos de la Crozada). Ed. and trans. Eugène Martin-Chabot. Vol. 1 of *La Chanson de Guillaume de Tudèle*. Paris: 1976.

Christian Dualist Heresies in the Byzantine World c. 650–c. 1405. Selected sources translated and annotated by Janet Hamilton and Bernard Hamilton. Manchester and New York: 1998.

Chronicon Henrici Knighton vel Cnitthon Monachi Leycestrensis. Ed. J. R. Lumby, D.D. Vol. 1. London: 1889.

Concilium Lateranse III. Cap. XXVII, "De hereticis." *Mansi*. Vol. 22.

"Confessio Johannis Tyssyngton de ordine Minorum." In *Fasciculi zizaniorum magistri Johannis Wycliff cum tritico,* ed. Walter Shirley. London: 1858.

"Confessio Magistri John Wycliff." In *Fasciculi zizaniorum magistri,* ed. Walter Shirley. London: 1858.

Corbian, P. de. "Prière à la Vierge." In *Anthologie des troubadours XIIme–XIIIme siècles*. Edition refondue. Paris: 1974.

Cursor mundi. Ed. R. Morris. Four versions: British Museum Ms Cotton Vespasian. A.III; Bodlean Ms Fairefax; Göttingen University Library Ms. Theol. 107; Trinity College Cambridge Ms R.3.8/Seven parts. London: 1874/1961.

Dante. "Il convivo." Trat. II, cap. VI, in *Dantis Alagherii Opera Omnia II*. Leipzig: 1921.

_____. *La Divina Commedia: Le rime, i versi della vita nuova e le canzoni del convivo.* Ed. G. Einaudi. 1954.

_____. *Vita nuova*. Canzone II in *Dantis Alagherii Opera Omnia II*. Leipzig: 1921.

Delmaire, B. "Un Sermon arrageois inédit sur les 'Bougres' du Nord de la France (Vers 1200)." *Heresis* 17 (1991).

Dondaine, A. "Hiérarchie cathare en Italie. I. De heresi Catharorum." In *Archivum fratrum Praedicatorum*, vol. 19. Rome: 1949.

_____. "Hiérarchie cathare d'Italie. II. Le Tractatus de hereticis d'Anselme d'Alexandrie. O.P." In *Archivum fratrum Praedicatorum*, vol. 19. Rome: 1950.

_____. *Un traité néomanicheen du XIII siècle, Le liber de duobus principiis*. Rome: 1939.

Döllinger, Ign. v. *Beiträge zur Sectengeschichte des Mittelalters*. Vol. 2. *Dokumente vornehmlich zur Geschichte der Valdesier und Katharer*. Munich: 1890.

Douais, C. *La Somme des autorités à l'usage des prédicateurs méridionaux au XIIIe siècle*. Paris: 1896.

Du Cange. *Glossarium mediae et infimae latinitats*. Vols. 1, 5. Niort: L. Fabre imprimeur-éditeur, 1884.

Duvernoy, J. *Le Régistre d'inquisition de Jacques Fournier 1318–1325*. Vol. 1. Toulouse: 1965.

"Euthymii Zigabeni de haeresi bogomilorum narratio." In G. Ficker. *Die Phundagiagiten*. Leipzig: 1908.

Euthymius Zigabenus. "Selected Writings." In *Patrologia Graeca*, vol. 130. Compiled and edited by A.P. Migne. Paris: Imprimerie Catholique, 1857–1858.

"L'Evangile de l'enfance." In *Dictionnaire des apocryphes ou collection des tous les livres apocryphes,* J. P. Migne, vol. 1. Paris: 1856.

Ficker, G. *Die Phundagiagiten*. Leipzig: 1908.

Fosdick, H.E., ed. *Great Voices of the Reformation (Anthology)*. New York: Random House, 1952.

Foxe's Christian Martyrs of the World. Westwood, New Jersey: 1985.

Gouillard J., *Quatre procès de mystiques à Byzance*. Vol. 4. *Les évêques "bogomiles"de Cappadoce*. Paris : Institut des études Byzantines, 1978.

Gui, Bernard. *Manuel de l'inquisiteur*. Vol. 1. Paris: 1926.

Heresy Trials in the Diocese of Norwich, 1428–31. Ed. Norman Tanner. Camden Fourth Series, Vol. 20. London: 1977.

The Holy Bible. New revised standard version. Oxford: 1989.

The Holy Bible, containing the Old and New Testament with apocryphal books, in the earliest English versions made from the Latin Vulgate by John Wycliffe and his followers. Ed. J. Forshall and Fr. Madden. London: 1850.

"L'Homélie d'Epiphane sur l'ensevelissement du Christ." Ed. A. Vaillant. Zagreb: Radovi Staroslavenskog instituta, 1958.

"Ingressus fratris Jonahhis Kynyngham Carmelitae contra Wicclyff." In *Fasciculi zizaniorum*, ed. Walter W. Shirley. London: 1858.

Langland, W. *Piers the Plougman*. Translated into modern English with an introduction by J. F. Goodridge. New York etc.: 1959/1977.

_____. *The Vision of Piers Plowman: A Complete Edition of the B-text*. A critical edition of the B-text based on Trinity Colledge Cambridge MS B.15.17 with selected variant readings, an introduction, glosses, and textual and literary commentary by A.V.C. Schmidt. London, Melbourne, Toronto, New York: 1978.

Langland's Vision of Piers the Plowman (Text B). Ed. W.W. Skeat. London, New York, Toronto: Original series 1869, reprinted 1881, 1898, 1930, 1950, 1964, 1971.

Lazar, M. "La Légende de 'l'Arbre de Paradis' ou 'bois de la croix': poème anglo-normand du XIIIe siècle et sa source latine, d'après le Ms.66. Corpus Christi College, Cambridge (Inédit)." In *Zeitschrift fur Romanishe Philologie* 76 (1960).

Livre des deux principes. Introduction, text critique, traduction, notes and index by Christine Thouzhellier. Paris: 1973.

Lollards of Coventry 1486–1522. Ed. and trans. Shannon Mc Sheffrey and Norman Tanner. London: Cambridge University Press, 2003.

Meung, J., and G. Lorris. *Le roman de la Rose*. Set in modern French by André Maury. Paris: 1949.

Michel, D. *Ayenbite of Inwit or Remorse of Conscience*. Vol. 1. Text from the R. Morris transcription now newly collated with unique manuscript British Museum Ms Arundel 57 by Pamela Gradon. London, New York, Toronto: 1886/1965.

Migne, J. P. *Dictionnaire des apocryphes*. Vols. 1, 2. Paris: 1856.

Millet, B., and J. Wogan-Browne, eds. *Medieval English Prose for Women*. Oxford: 1990.

Milton, J. *Areopagitica: A Speech of Mr. John Milton for the Liberty and Vnlicenc'd Printing to the Parliament of England*. London: 1644.

_____. *Areopagitica and Other Prose Works by John Milton*. London, New York: 1927.

_____. *Complete English Poems, Of Education, Areopagitica*. London: 1909/1990.

_____. "Considerations Touching the Likeliest Means to Remove the Hirelings out of the Church where is also Discoursed of Tithes, Church Fees, and Church Revenues; whether any Maintenance of Ministers Can Be Settled by Law...." In *The Prose Works of John Milton*, vol. 3. London: 1883.

_____. *Eikonoklastes, in Answer to a Book Intitul'd Eikonobasilike, the Portracture of his*

Sacred Majesty King Charles the First in his Solitudes and Sufferings. Amsterdam: 1690.

_____. *Latin Writings: A Selection.* Ed. J.K. Hale. Medieval and Renaissance Texts and Studies, vol. 191. Tempe, AZ: Van Gorcum, 1998.

_____. "Of the Reformation in England and the Causes That Hitherto Have Hindered It. In Two Books." In *Areopagitica and Other Prose Works of John Milton.* London, New York, Toronto: 1927.

_____. "On the late massacre on Piedmont" In *Selected Shorter Poems and Prose.* London, New York: 1988/9.

_____. *Paradise Lost.* In *The Poetical Works of John Milton.* London, New York, Toronto: 1958.

_____. *Paradise Regained.* In *Complete English Poems.* London: 1909/1990.

_____. *The Prose Works of John Milton.* Vols. 1–5. London: 1883.

_____. "The Reason of Church Government urged against Prelaty." In *The Prose Works of John Milton.* Vol. 3. London: 1883.

_____. *Selected Shorter Poems and Prose.* London, New York: 1988/9.

_____. "The Tenure of Kings and Magistrates." In *The Prose Works of John Milton,* vol. 2. London: 1883.

_____. "To Benedetto Buonmattai." In *The Prose works of John Milton,* vol. 3. London: 1883.

_____. "To the Accomplished Emeric Bigot." In *The Prose Works of John Milton,* vol. 3. London: 1883.

_____. "A Treatise of Christian Doctrine Completed from the Holy Scriptures Alone." In *The Prose Works of John Milton,* vol. 5. London: 1883.

_____. "A Treatise of Civil Power in Ecclesiastical Causes." In *Milton's Prose.* Oxford, London, New York, Toronto: 1925/1949.

"MS Bodley 959 Genesis-Baruch 3.20 in Earlier version of the Wycliffite Bible." Ed. C. Linderg. In *Stockholm Studies in English* 6 (1959), 10(1963), 13(1965), 20 (1969).

New Testament, translated out of the Latin Vulgat by John Wyclif, about 1378. Ed. John Lewis. London: 1731.

New Testament, translated from Latin, in the year 1380 by John Wiclif, D.D. To which are prefixed Memoirs of the Life, Opinions, and Writings of Dr. Wiclif, and the Historical Account of the Saxon and English Versions of Scriptures, previous to opening of the fifteenth century. 4to. London: 1810.

Petrarca, F. *Le Rime del Petrarca.* Vol. 2. Florence: 1832.

Plotin. *Ennéades.* Vol. 1. Paris: 1924.

Puech, H., and A. Vaillant. *Le Traité contre les Bogomiles de Cosmas le Prêtre.* Paris: 1945.

Rački, Fr. "Prilozi za povjest bosanskih patarena." In *Starine* (University of Zagreb) 1 (1869).

"Raynerus Sacconi O.P.," by F. Saniek O.P. In *Archivum Fratrum Praedicatorum,* vol. 44. Rome: 1974.

Sacconi, R., O.P. "Summa de catharis par Fr. Sanjek O.P." In *Archivum fratrum praedicatorum,* vol. 44. Rome: 1974.

Salve, Burce. "Supra stella." In *Dokumente vornehmlich zur Geschichte der Valdesier und Katharer herausgegeben,* by Ign. v. Döllinger. Munich: 1890.

Scriptorum veterum (quorum pars magna nunc primum e MSS. Codibus in lucem prodit) qui Ecclesiae Rom. Errores & Abusus detegunt & damnant necessitatem que Reformationis urgent. London: 1690.

Shirley, Walter W., ed. *Fasciculi zizaniorum magistri Johannis Wycliff cum tritico.* London: 1858.

Tanner, N., ed. *Kent Heresy Proceedings 1511–12.* Kent: 1997.

"Theophylacti Constantinopolis patriarcha epistola." In *Fontes graecae historiae bulgaricae.* V. 1964.

Thomae Aquinatis. *Summa Theologica.* Pars Tertia, Quaestio LII, Articulus VIII. Rome: Ex Typographia Forzani et S.: 1894.

Tischendorf, K. *Evangelia apocrypha.* Leipzig: 1852.

"[Twenty-four] XXIV conclusiones Wycclyf damnatae Londoniis in synodo." In *Fasciculi zizaniorum magistri Johannis Wycliff cum tritico,* ed. Walter W. Shirley. London: 1858.

Tyndale, W. *Doctrinal Treatises and Introduction to Different Portions of the Holy Scriptures by William Tyndale, Martyr, 1536.* Cambridge University Press, 1848.

_____. *An Exposition upon the V, VI, VII Chapters of Matthew.* Antwerp: 1533.

_____. *Expositions and Notes on Sundry Portions of the Holy Scriptures together with the Practice of Prelates by William Tyndale, Martyr 1536.* Cambridge: 1849.

_____. *The Independent Works of William Tyndale: An answer unto sir Thomas More.* Dialogue. Washington: 2000.

_____. *The Obedience of a Christian Man.* London: 2001.

_____. *The Parable of the Wicked Mammon.* Antwerp: 1528.

_____. *Practice of Prelates by Wylliam Tyndale, Martyr, 1536.* Cambridge University Press, 1849.

Voragine, J. de. *La légende dorée.* Trans. from the Latin by T. de Wyzeva. Paris: 1920.

Wycliff, J. "The Anticrist labour to destroy the holy Writ." In Fosdick, *Great Voices of the Reformation (Anthology).* New York: Random House, 1952.

_____. *De compositione hominis.* London: 1884.

_____. *Johannis Wyclif Operis evangelici.* Books 3 and 4. London: 1896.

_____. *Miscellanea Philosophica.* Vol. 2. London: 1905.

_____. *Opus evangelicum.* Vols. 1, 2. London: 1895.

_____. *Summae in theologia (Tractatus tertius). De civile domino (Liber primus).* London: 1835.

_____. *Tractatus de Benedicta Incarnatione.* London: 1886.

Wycliffite Manuscript. The New Testament. England, 1400–1450. CD. Edited by Bridwell Library, Dallas. Oakland, CA: Octavo Corp., 1999.

Secondary Sources

CYRILLIC (TRANSLITERATED)

Aleksiev, M. *Iz istorii angliyskoy literatury (Videnie o Petre Pahare).* Moskow-Leningrad: 1960.

Angelov, D. *Bogomilstvoto.* Sofia: 1993.

_____. "Bogomily i katary." In *Slavyanskie kul'tury i Balkany.* Vol. 1. Sofia: 1978.

_____. *Bulgarinat v Srednovekovieto. Svetogled, ideologia, dushevnost.* Varna: 1985.

_____. *Istoria na Vizantiya.* I chast. Sofia: 1976.

Barlieva, Sl. "Agiografskite tvorbi za sv.sv. Kiril i Metodiy v Legenda Aurea na Yakov Voraginski." In *Kirilo-Metodievski studii,* Kn. 11. Sofia: 1998.

Duychev, I. *Prouchvanyia varhu srednovekovnata bulgarska istoriya i kultura.* Sofia: 1981.

Eldarov, G. "Sv. Frantsisk i islyama." *Abagar* 1 (January 1997).

Franko, I. "Peredmova." In *Apokrifi i legendi z ukrainskih rukopisisv,* vol. 2. Lviv: 1899.

Galahov, A. *Istoriya ruskoy slovesnosti — drevney i novoy.* Vol. 1. St. Petersburg: 1880.

Gechev, St. *Golgotata na Varava. Piesi.* Sofia: 1999.

_____. *Kam vaprosa za slaviyanskiya fiziolog.* Sofia: 1938.

_____. "Predgovor za Palatinskata antologiya i za drugi drevni nesta." In *Palatinska antologiya.* Sofia: 1994/1996.

Gecheva, Kr. *Bogomilstvoto. Bibliografia.* Sofia: 1997.

Ginchev, Ts. *Po nyakolko dumi.* Sofia: 1988.

Golenishchev-Kutuzov, I. *Srednevekovaya latinskaya literatura Italii.* Moskva: 1972.

Hadzhikosev, S. "Kam izvorite na novoevropeyskata poezia." In *Snegat zelenina sanuva.* Sofia: 1990.

Ilchev, St. *Rechnik na lichnite i familnite imena u bulgarite.* Sofia: 1969.

Ivanov, Y. *Bulgarskite narodni pesni.* Sofia: 1959.

Jirecek, K. *Istoria na bulgarite.* Sofia: 1999.

Jusserand, J. *Istoriya angliyskago naroda v ego literature.* St. Petersburg: 1898.

Karsavin, L. *Ocherki religioznoy zhizni v Italii XII–XIII vekov.* St. Petersburg.

Kenanov, D. "Yordan Ivanov i Taynata kniga na bogomilite." In *Izvestia na istoricheskia muzey.* Vol. 4. Kyustendil: 1992.

Kirilo-Metodievska entsiklopedia. Vol. 1. 1985.

Klibanov, A. "Bogomilstvoto kato svetovno yavlenie (razgovor s V. Velchev i K. Mechev)." *Problemi na kulturata* 1 (1981).

Kodov, Hr. "Notes." In Kliment Ohrisdki, *Complete Works. Sabrani sachinenia.* Vol. 2. Sofia: 1997.

Krastanov, Tr., A. M. Totomanova, and I. Dobrev. *Vatikanski palimpsest.* Sofia: 1997.

Krastev, K. "Bulgarskiat prinos v Boyianskite stenopisi." *Izkustvo* 4–5 (1965).

Lavrov, P. *Materialy po istorii vozniknoveniya drevneshey slavyanskoy pismennosti.* Leningrad: 1930.

Lazarov, St. *Prouchvania varhu kulturata na bogomili i katari: teatar, muzika (aftoreferat na disertatsiya).* Sofia: 1989.

Le Goff, J. *Intelektualtsite prez Srednovekovieto.* Sofia: 1993.

Lur'e, A. "Komentarii k Poslanie Genadiya k Yoasafu." In *Pamyatniki literatury drevney Rusi (vtoraya polovina XV veka).* Moskva: 1982.

Miltenova, A. "Belezhki." In *Bulgarskata literatura i knizhnina prez XIII.* Sofia: 1987.

_____. "Tekstologicheski nablyudenia varhu dva apokrifa (Apokrifen tsikal za krastnoto darvo, pripisvan na Grigoriy Bogoslov i apokrifa za Adam I Eva)." In *Starobulgarska literatura* 2 (1982).

Mishev, D. *Bulgaria v minaloto.* Sofia: 1918.

Nikolov, Y. *Eresite v Zapadna Evropa XII–XIII vek (sotsialno politicheski problemi).* Sofia: 1989.

Osokin, N. *Istoriya al'bigoytsev i ih vremeni.* Moskva: 2000. Kazan: 1869.

_____. *Istoriya al'bigoytsev do konchiny papy Innokentiya III.* Vol. 1. Kazan: 1869.

Panayotov, V. "Svedenia za bogomilstvoto v Pismoto do Panko na Atanasiy Yerusalimski." In *Starobulgaristika* 3 (1981).

Peev, P. *Prezviter Eremia (avtoreferat za prisazhdane na nauchna stepen kandidat na filologicheskite nauki).* Shumen: 1991.

Petkanova, D. "Apokrifnata literature i lichnoto tvorchestvo na starobulgarskite pisateli." In *Starobulgaristika* 3 (1981).

_____. "Apokrifni motivi v tvorchestvoto na Kliment Ohridski." In *Kirilo-Metodievski studii*. Vol. 8. Sofia: 1991.

_____. "Kam vaprosa za vrazkata na folklore s bogomilstvoto." *Izvestia na Instituta za bulgarska literatura*. Vol. 6. Sofia: 1958.

Peychev, B. "Yoahim ot Fiore i Bulgaria." In *Bulgaria, Italiya i Balkanite*. Sofia: 1988.

Polniy pravoslavnyy bogoslovskiy slovar.' Izd. P. Soykina. Vol. 2. N.p., n.d.

Popov, G., and Kr. Stanchev. *Kliment Ohridski*. Sofia: 1988.

Primov, B. *Bugrite (Kniga za pop Bogomil i negovite posledovateli)*. Sofia: 1970.

_____. "Bulgarskoto narodno ime v Zapadna Evropa vav vrazka s bogomilite." In *Izvestia na institute za bulgarska istoria* 6. Sofia: 1956.

Radchenko K. "Etyudi po bogomil'stvu." *Izvestia otdeleniya ruskogo yazika i slovesnosti*. Vol. 15. SPb.: 1910.

Runciman, S. *Istoriya na parvoto bulgarsko tsarstvo*. Sofia: 1993.

Saprykin, Yul. "Vzglyady Dzhona Uiklifa na obstnost' imustestva i ravenstva." In *Srednie veka* 34. Moskva: 1971.

Seifert, L. *Svetovnite revolyutsioneri (ot pop Bogomil do Lenin)*. Sofia: 1994.

Shishmanov, I. *Literaturna istoria na Vazrajdaneto v Italia*. Sofia: 1934.

Shurbanov, A. "Svetotvorchestvoto na Milton." In *Izgubenia ray,* trans. A. Shurbanov. Sofia: 1981.

Sofiyski, St. *Bulgarskata tsarkva*. Sofia: 1932.

Sokolov, M. *Materialy i zametki po starinnoy slavyanskoy literature*. Vol. 1. Moskow: 1888.

Starobulgarskata literatura: Entsiklopedichen rechnik. Ed. D. Petkanova. Sofia: 1992.

Stoilov, A. "Legendata za greshna mayka." In *Bulgarska sbirka*. God. VIII. 1901.

Todorov, E. *Drevnotrakiyskoto nasledstvo v bulgarskia folklor*. Sofia: 1972.

Valchanov, Sl. "Otrazhenia na starozavetnata apokrifna traditsia v srednovekovnata bulgarska literatura." In *Godishnik na Duhovnata akademiya "Sv. Kliment Ohridski."* T.XXVIII. Part 3. Sofia: 1978/1979.

Vargov, Hr. *Revolyutsioneri*. Sofia: 1924.

Vasilev, G. "Bogomili, katari i lolardi — provodnitsi na visoka pozitsia na zhenata v Srednovekovieto." In *Rodina. Spisanie za bulgarska istoricheska kultura* 4, 1996.

_____. "Bogomilski idei i obredi v tvorchestvoto na William Tyndale." *Mezhdunarodni otnoshenia*. May-June 2002.

_____. *Bulgarski bogomilski i apokrifni predstavi v angliyskata srednovekovna kultura (Obrazat na Hristos Orach v poemata na William Langland "Videnieto na Petar Oracha")*. Sofia: 2001.

_____. "Dualistkata filosofia i obraznost u Milton." *Vezni* 10, 2003.

_____. "Elementi na orfizam v bogomilstvoto." In *Izvestiya na istoricheskia muzey*. Vol. 5. Kyustendil: 1998.

_____. "Ima li predpostavki edno novo Vazrazhdane?" *Filosofska missal*. March-April 1996.

_____. "Orfizam i bogomilstvo." *Savremennik* 1, 1994.

_____. "Otglasi ot bogomilstvoto v angliyskia ezik." *Letopisi*. March–April 1996.

Vasiliev, A. *Ermenii: Tehnologia i ikonografia*. Sofia: 1976.

_____. *Soctsialni i patriotichni motivi v staroto bulgarsko izkustvo*. Sofia: 1973.

Veselovski, A. "Kaliki perehozhie i bogoml'skie stranniki." In *Vestnik Evropy,* vol. 2. 1872.

_____. *Solomon i Kitovras."* St. Petersburg: 1872.

Yagich, V. *Istoria serbohorvatskoy literatury.* Kazan: 1879.

Yoan-Pavel II. "Da si priznaem grehovete." In *Abagar* 10 (October 1999).

_____. *Kiril i Metodiy (Blagovestie i ekumenizam).* Sofia: 1996.

Zaytsev, V. *Bogomil'skoe dvizhenie i obstestvennaya zhizn' Severnoy Italii epohi Duecento.* Minsk: 1967.

OTHER SECONDARY SOURCES

Abels, R., and E. Harrison. "The Participation of Women in the Languedocien Catharism." In *Medieval Studies.* Vol. 41. 1979. 215–251.

Aers, D. *Chaucer, Langland and the Creative Imagination.* London: Routledge & Kegan Paul, 1980.

Ancelet-Hustache, J. *Maître Eckhart et la mystique rhénane.* Paris: 1971.

Aston, M. *Lollards and the Reformers (Images and Literacy in Late Medieval Religion).* London: Hambledon Press, 1984.

Aston, M. A. "Lollardy and Sedition 1381–1431." In *Past and Present*, Apr. 1960.

Baggiolini, C. *Dolcino e i patareni.* Novara: 1837.

Baugh, A., and K. Malone. *A Literary History of England.* Vol. I. *The Middle Ages (the Old English Period to 1100).* London: Routledge & Kegan Paul, 1985.

Bayet, M. C. "L'Empire Byzantin." In *Histoire générale du IVe siècle à nos jours (sous la direction de M.M. E. Lavisse et A. Rambaud).* Vol. 1, *Les origines 395–1095.* Paris: 1893.

De Beausobre, M. *Histoire critique du Manichée e du Manichéisme.* Amsterdam: 1734.

Biller, P. "Women and Texts in Languedocian Catharism." In *Women, the Book and the Godly: Selected Proceedings of St Hilda's Conference.* Vol. 1. Cambridge: 1993.

Borst, A. *Les Cathares.* Paris: 1978.

Brenon, A. *Les Archipels cathares: Dissidence chrétienne dans l'Europe médievale.* Cahors: 2000.

_____. *Localisation des manuscrits vaudois: Centro studi piemontesi.* Torino: 1978.

Brockett, L. P. *The Bogomils of Bulgaria and Bosnia: The Early Protestants of the East: An Attempt to Restore Some Lost Leaves of Protestants History.* Philadelphia: 1879.

Bruffaut, R. *Les Troubadours et les sentiments romanesques.* Paris: 1945.

The Cambridge History of English literature. Vol. I (from the beginnings to the cycles of romances). Cambridge: Cambridge University Press, 1932.

The Cambridge History of English and American Literature in 18 volumes (1907–1921). Vols. 2, 4.

Cantu, C. *Les Hérétiques d'Italie — discours historique de César Cantu (Les précurseurs de la Réforme).* Paris: 1869.

The Catholic Encyclopedia. Vol. 2. Robert Appleton Company, 1907.

Daniell, D. *William Tyndale: A Biography.* New Haven and London: 2001.

Deanesly, M. A. *The Lollard Bible (and Other Medieval Biblical Versions).* Cambridge: 1920/1966.

Delaruelle, E. "L'État actuel des études sur le catharisme." In *Cahiers de Fanjeaux,* vol. 3. Toulouse: 1986.

Delmaire, B. "Un Sermon arrageois sur le 'bougres' du Nord de la France (vers 1200)." *Heresis* 17 (1991).

Dobranski, Stephen P., and John P. Rumrich, eds. *Milton and Heresy.* New York: Cambridge University Press, 1998.

Doane, A. *The Saxon Genesis: An Edition of the West Saxon Genesis B and the Old Saxon Vatican Genesis.* Madison: University of Wisconsin Press, 1991.

Drout, M. "Piers's Good Will: Langland's Politics of Reform and Inheritance in the C-text." In *Social Practice in the Middle Ages. Essays in Medieval Studies*, vol. 13. Pp. 51–59.

Duvernoy, J. "L'Acception 'haereticus' (iretge)." In *The Concept of Heresy in the Middle Ages.* Vol. 1. Paris-La Haye: 1967.

_____. "Météorologie et Bulgarie." *Bulgarian Historical Review* 1–2 (2003).

_____. "Les Origines du movement Vaudois." *Heresis* 13–14 (1990).

Dzhonov, B. "Le Modèle de confession chez les Bogomiles et les Cathares." *Paleobulgarica* 4 (1980).

Eames, Elizabeth. *English Medieval Tiles.* Cambridge, MA: Harvard University Press, 1985.

Enciclopedia Italiana. Vol. 27. Rome: 1945–47.

Encyclopaedia Britannica. Vols. 3, 14. 1970.

Enev, M. *The Apocalypse.* Sofia: 1996.

Fines, J. "Heresy Trials in the Diocese of Coventry and Lichifield, 1511–12." *Journal of Ecclesiastical History* 14 (1963).

Forsyth, N. *The Satanic Epic.* Princeton University Press, 2003.

Foxe, J. *Acts and Documents.* London: 1563.

Foxe's Christian Martyrs of the World. Westwood, New Jersey: 1985.

Fueslin, H. *Dissertatio de fanaticis seculo XII in Anglia repertis.* Bern: 1761.

Fuessly, J. K. *Neue und unparteische Kirchen und Ketzerhistorien der mittler Zeit.* Vols. 1–3. Frankfurt am Main etc: 1770–1774. Quoted according to the bibliography: Kr. Gecheva. *Bogomilstoto.* Sofia: 1997.

Funk and Wagnalls. *New Standard Dictionary of the English Language.* New York, London: 1933.

Gairdner, J. *Lollardy and Reformation.* Vols. 1–4. London: 1908–13. Repr. 1968.

Gaster, M. *Ilchester Lectures on Graeco-Slavonic Literature and Its Relation to the Folklore of Europe During the Middle Ages.* London: 1887.

Gillet, L. *Dante.* Paris: 1941.

Godwin, W. *A Greek Grammar.* London: 1910.

Goodridge, F. *Piers the Ploughman.* Translated into modern English with an introduction and notes by J. F. Goodridge. New York, etc.: 1959/1977.

Grand Larouse encyclopédique. Vol. 8. Paris: 1963.

Gray, M. *A Chronology of English Literature: From Anglo-Saxon Times to Present Day.* Longman and York Press, 1989.

Guéorgiev, St. *Les Bogomiles et Presbiter Kosma.* Lausanne: 1920.

Guiraud, J. *Cartulaire de Notre Dame de Prouille, précédé d'une étude sur Albigéisme languédocien au XII et XIIIe siècles.* 2 vols. Paris: 1907.

Gurteen, S. H. *The Epic of the Fall of Man: A Comparative Study of Caedmon, Dante, and Milton.* New York: 1896.

Guzelev, V. "The Bulgarian Version of the Apocalypse: The 'Secret book' of the Bogomils or John's Gospel." In *The Apocalypse.* Sofia: 1996.

Hamilton, Bernard, and Janet Hamilton. Notes in *Christian Dualist Heresies in the Byzantine World, c. 650–c. 1450.* Manchester University Press, 1998.

Hamilton, B. "Wisdom from the East: The Reception by the Cathars of Eastern Dualist Texts." In *Heresy and Literacy, 1000–1530,* ed. P. Biller and A. Hudson. Cambridge: 1994/1996.

Hargreaves, H. "The Marginal Glosses the Wycliffite New Testament." *Studia Neophilologica* (Upsalla) 33 (1961).

Härtel, H. *Lollardische Lehrelemente im 14. und 15. Jahrhundert.* Doctoral dissertation, Georg August University, Göttingen. 1969.

Haskins, Ch. *The Renaissance of the Twelfth Century.* Cambridge, Mass.: 1927.

Hearnshow, F. *Some Great Political Idealists of the Christian Era.* London, Bombay, Sidney: (s. a.).

Hotchkiss, V. "Outlawed English." In *Formatting the Word of God,* ed. V. Hotchkiss and Ch. Ryrie. Dallas: 1998.

Hristova, R. *The Influence of Ancient Unofficial Religious Doctrines on William Blake's Art and Writings.* Paper presented at the 34th annual conference of the British Society for Eighteenth-Century Studies (BSECS), 6–8 January 2005, St. Hugh's College, Oxford.

Hudson, A. "'Laicus literatus': The Paradox of Lollardy." In *Heresy and Literacy, 1000–1530.* Ed. P. Biller and A. Hudson. Cambridge: 1994/1996.

_____. The *Premature Reformation: Wycliffite Texts and Lollard History.* Oxford: Clarendon, 1988.

Hupe, H. "The Filiation and the Text of the Mss." In *Cursor Mundi,* part 7. London: 1874/1961.

Jackson, A. *Zoroaster, the Prophet of Ancient Iran.* New York: 1898/1926.

James, M. R. "Rare Medieval Tiles and Their Story." In *The Burlington Magazine for Connoiseurs* (London) 42 (Jan.–June 1923).

Jeanroy, A. "Avant-propos." In *Anthologie des troubadours XIIme–XIIIme siècles.* Edition refondue. Paris: 1974.

John, J. A. S. "Editor's Preliminary Remarks." In *The Prose works of John Milton.* Vol.II. London: 1883.

_____. "Preface to 'Considerations Touching the Likeliest Means to Remove the Hirelings out of the Church where is also Discoursed of Tithes, Church Fees, and Churche Revenues; whether any Maintenance of Ministers Can Be Settled by Law....'" In *The Prose Works of John Milton.* Vol. 3. London: 1883.

Jolliot, A. "Les Communautés vaudoises des Hautes Vallées alpines aux XVe et XVIe siècles." Fédération historique du Languédoc méditerranéen et du Roussillon. XLIVe Congrès (Privas, 22–23 mai 1971). Université Paul Valéry. Montpellier: 1972.

_____. *Les Livres des Vaudois.* Catalogue. Ecole pratiques des hautes études. V^e section — sciences religieuses. Annuiare. Vols. 80–81. Extraits du fascicule II.

Jorgenson, J. "The Debate over the Patristic Texts on Purgatory at the Council of Ferrara-Florence, 1438." In *St. Wladimir's Theological Quarterly* (New York) 4 (1986).

Jusserand, J. *L'Épopée mystique de William Langland.* Paris: 1893.

_____. *Histoire abregée de la littérature anglaise.* Paris: 1896.

Knowles, M. D., and D. Obolenski. *Nouvelle histoire de l'Eglise.* Vol. 2. *Le Moyen âge.* Paris: 1968.

Kurth, B. *Milton and Christian Heroism.* Berkeley and Los Angeles: 1959.

Laffont, Robert, and Valentino Bompiani. *Dictionnaire des oeuvres de tous les temps.* 5 vols. Paris: Bompiani, 1952–1955.

Lagarde, G. *La Naissance de l'esprit laïque au déclin du Moyen âge.* Vienna: 1934.

Lambert, Malcolm. *The Cathars.* Oxford: Blackwell, 1998.

_____. *Medieval Heresy: Popular Movements from the Gregorian Reform to the Reformation.* 3rd ed. Oxford: Blackwell, 2002.

Larsen, A. "Are All Lollards Lollards?" In *Lollards and Their Influence in Late Medieval England*. Ed. Fiona Somerset, Jill Havens and Derrick Pitard. London: Boydell and Brewer, Ltd., 2003.

Lazar, M. "La Légende de 'l'Arbre de Paradis' ou 'bois de la croix' (poème anglonormand du XIIIe siècle et sa source latine, d'après le Ms.66. Corpus Christi College. Cambridge. (Inédit)." In *Zeitschrift fur Romanishe Philologie* 76 (1960).

Lea, H. Ch. *A History of the Inquisistion of the Middle Ages*. Vol. 2. London: 1888.

Léger, J. *Histoire des Eglises Evangéliques des vallées de Piémont*. Leiden: 1669.

Le Goff, J. *Un Autre Moyen-Age*. Paris: 1999.

———. *La Naissance du Purgatoire*. Paris: 1981.

Legouis, E. *A History of English Literature: The Middle Ages and the Renaissance*. Revised edition. London: J. M. and Sons, Ltd., 1967.

Le Roy Ladurie, E. *Montaillou, village occitan de 1294 à 1324*. Paris: 1975/1982.

Life and Times of John Wycliffe: The Morning Star of the Reformation. London: 1884.

Lombard, A. *Pauliciens, Bulgares et Bons-hommes en Orient et Occident (Etude sur quelques sectes du Moyen âge)*. Geneva, Basel, Paris: 1879.

Long, E. "Feminism and Cultural Studies," *Cultural Perspectives on Media and Society*, ed. R.K. Avery and D. Eason. New York: The Guilford Press, 1991.

Loos, M. *Dualist Heresy in the Middle Ages*. Prague: 1974.

Mâle, E. *L'Art religieux du XIIIe siècle en France (étude de l'iconographie du Moyen âge et sur ses sources d'inspiration)*. Paris: 1919.

Maury, A. *Essai sur les légendes pieuses du Moyen-âge*. Paris: 1843.

Manly, J. "Piers the Plowman and Its Sequence." In *The Cambridge History of English Literature*, vol. 2, *The End of the Middle Ages*. Cambridge: 1932.

Manselli, R. "Dolore e morte nella esperienza religiosa catara." In *Todi*. Presso di l'Academia Tudertina: 1967.

McSheffrey, Sh. "Literacy and the Gender Gap in the Late Middle Ages: Women and Reading in Lollard Communities." In *Women, the Book and the Godly*, Vol. 1. Cambridge: 1995.

———. "Women and Lollardy: A Reassessment." *Canadian Journal of History* 26 (1991).

Merrifield, J. *The Perfect Heretics: Cathars and Catharism*. With contributions from Yves Rouquette, Michel Roquebert and Anne Brenon. Lyme Regis, 1995.

Mincoff, M. *A History of English Literature*. Part I: *From the Beginnings to 1700*. Sofia: 1970.

Monnier, J. *La Descente aux enfers*. Paris: 1904.

Moore, R. *The Origins of the European Dissent*. New York: 1977/85.

Morghen, R. "Problèmes sur l'origine de l'hérésie au Moyen âge." *Revue historique* 236, 90th year (1966).

Morris, R. "Preface, Notes and Glossary." In *Cursor mundi*. Part 6. London: 1874/1961.

Mosheim, J. *Ecclesiastical History from the Birth of Our Saviour to the Eighteenth Century*. Book 3, part 2, chap. 2. Boston and London: 1802. Original title: *Institutionum Historiae Ecclesiasticae antiquioris et recentioris, libri IV*. Frankfurt and Leipzig: 1726.

Nauert, G. Jr. Editor's preface in "Lollard Themes in the Reformation Theology of William Tyndale." In *Sixteenth Century Essays and Studies*, vol. 6. 1986.

Naumov, Al. *Apocryfy w systemie literatury cerkiewnosc owianskiej*. Wroclaw, Warsaw, Krakow, Gdansk: 1976.

Nelli, R. "Contribution à l'Iconographie du Catharisme: La Croix Cathare." *Revue d'ethnographie méridionale* 16, no. 3, 26th year (Autumn 1963).

_____. *Dictionnaire des hérésies méridionales et mouvements hétérodoxes, apparues dans le Midi de la France depuis l'établissement du Christianisme.* Toulouse: 1968.

_____. *Le Phénomène cathare (perspectives philosophiques et morales).* Toulouse: 1988.

_____. "Préface vers J. Ivanov " In *Livres et légendes bogomiles (aux sources du Catharisme).* Paris: 1976.

_____. *La Vie quotidienne des Cathares du Languedoc au XIIIe siècle.* Paris: 1969.

Nelson, D. "Society, Theodicy and the Origins of Medieval Heresy." In *Schism, Heresy and Religious Protest.* Cambridge: 1972.

Niel, F. *Albigeois et cathares.* Paris: 1959.

Nuttall, A. *The Alternative Trinity: Gnostic Heresy in Marlowe, Milton, and Blake.* Oxford: 1998.

Obolensky, D. *The Bogomils: A Study in Balkan-Neo-manichaeism.* Cambridge: 1948.

_____. "Papas Nicetas: A Byzantine Dualist in the Land of the Cathars." *Harvard Ukrainian Studies Okeans* 7 (1983).

Olivieri, D. *Dizionario etimologico italiano (concordato coi dialetti, le lingue straniere e la topo-onomastica).* Milano: 1953.

Onions, T. *The Oxford Dictionary of English Etymology.* Oxford: Oxford University Press, 1966.

The Oxford English Dictionary. Vol. 1. Oxford: 1933.

The Oxford English Dictionary. Vols. 1, 2, 6. 1989.

Partridge, E. *A Short Etymological Dictionary of Modern English.* London: 1958/1966.

Paterson, L. *Chaucer and the Subject of History.* London: 1991.

Pelikan, Y., with Valerie R. Hotchkiss and David Price. *The Reformation of the Bible. The Bible of the Reformation.* New Haven: Yale University Press, 1996.

Perrin, J. *Histoire des vaudois et des albigeois.* Geneva: 1619.

Perrin, J. P. *Histoire des chrétiens albigeois, contenant les longues guerres et persécutions qu'ils on souffert à cause de la doctrine d'Evangile.* Geneva: 1618.

du Perron, A. *Zend-Avesta, ouvrage de Zoroastre.* Vol. 2. Paris: 1771.

Planiscig, L. *Luca della Robia.* 2nd ed. Vienna: 1940.

Pitard, D. "A Selected Bibliography for Lollard Studies." In *The Lollards and Their Influence in Late Medieval England,* ed. Fiona Somerset, J. Havens, and D. Pittard. Boydell and Brewer, 2003.

Poole, R. *Wycliffe and Movements for Reform.* New York: 1978 (reprint of the 1889 ed.).

Prati, A. *Vocabulario etimologico italiano.* Torino: 1951.

Puech, H. Ch. *Le Manichéisme (Son fondateur. Sa doctrine).* Paris: 1949.

Puech, H., and A. Vaillant. *Le Traité contre les Bogomiles de Cosmas le Prêtre.* Paris: 1945.

Renwick, W. L., and H. Orton. *The Beginnings of English Literature to Skelton 1509.* Vol. 1. London: 1939/1952.

Resnicov, S. "The Cultural History of a Democratic Proverb." *Journal of English and German Philology* 3 (1937).

Robinson, F. "Commentary." In *Wycliffite Manuscript: The New Testament: England, 1400–1450.* CD. Ed. By Bridwell Library, Dallas. Oakland, CA: Octavo Corp., 1999.

Rosén, T. *The Slavonic Translation of the Apocryphal Infancy Gospel of Thomas.* Uppsala: 1997.

(Le) Robert. *Dictionaire de la langue française.* Vol. 7. Paris: 1985.

Roubaud, J. Introduction to *Les Troubadours (anthologie bilingue).* Paris: 1971.

De Rougemont, D. *L'amour et l'Occident*. Paris: 1939/1970.

Rousseau, J. J. *Discours sur l'origine et les fondements de l'inégalité parmi les hommes*. Paris: 1903.

Runciman, St. "Bogomil and Jeremiah." In *Sbornik v pamet na prof. Petar Nikov*. Sofia: 1940.

Sanders, A. *The Short Oxford History of English Literature*, rev. ed. Oxford: Clarendon Press, 1996.

Schmidt, C. *Histoire et doctrine de la secte des Cathares ou Albigeois*. Vol. 1, 2. Paris-Geneva: 1849.

Seifert, L. *Die Welte revolutionäre. Von Bogomil über Huss zu Lenin*. Vienna: 1931.

Skeat, W. *An Etymological Dictionary of the English Language*. Oxford: 1956 (reproduction of the 1879–1882 edition).

Smeeton, D. D. "Lollard Themes in the Reformation Theology of William Tyndale." *Sixteenth Century Essays and Studies*. Vol. 6. Kirksville, MO: Sixteenth Century Journal Publishers, 1986.

Solovjev, A. "Svedocanstva pravoslavnih izvora o bogomilstvu na Balkanu." In *Godisnjak istorikog drustva Bosne i Hercegovine. godina*, vol. 5. Sarajevo: 1953.

Somerset, Fiona, J. Havens, and D. Pittard, eds. *The Lollards and Their Influence in Late Medieval England*. London: Boydell and Brewer, Ltd., 2003.

Stoyanov, Y. *The Hidden Tradition in Europe: The Secret History of Medieval Christian Heresy*. Penguin books/Arkana, 1994.

_____. *The Other God: Dualist Religions from Antiquity to the Cathar Heresy*. New Haven and London: 2000.

Summers, W. *The Lollards of Chiltern Hills*. London: 1906.

_____. *Our Lollard Ancestors*. London: 1904.

Thomov, T. "Les appellations de 'bogomiles' et de 'Bulgares' et leur variantes et équivalents en Orient et Occident." In *Etudes Balkaniques* no. 1, 1973.

Thomson, A. *Morning Star of the Reformation: The Life of John Wycliffe*. Greenville, SC: Bob Jones University Press, 1988.

Thomson, Cl. "Ch. XVI. Later transition English. I. Legendaries and Chroniclers." In *Cambridge History of English Literature*, vol. 2. London: Cambridge University Press, 1933.

Thomson, J. *The Later Lollards 1414–1520*. Oxford University Press, 1965.

Thode, M. *Saint François d'Assise et les origines de l'Art de la Renaissance*. Paris: 1885.

Thouzellier, Chr. *Hérésie et hérétiques (Vaudois, Cathares, Patarins, Albigeois)*. Rome: Edizione de Storia e Letteratura, 1969.

Tischendorf, K. "Nota." In *Evangelia apocrypha*. Leipzig: 1852.

Vaillant, A. Preface to *L'Homélie d'Epiphane sur l'ensevelissement du Christ*. Zagreb: Radovi Staroslavenskog instituta, 1958.

Vasilev, G. "Une Bibliographie attendue (Guetcheva, Kr. Le Bogomilisme. Bibliographie, Sofia: 1997, 232 pages)." In *Etudes Balkaniques* 3–4, 1997.

_____. "Bogomils and Lollards: Dualistic Motives in England during the Middle Ages." *Etudes Balkaniques* 1, 1993.

_____. "Bogomils, Cathars, Lollards and the High Social Position of Women during the Middle Ages." *Facta Universitatis. Philosophy and Sociology*. Vol. 2, no. 7, 2000.

_____. *Dualist Ideas in the English Pre-Reformation and Reformation: Bogomil-Cathar Influence on Wycliffe, Tyndale, Langland and Milton*. Sofia: Bul Koreni, 2005.

_____. "Idées et images dualistes dans l'oeuvre de William Tyndale." In *Bogomiles, patarins et cathares* no. 16. Toulouse: Slavica Occitanica, 2003.

_____. "Les Innovations bogomiles et la protorenaissance italienne (il Duecento)." In *Etudes Balkaniques* 2, 1992.

_____. "John Wycliffe, the Dualists and the Cyrillo-Methodian Version of the New Testament." In *Etudes Balkaniques* 1, 2001.

_____. "Orphisme et Bogomilisme." In *Thracia* 11. Serdicae: 1995.

_____. "Traces of Bogomil movement in English." In *Etudes Balkaniques* 3, 1993.

_____, and T. Totev. "Jean Duvernoy, un savant d'autorité internationale et un bon ami de la Bulgarie — Docteur honoris causa de l'Université de Choumen." *Bulgarian Historical Review* 1–2: 2003.

Vattier, V. *John Wyclyff, D.D.: Sa Vie — ses Oeurvres — Sa Doctrine.* Paris: 1886.

Vaughan, C. Introduction to *Areopagitica and Other Prose Works of John Milton.* London, New York: 1927.

Vaughan, R. *The Life and the Opinions of John de Wycliffe, D.D.* 2 vols. London: 1831.

Venckeleer, T. "Un Recueil cathare: le manuscrit A.6.10 de Dublin. Une apologie." *Revue Belge de Philologie et d'Histoire* 38 (1960).

_____. "Une Glose sur le Pater." *Revue Belge de Philologie et d'Histoire* 39 (1961).

Walker, W. "Review of Stephen P. Dobranski and John P. Rumrich, eds., Milton and Heresy." In *Early Modern Literary Studies* 7, no. 1 (May 2001), Special Issue 8.

Webster's Third International Dictionary. Massachusets: 1961.

Weis, R. *The Yellow Cross: The Story of the Last Cathars' Rebellion against the Inquisition 1290–1329.* New York: 2002.

White, H. "Langland, Milton and felix culpa." *Review of English Studies* 45, no.1 (1994).

Wilks, M. "Reformatio regni: Wyclif and Hus as Leaders of Religious Protest Movements." In *Schism, Heresy and Religious Protest.* Edited by Derek Baker. London: Cambridge University Press, 1972.

Workman, H. *The Dawn of the Reformation.* Vol. 4. *The Age of Wyclif.* London: 1901.

_____. *John Wyclif: A Study of the English Medieval Church.* Vols. 1 and 2. Hamden, Connecticut: Archon Books, 1966.

Index

199